GROWING VEGETABLES
THE BIG YIELD/SMALL SPACE WAY

DUANE NEWCOMB

Illustrations by Lynn Lieppman

J. P. Tarcher, Inc.
Los Angeles
Distributed by Houghton Mifflin Company
Boston

Library of Congress Cataloging in Publication Data

Newcomb, Duane G
 Growing vegetables the big yield/small space way.

 Bibliography: p. 213
 Includes index.   1. Vegetable gardening.   I. Title.
 II. Title: Big yield/small space way.
SB321.N445   635   80–53150
ISBN 0–87477–170–6

Copyright © 1981 by Duane Newcomb

J. P. Tarcher, Inc.
9110 Sunset Blvd.
Los Angeles, CA 90069
Library of Congress Catalog Card No.: 80–53150

Design by Jane Moorman

MANUFACTURED IN THE UNITED STATES OF AMERICA

Q   10 9 8 7 6 5 4 3 2 1

First Edition

CONTENTS

PREFACE

Growing Vegetables the Big Yield/Small Space Way is more than just another garden book: it's a cornucopia of information telling you how to grow vegetables abundantly even if your growing space is very limited.

Many of us feel a strong need to reduce living costs and to improve our diets by growing at least some of our own food, yet a well-fed family of four requires a minimum of 1,000 square feet of yard space for a conventional garden. Even the newer intensive-gardening methods, when used alone, take too much space and work to provide a convenient supplemental food source.

For some years now, agricultural experts and veteran gardeners have agreed that what America needs most to solve the home food problem is a small-space garden that will produce abundantly and take minimum amounts of water and work.

Without a doubt, we're now heading in that direction in a big way. Small-space gardening is a rapidly growing specialty. Gardening-supply firms are turning out myriad devices to assist in this approach to home growing, including plant tents, instant greenhouses, vertical grow trees, tomato ladders, and automatic cold frames, to name just a few.

Moreover, in the last few years agricultural experiment stations have stopped devoting all their research to big, commercial-level agriculture and have begun to turn their attention toward small-space-gardening techniques. Out in Utah, for instance, Dr. Frank Williams of Brigham Young University has led the way with research on tiny garden plots ranging in size from 5 by 5 feet to 50 by 50 feet. In universities across the country, many others have followed suit, concentrating on both standard and intensive techniques. And several years ago in South Africa, Pauline Raphaley saved millions from starvation with her door-yard-gardens concept.

I myself became interested in small-space gardening about ten years ago, when I started to investigate the bio-dynamic/French Intensive techniques pioneered by Alan Chadwick. While the Chadwick method certainly increased production many times over, I realized that the orthodox intensive methods were too time-consuming for the average gardener. As a result, in 1975 I modified these techniques for backyard use in *The Postage Stamp Garden Book*. Since that time, thousands have written to tell me that they really are growing a lot more vegetables in a lot less space.

But it was clear to me that even these techniques wouldn't create the home food-growing revolution for which I had hoped. The answer: Make the garden smaller, much smaller; cut down drastically on the work required; and increase production dramatically.

I began to comb the new agricultural experiment station reports. I talked to hundreds of gardeners who were pioneering small-space gardening on their own. I went after bits and pieces of relevant information wherever I could find them.

The results of my search are in this book. It is, in effect, a systematic approach to small-space gardening using wide-row intensive methods (broadcast planting across the bed instead of planting in traditional straight rows), protective devices as season stretchers, and the new vertical-gardening techniques. Put all together, these helpmates easily turn even a 5-by-5-foot flower bed into a family-sized groaning board.

Intensive methods alone can double and triple production. Plant protectors and inexpensive, easy-to-make instant greenhouses will extend the growing season several months on either end. And many of the new vertical devices allow you to grow hundreds of pounds of produce above the ground.

Small-space gardening also has a number of attributes that can't be measured by the pound or by the number of tomatoes or cucumbers produced. Since this approach reduces the amount of work and space involved to child-sized dimensions, it is especially suited to family gardening. Kids quickly lose interest in the tedious work of planting a 15- or 20-foot row of radishes, but they don't at all mind helping to plant a 1-foot-square bed.

Big Yield/Small Space gardening could also become useful to schools that wish to use the vegetable garden as a teaching tool. This type of garden doesn't require as much space or work as a larger conventional or intensive garden; and if protective devices are used, the garden can be planted early enough in the spring to produce a harvest of many vegetables before the end of the term in June.

One of the biggest pluses of small-space gardening, however, may well be the psychological benefits it offers people who ordinarily wouldn't have enough room to grow vegetables. I found this aspect of it invaluable just a few years ago, when I moved a thousand miles from home and rented an old house in a crowded residential area. The only gardening space available was a 4-by-20-foot flower bed spanning the south side of the house. In the spring I dug up 14 feet of this, added massive amounts of organic ingredients and other materials, and proceeded to grow a Big Yield/Small Space intensive garden. In that tiny area I planted over 20 vegetables—corn, acorn squash, tomatoes, zucchini, cucumbers, herbs, and many others. And out of that garden I took a tremendous harvest.

Every day I watered my garden, and sometimes I pulled a few weeds. I frequently started my gardening feeling tense and concerned about mundane problems, but within a few minutes I would completely relax. Over the next few months, as I harvested each crop, I began to feel a deep sense of accomplishment, something I don't always get from day-to-day living. In addition, the garden itself gave me the sensation of being back in step with nature, despite the crowded city conditions around me. Since that time, harried businessmen and businesswomen, overworked homemakers, people from all walks of life have all told me of similar experiences they've had.

Big Yield/Small Space gardening, then, offers many more advantages than just high yields for small areas: it adds a whole new dimension to the efforts of the veteran gardener, yet involves simple techniques for the first-season vegetable grower; and for the millions of us who are feeling the bite of rapidly rising food costs or are faced with very special gardening needs, this approach can become not only the answer to many of our gardening problems but also a supremely satisfying way of life.

CHAPTER ONE

LEADING YOU DOWN THE BIG YIELD/SMALL SPACE GARDEN PATH

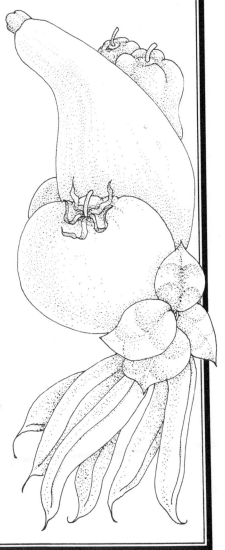

Thanks to much agricultural research and the work of a number of innovative gardeners, home vegetable gardening has undergone a space, method, and quantity revolution. It is now possible for you to duplicate the kinds of harvests previously associated only with suburban or country estates, even if you're a city dweller with a tiny backyard. There are scores of techniques from which to choose; applied in various combinations, they can allow you to fulfill this promise. What follows is a description of the small-space system and its component parts, with an emphasis on the options available to you at each step down the Big Yield/Small Space garden path.

WHAT MAKES THE SYSTEM WORK?

A Good Start   Advance planning along with the proper selection of seed and seedling plants is an initial must. I focus on the various ways to get your vegetables started—indoors and out—since this is the first means by which you can stretch the growing season.

Superfertile Garden Soil   By incorporating massive amounts of organic additives and either organic or inorganic nutrients, you create a special soil that will support maximum growth.

Intensive Planting   Seed is sown across the bed instead of being planted in rows to use every last inch of soil and to grow up to 30 times as many vegetables as you can in the same space in a conventional garden.

Season Extension A variety of protective devices, ranging from inexpensive plastic jugs to elaborate bed-wide greenhouses, enables you to more than double production by extending the season a month or two in both the spring and the fall. And in some areas you can grow crops under simple protective devices all year long.

Full Use of Vertical Space A wide range of innovative supports allows you to take advantage of the unused space above the garden to double and triple vine-crop production.

Container Gardening The dual emphasis here is on personal creativity (identifying nontraditional growing sites on your property where containers can be placed—a patio, for instance) and on the needs of vegetables raised in this manner.

Planting Timetable An overall planting schedule tailored to your individual garden permits you to start seed indoors and transplant or plant at just the right time to obtain maximum production of all vegetables.

Proper Watering and Disease and Pest Control Vegetable gardens thrive when they're cared for properly. I provide basic information on watering and the control of disease and pests, describing also the techniques that are best suited to Big Yield/Small Space gardens.

Growing Your Favorites In this final section you will find advice about the cultivation of more than 40 of the most popular homegrown crops, with an emphasis, once again, on how to raise these the Big Yield/Small Space way. Accompanying tables list hundreds of varieties and suggest catalog seed sources.

THERE'S ALWAYS ROOM FOR VEGETABLES

Now let's take a walk through your yard. Say you have a small house on a narrow lot with a 4-by-10-foot strip of hard-packed dirt down the side of the drive and two 4-by-6-foot sections on either side of the front steps. Or you have a paved-over front yard with three round flower beds, each 4 feet in diameter, a shady, 7-by-20-foot side yard, and a 6-by-10-foot south-facing patio. Nothing here offers any gardening possibilities. Right? Absolutely wrong.

The larger yard has a spacious 88 square feet available for vegetables, the paved yard offers 38 square feet of area, the shady side yard 140 square feet of space that needs help, and the patio enough room for a large raised bed or a whole array of extremely productive containers.

What this example illustrates is that you don't have to grow vegetables in one continuous area. You can break your garden into two, three, or more small plots scattered here and there around the yard. All space counts and, in the long run, can add up to an extremely abundant harvest.

If you take inventory of your outdoor vegetable-gardening space, you should unearth many possibilities. Look first at all the bare areas. These may include a small strip alongside the garage, the middle of a driveway, an unused side yard, or small bare spots around the steps. Next, look at your flower beds. Are you disposed toward replacing your flowers with vegetables or combining the two in the same growing space? Finally, consider your front and back lawns. Are you willing to convert a portion or all of this area to vegetables?

Now calculate the size of each piece of available gardening space in square feet and add these figures together. This is the total area you have for in-the-ground Big Yield/ Small Space gardening.

THINK BEFORE YOU DIG

Before you turn over one spadeful of dirt, you should give careful thought to how big or how small your garden should be and to the types and quantities of vegetables you intend to plant. Consider the number of people in your family, the amount of fresh vegetables you'll consume, your desire for an additional supply to can or freeze, and the amount of work you want to do.

These extra planning moments can save you a whole peck of trouble later on. One gardener I know sat down with a seed catalog in January and ordered her vegetables from the pictures without considering the space she had available. When I saw her in early April, she was standing beside her 6-by-5-foot garden plot trying to decide where to plant the 145 packets of seed she had ordered. Another friend planted 62 zucchini plants in her garden. Later she and her children found themselves peddling "free" zucchini door to door in a wheelbarrow. Still another acquaintance planted his garden with such delicacies as parsnips,

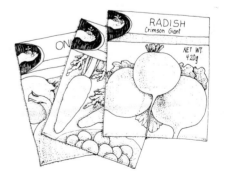

turnips, and kohlrabi. When last heard from, he was trying to dream up exotic recipes for parsnip cookies, turnip cake, and kohlrabi pie so his crops wouldn't go to waste.

As a rule of thumb, a 400-square-foot Big Yield/Small Space garden will produce all the vegetables a family of four to six can use in a year (about 2,000 pounds). You'll also have a surplus of vegetables for canning, freezing, and sharing with friends. A 200-square-foot garden will produce about 1,000 pounds of vegetables—all the fresh produce a family of four can eat during the growing season.

For smaller families, cut your space proportionally, recognizing that if you intend to grow a variety of vegetables, 25 square feet should be the absolute minimum. A 25-square-foot garden will produce between 100 and 200 pounds of vegetables. This will include all the salad fixings a person can eat, plenty of tomatoes in season, and lots of extras besides.

As a general rule, start small. A 25-square-foot garden (5 by 5 feet) makes a good-sized plot for the first year or two. Salad, tomato, and other specialty gardens, of course, can be grown in much smaller areas. After that, let your experience and preferences be your guide as to exactly what size area is right for you.

CONSIDERING THE COSTS

Big Yield/Small Space gardening can be an inexpensive or a costly endeavor, depending on your personal needs and financial situation.

Since I am essentially thrifty, I try to keep my costs as low as possible. In my last garden I spent a total of $11 for both seed and necessary materials. To protect my plants from frost, I used cutoff 1-gallon plastic milk jugs.

If you're starting from scratch, of course, you'll have to anticipate a more substantial investment than this. Figure a minimum of $6 to $20 for seed, depending on the size of your garden and the number of vegetables you intend to plant, and another $5 to $20 for materials to improve your soil (see Chapter 3). These are rock-bottom costs for starting a vegetable garden if you already own your tools and use scrap materials for other Big Yield/Small Space needs.

As you will see in this book, however, many commercial products to save you time or help you garden more efficiently are now on the market. Such items as seedling start-er kits, grow lights, plastic protective devices, power tools, and elaborate vertical structures can easily run the cost of gardening up to a one-time expense of several hundred dollars.

In reality, it's all a trade-off. Some gardeners want to spend the least amount of money possible and are willing to put in the additional work this might entail. Others would rather invest in sophisticated equipment so they have time to pursue other interests. Still others will spring for such items as raised beds, expensive watering systems, and elaborate vertical structures to simplify the gardening process or to improve their gardens' appearance or yield.

In the remainder of this book, you will be offered many alternatives. All will help you grow an extremely pro-ductive Big Yield/Small Space garden, regardless of how much money you spend. You alone will have to decide what you want to do with your own garden and which methods or pieces of equipment best fit your individual require-ments.

THE TIME INVESTMENT

Most of your gardening time will be devoted to preparation and planting. As a rough guide, figure on spending about 40 minutes to 1 hour to prepare a 100-square-foot garden by hand, 20 minutes with a power tool. Allow 1 hour for initial intensive planting and 30 minutes a week for culti-vation and watering. These tasks will take about three or four times longer for a 400-square-foot garden.

Because of its size, the Big Yield/Small Space garden takes less time to dig and plant than a conventional garden. Moreover, it needs less weeding because the intensive plant-ing of vegetables creates a leafy canopy that shades out most weeds as the vegetables approach maturity. I like to spend a little time each day in my garden as a break from other activities, but this isn't necessary except under un-usual circumstances.

WHAT WILL YOUR GARDEN GROW?

To determine what vegetables to plant and in what quan-tities, consider first what your family likes to eat. It's amaz-ing how many gardeners have ignored this commonsense approach. They've ended up with great quantities of brussels sprouts, for instance, that only one family member enjoys.

In addition, plant small quantities of those vegetables that outproduce your capacity to consume them. Lettuce, radishes, and summer squash typically fall into this category. A few leaf lettuce plants will easily stay ahead of your needs if you harvest a few leaves as you need them; and just three or four zucchini plants will produce enough fruits to drive you out of house and home. Appendix D lists information about the yields and space requirements of specific vegetables. Consider your family's preferences and subtract or add to these amounts accordingly.

LOCATION LOGISTICS

Here are some basics to consider when you're deciding where to do your actual growing.

First, locate your vegetable plots where they are not shaded by buildings or trees. They'll do best if they receive full sun for at least 6 hours a day. It is especially important for vegetables that produce "fruit," such as tomatoes, cucumbers, squash, eggplant, peppers, and corn, to receive this kind of exposure. (Just think of them as sun worshipers.) Many of the leafy vegetables, such as spinach and lettuce, can get by in semishade. If out of necessity you must garden in areas that are shaded most of the day, see Chapter 5 for a discussion of ways to reflect light and heat in such locations.

When possible, keep your garden at least 20 feet away from tall trees. They cast unwanted shade and compete for many needed nutrients as well. Generally, tree roots take food from the soil in a circle as far out as the tree's widest-reaching branches. Within this circle, plants often do poorly.

Avoid low, wet areas that are slow to dry in the spring, those that have a serious weed problem (such as a heavy infestation of crabgrass), and steep slopes. If you must garden on a slope, terrace and run the rows at right angles to the slope. In an uneven area, the rows should follow the contour of the slope.

Place your garden as close to the water supply as possible. It's also sensible to locate it near your tool-storage area and not too far from the house.

A major key to your success will be locating your Big Yield/Small Space garden along a fence or against the side of a building if possible. This will provide a ready-made vertical support for the vine crops that can double and triple your harvest.

The Big Yield/Small Space system provides ways to use virtually any available space regardless of the problems it presents, even if you have to violate one or several of the above rules. The solutions to many location dilemmas are described in Chapters 5 and 6.

START WITH A PAPER GARDEN

Your Big Yield/Small Space garden should turn out an almost endless supply of food 6 to 12 months out of the year. Before you plant you should decide such basics as the amount of space you intend to devote to each vegetable, where each will be located, the quantities you want to grow of each vegetable, the size and shape your garden will be, and when you intend to plant.

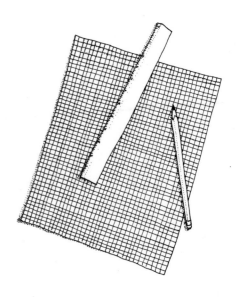

Always begin by putting your garden plan on paper. Some gardeners draw this plan to scale (for example, making ¼ inch equal 1 foot), which allows them to allocate space accurately. Others simply draw a rough sketch and go from there. Personally, I like to use graph paper because it enables me to see at a glance precisely how much space I'm using.

Sample Gardens

Figures 1–1, 1–2, and 1–3 show three plans you can use in your own garden. Each plan has a design for spring/summer and one for fall/winter. They are included here to help you start putting the basic Big Yield/Small Space concept to use right now. There are, however, many possible variations. The size, shape, and quantities of vegetables you grow, the types of vertical support you use, and the ways you choose to modify climate conditions all depend on your own individual circumstances. These variables will be covered in detail in Chapters 2, 5, and 6.

VEGETABLE FACTORY 25 SQ. FT. GARDEN

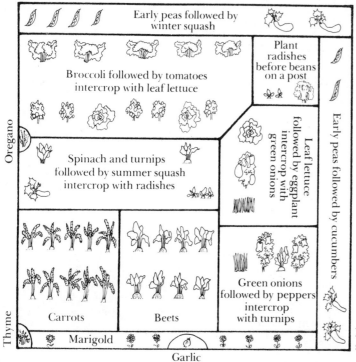

Oregano

Thyme

Early peas followed by winter squash

Broccoli followed by tomatoes intercrop with leaf lettuce

Plant radishes before beans on a post

Leaf lettuce followed by eggplant intercrop with green onions

Early peas followed by cucumbers

Spinach and turnips followed by summer squash intercrop with radishes

Carrots

Beets

Green onions followed by peppers intercrop with turnips

Marigold

Garlic

Fig. 1–1 Sample 25-sq.-ft. garden— spring/summer.

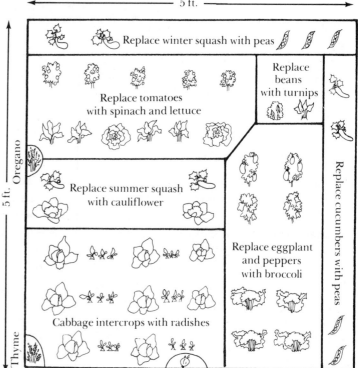

5 ft.

5 ft.

Oregano

Thyme

Replace winter squash with peas

Replace tomatoes with spinach and lettuce

Replace beans with turnips

Replace summer squash with cauliflower

Replace eggplant and peppers with broccoli

Replace cucumbers with peas

Cabbage intercrops with radishes

Garlic

Fig. 1–1 Sample 25-sq.-ft. garden fall/winter.

VEGETABLE FACTORY 100 SQ. FT. GARDEN

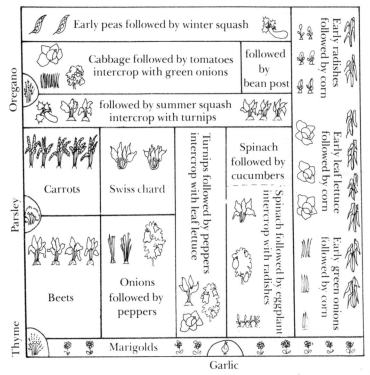

Fig. 1–2 Sample 100-sq.-ft. garden spring/summer.

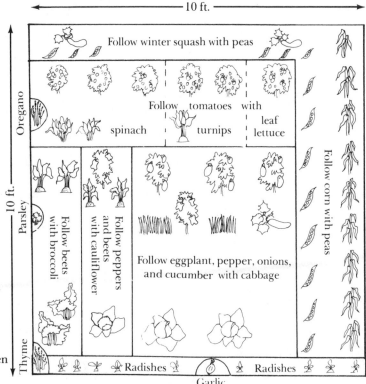

Fig. 1–2 Sample 100-sq.-ft. garden fall/winter.

VEGETABLE FACTORY 80 SQ. FT. GARDEN

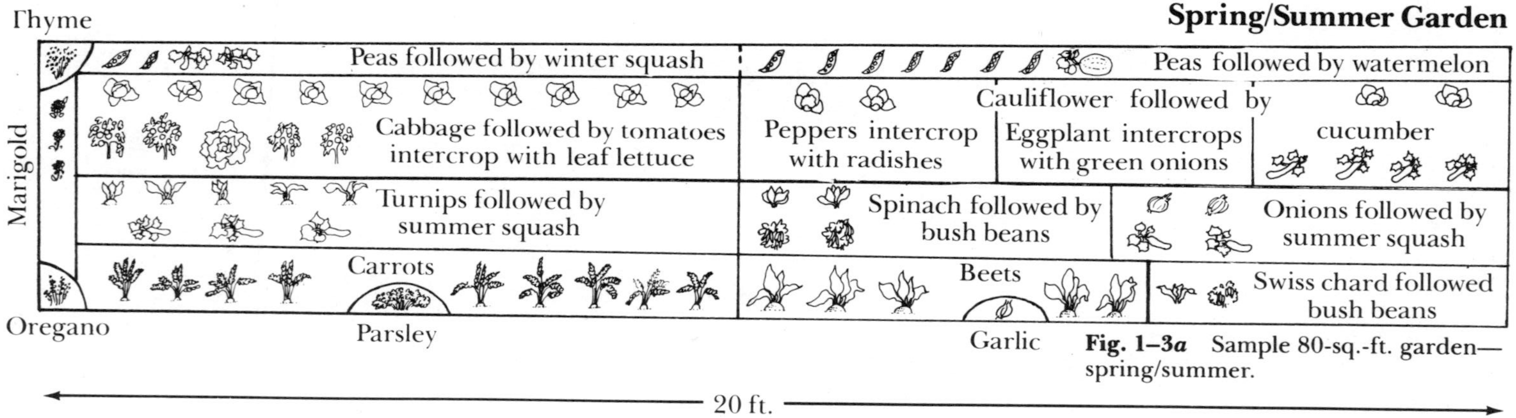

Spring/Summer Garden

Thyme

Marigold

Oregano

Peas followed by winter squash

Cabbage followed by tomatoes intercrop with leaf lettuce

Turnips followed by summer squash

Carrots

Parsley

Peas followed by watermelon

Cauliflower followed by cucumber

Peppers intercrop with radishes

Eggplant intercrops with green onions

Spinach followed by bush beans

Onions followed by summer squash

Swiss chard followed by bush beans

Beets

Garlic

Fig. 1–3a Sample 80-sq.-ft. garden—spring/summer.

20 ft.

In between Fall/Winter Garden

Thyme

Oregano

Follow tomatoes with cabbage

Follow summer squash, carrots with broccoli

Parsley

Follow summer squash and watermelon with peas

Follow eggplant, pepper, onions, and cucumber with cabbage

Follow bush beans with chinese cabbage

Follow beets with lettuce

Follow summer squash with turnips

Follow bush beans with spinach

Garlic

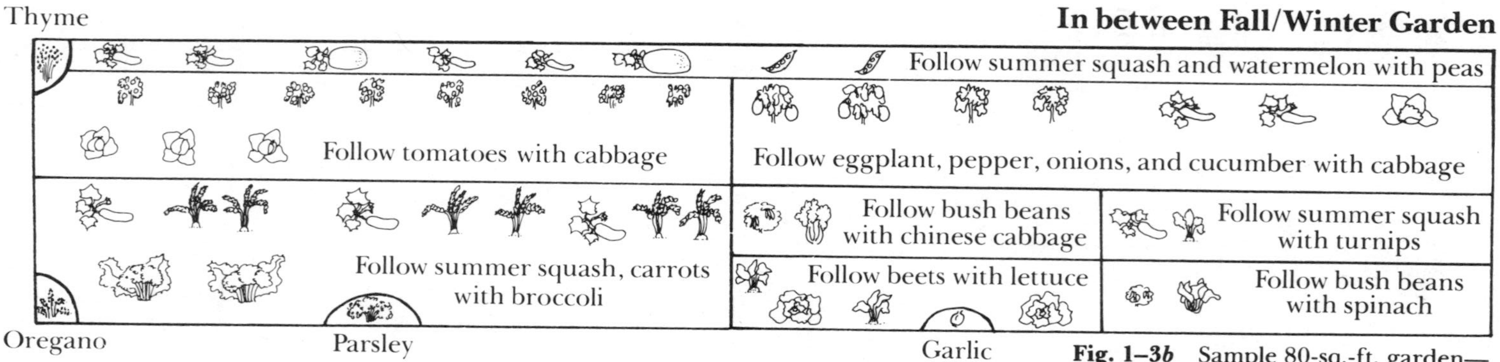

Fig. 1–3b Sample 80-sq.-ft. garden—fall/winter.

BIG YIELD/SMALL SPACE CHRONOLOGY

You enter the Big Yield/Small Space garden path one step at a time, so here, in general outline, is the basic production schedule that makes this approach work:

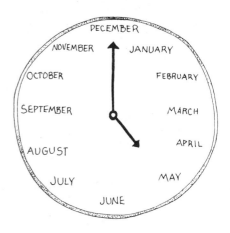

Step 1: Plan your garden. Lay out your space exactly. Decide how many plants of each vegetable you need.

Step 2: Check your catalogs and order the appropriate varieties or buy from the seed racks at your local nursery.

Step 3: Create your planting timetable, taking into consideration in-the-ground, vertical, and container possibilities.

Step 4: Begin indoor planting.

Step 5: Make up your Big Yield/Small Space soil or reconstitute your beds.

Step 6: Plant seeds and seedlings the intensive way on the dates you have established.

Step 7: Put protective season-stretching devices in place to get an early start or to provide optimum growing conditions for certain vegetables.

Step 8: Remove devices as the weather warms up.

Step 9: Harvest, reconstitute the beds, and replant.

PLANTING POINTERS

Following the aforementioned instructions puts the system into successful operation, but you can do even more to guarantee a maximum yield from the space you use. I advise three specific planting techniques that home growers have perfected over the years. These are effective because they keep your entire gardening space in production throughout the full growing season:

1   *Interplanting,* or placing quick-maturing vegetables between more widely spaced, slower-maturing varieties (see Chapter 11 for days to maturity and spacing advice for each vegetable)
2   *Succession planting,* which means sowing a new crop as soon as the first one is harvested

3 *Catch cropping,* which consists of planting quick-maturing vegetables in a spot where you have just harvested slower-maturing varieties

It's also wise to rotate your crops (for example, plant beans where you've just harvested cabbage) to protect your soil. Some vegetables, known as *heavy feeders,* make especially substantial demands on the basic soil nutrients, while others actually enrich your growing environment. (See Table 1–1 for a listing of heavy, medium, and light feeders so you can plan accurately.)

What you now have is a sense of the basics. Some of these are age-old approaches. Others, such as intensive planting, vertical gardening, and season stretching, are just beginning to come into popular use, especially in various combinations.

In the succeeding chapters you will find detailed instructions and suggestions about each of these topics, all meant to ease your journey down the Big Yield/Small Space garden path. So let's begin—as your vegetables will—with seeds and seedlings.

TABLE 1–1. VEGETABLE FERTILIZER REQUIREMENTS

HEAVY FEEDERS	MEDIUM FEEDERS	LIGHT FEEDERS	SOIL RESTORERS
Artichokes	Asparagus	Beets	Beans*
Cabbage	Broccoli	Carrots	Peas*
Celery	Cantaloupes	Radishes	
Sweet Potatoes	Corn	Rutabagas	
Tomatoes	Cucumbers	Turnips	
	Eggplant		
	Herbs		
	Kale		
	Mustard		
	Okra		
	Onions		
	Pumpkins		
	Rhubarb		
	Squash		
	Swiss Chard		
	Watermelons		

*Beans and peas help improve soil fertility. The bacteria living in the nodules on the roots of legumes take soil nitrogen in unusable forms and combine it with sugars from the legumes to produce ammonia, a nitrogen compound that plants can use. Legumes thus conserve and restore the soil.

CHAPTER TWO
SEED AND
SEEDLING SORCERY

Many people find that getting vegetables started from seed and seedlings is the most difficult part of the entire growing process. Therefore, this initial step deserves our full attention. I'll be describing the alternatives open to you in terms of where and what to buy. Then you'll find guidelines on the planting methods available, each of which is suitable for a specific set of vegetables.

There are three basic ways to begin the planting process:

1   By sowing seeds directly into the soil
2   By starting your vegetables as seedlings purchased at the nursery and then placed in the garden
3   By starting seeds indoors and then transplanting the seedlings when the weather warms up

Since this last method is generally the most unfamiliar and serves as an ideal season stretcher, I'll describe it in some detail.

If you follow the directions in this chapter, you'll be well on your way to harvesting an initial crop of root and leafy vegetables just at the time your neighbors are turning over their first shovelfuls of dirt for their conventional spring gardens.

IT ALL BEGINS WITH SEED AND SEEDLINGS

It's best to purchase *nursery seedling plants* if you want to cut several weeks off the required growing time and do not need a wide selection of varieties (see Table 2–1). Most nurseries offer tomatoes, cabbage, cauliflower, brussels sprouts, eggplant, peppers, onions, lettuce, squash, melons, cucumbers, and similar seedlings, but have restricted their selection to one or two varieties of each vegetable.

Fortunately, this situation is improving. Some nurseries now sell, for example, 10 to 15 tomato varieties, but the selection in many places is still severely limited. Many growers and garden centers now label plants with variety names; others simply label their plants "cabbage," "watermelon,"

TABLE 2–1. METHODS OF STARTING VEGETABLES

METHOD	TYPE OF VEGETABLE	
Start directly from seed in garden	Beets Carrots Corn Salad Cress, Garden Okra	Parsnips Rutabagas Salsify Turnips
Start indoors, transplant to garden	Broccoli Brussels Sprouts Cabbage Cardoon Cauliflower Celeriac	Celery Eggplant Florence Fennel Peppers Tomatoes
Start indoors or outdoors	Chinese Cabbage Chard Collards Corn, Sweet Dandelion Endive/Escarole	Kale Kohlrabi Leeks Lettuce Mustard
Start from seed in garden or start indoors *individually* in biodegradable containers to protect sensitive root systems	Beans Cucumbers Muskmelons Peas	Pumpkins Squash Watermelons
Start in other ways	Artichokes: start from root divisions Asparagus: start from 1-year-old roots Garlic: start from cloves Horseradish: start from root cuttings Onions: start from sets, seeds, or small plants Potatoes: start from potato pieces	Rhubarb: set out root crowns Shallots: start from cloves Sweet Potatoes: start from slip transplants obtained from nurseries or seed catalog firms

and so on. These "generic" vegetables will usually produce good results in local gardens, though, so go ahead and buy them unless you are looking for vegetables with specific qualities (tomatoes suited for growing in containers, for instance).

When you buy seedling plants, select healthy-looking, compact, dark green, full-foliage specimens with well-branched stems. Yellow or pale plants indicate a nutrition deficiency, neglect, or overhardening. Wilted plants or plants with dead leaf tips indicate that the plants have been allowed to dry out. Torn leaves and damaged plants indicate poor handling. Insect-infested plants (look under the leaves) can infest other plants in your garden. Tall, spindly plants generally have root systems that are poor in relation to their top growth.

Plants purchased from a flat or in plant packs generally cost less than, and grow just as well as, seedlings grown singly in pots. Squash, melons, cucumbers, and similar seedling plants must be started individually in peat pots, however, so they can be transplanted into the ground without their roots being disturbed.

Shop the *seed racks* if you need a wider choice than is available in seedlings but still intend to plant fairly standard varieties. Since the vegetable-garden explosion, seed-rack selections have improved. You can often find the more unusual varieties, the new hybrid seeds, and even a wide selection of oriental vegetables in the racks.

Local seed racks usually contain varieties that grow nicely in your area. Companies sometimes include nationally known varieties, however, that may not adapt well to your climate (see the discussion of variety selection in this chapter).

Every seed-rack package lists the variety name, the disease resistance (if any), the number of days to maturity, bare-bones planting instructions, and an expiration date. Make sure you check this expiration date before purchasing your seed. Companies usually change the seed packages seasonally, but sometimes old seed can stay on the rack. In addition, some seeds, such as onions, are short-lived and should be planted as soon as possible.

Most seed is chemically treated with a fungicide to prevent damping off (rotting of the seed or emerging seedlings) and other problems. If you garden organically and

want untreated seed, you can obtain it from Johnny's Selected Seeds, Nichols Garden Nursery, and several other firms (see Appendix E).

You can also obtain pelleted seed, which has been coated with fertilizer, fungicide, and inert material to make the seed larger and easier to handle. Pelleted seed is available from catalog firms and some seed racks.

Seed tapes are gaining in popularity. These are made from a water-soluble material into which the seeds are inserted at equal intervals. The distance between the seeds depends on the spacing needs of that particular vegetable. Available in 10- to 15-foot lengths for outdoor planting, seed tapes allow vigorous seedlings to emerge without crowding, eliminate the need for thinning, and permit sowing in straight rows. You can purchase tapes featuring such special collections as a full-season lettuce garden (a set of lettuce varieties that reach maturity over an extended period of time) or a children's minigarden (an assortment of easy-to-grow vegetables for kids).

Tapes for sowing seeds in flats (shallow boxes in which plants are grown together) are also available in 3-foot lengths with seeds spaced at ½- or 1-inch intervals. This prespacing reduces the difficulty of sowing seeds evenly and gives each plant adequate growing space.

Shop *seed stores* if you want a wide selection and a different experience. Although you won't find as many bulk-seed stores around today as you did a few years ago, they still exist in some areas. These stores offer a far greater variety than is available from nursery seed racks; they generally sell in bulk from rows and rows of drawers and seed bins. Many offer seed through catalogs. Two of the better-known firms are Rocky Mountain Seed Company and Nichols Garden Nursery (see Appendix E).

Mail-order seed companies that also have seed stores are designated by *R* (retail store) in the catalog seed sources list in Appendix E. You'll find seed stores in your area listed under "Seeds" in the telephone-directory yellow pages. Unfortunately, many metropolitan areas no longer have a seed store in the vicinity. If yours does, it is well worth a visit.

Order from *seed catalogs* when you are looking for a large seed selection or a specialized variety. Catalog firms offer many specialties from which to choose.

New Introductions Plant breeders at the state experimental stations, the U.S. Department of Agriculture, and seed companies are constantly developing new varieties. Many of these have been bred for traits most useful to commercial agriculture (such as the ability to ship well) and are not offered to the home gardener, but those varieties deemed suitable for home gardens and offered for sale by seed companies (such as Sugar Snap peas) are often spectacular. Practically every seed company offers new varieties each year.

All-America Selections All-America Vegetable Selections are sponsored by an organization called All-America Selections. The 35 to 70 new vegetable varieties introduced each year are grown in 50 different test gardens across the United States, then are evaluated by a panel of judges. Every season, 3 or 4 of these new varieties are selected for the bronze, silver, and gold All-America medals. To be selected for All-America honors, a vegetable must have superior qualities and be adapted to a wide range of soil and climates. All-America Selections are noted in seed catalogs by the letters *AAS*.

Special-Quality Varieties and Catalog Specialties Many catalogs single out vegetable varieties with special qualities—the sweetest, the largest, the best flavored, the easiest to grow in home gardens, and so forth. Burgess Seed and Plant Company notes these special varieties as "Best of Burgess"; the W. Atlee Burpee Company marks theirs with a bull's-eye.

Most seed firms also feature special varieties sold exclusively by them. Examples are the large 1- to 2-pound Abraham Lincoln tomato sold exclusively by R. H. Shumway Seedsman and the Vigor Boy tomato, a heavy-yield variety offered only by Gurney Seed and Nursery Company.

Midgets, Novelties, Oriental Vegetables, Others Most firms now offer an extensive number of midget varieties of cabbage, cucumbers, carrots, corn, eggplant, melons, and tomatoes. Of special interest are the many new icebox-type (small) watermelons. Seed firms also feature an ever-growing list of oriental, French, Italian, and gourmet varieties.

Special Collections Many catalogs list special seed collections that you may want to investigate. Burgess Seed and Plant Company, for example, offers a small-space collection, a canning and freezing collection, an all-seasons pea collection, a carrot collection, and more.

Catalogs explain whether a variety is a hybrid (denoted by the word *hybrid* or *Fl. hybrid*). Hybrids are a cross between two parents of different types, each parent having its own particular qualities. Catalogs also note which varieties are disease resistant.

Each catalog has its own personality. The Burgess Seed and Plant Company offers many unusual vegetables; W. Atlee Burpee Company has one of the most complete catalogs. Thompson and Morgan, whose agents comb the world for seeds, lists some 3,000 varieties. J. A. Demonchaux offers French varieties; R. H. Shumway Seedsman publishes a catalog with an "old-time" format. Seed catalogs are listed and briefly described in Appendix E.

WHAT VARIETIES SHOULD YOU CHOOSE?

Obviously, you need to select the varieties of vegetables that grow best for you. This will require a certain amount of experimentation in your garden. Some general guidelines will help you to make wise choices from the beginning.

If you have a disease problem in your area, choose varieties that are disease resistant. This information is noted in most catalogs. The salesperson at the nursery can alert you to local disease problems.

In areas experiencing long, hot summers, stretch the season by planting both early- and late-maturing varieties. If you live in a northern area, choose short-season varieties of tomatoes, corn, peppers, and vine crops. Regional seed companies often specialize in varieties suited to particular areas. Stokes Seeds offers varieties for northern climates. Rocky Mountain Seed Company features varieties for the intermountain West. Roswell Seed Company sells varieties with special adaptability to the Southwest.

Also consider varieties with special qualities. There are, for example, over 500 tomato varieties. Some are especially suited to containers; some are small fruited; some have orange, yellow, white, or pear-shaped fruit; some have fruit in the large 1- to 2-pound range. Many other vegetables offer similar choices. You will find these varieties available through individual catalogs. Variety-comparison charts and sources can also be found in *The Complete Vegetable Gardener's Sourcebook.*

New varieties are listed in the catalogs each year. You should plan to try some of these along with the old standbys. Many are especially suited for home gardens, such as Sugar Snap peas, which can be eaten in the pod; early butternut squash, which matures in about 85 days and produces 3½-pound fruits; and Dutch Treat sweet yellow peppers, which are ready to eat before most other pepper varieties mature. These three are personal favorites of mine.

Another source of vegetable-variety information is the list published by each state of vegetables recommended for local gardens. You can obtain a copy of the list for your area by calling your local county extension agent (check the telephone-directory white pages) or by writing to your state's Cooperative Extension Service (see Appendix G). Your county agent can also recommend additional varieties especially suited to your particular climate.

STARTING SEEDLINGS INDOORS

You can get a jump on vegetable production by weeks and even months if you start as many vegetables as possible indoors ahead of the season and modify your outdoor climate so you can transplant the seedlings directly into your garden several months early. To use this system effectively, you must know exactly when to plant vegetables indoors; this way, you'll be sure to move them into your Big Yield/ Small Space beds at the best possible time.

There are two major methods by which to start your seedlings. Both are described in detail below.

The One-Step Method

With the one-step method, sow seeds directly in a small pot or cube made of biodegradable materials. When seedlings reach transplant size, they're placed in the garden, pots and all. The roots then grow through the pot walls and spread into the surrounding soil (see Figure 2–1).

This procedure prevents the root shock that can occur upon transplanting. Large-seeded plants, such as squash, cucumber, and melons, should always be planted this way,

Fig. 2–1   The One-Step Method

Sow seed into a small biodegradable pot or cube.

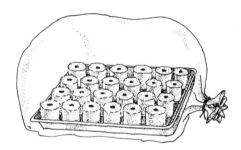

Keep damp but not soaked. Cover with plastic and keep at room temperature in a bright area out of direct sunlight.

When plants are 4 to 6 in. high, they are ready to harden off and transplant into the garden.

Fig. 2–2　Containers for Starting Seeds

Plantable cubes of peat moss are both pot and soil. Some also contain nutrients.

Pressed-peat pots come round or square, individually or in strips of 6 or 12.

Jiffy-7 pellets, peat cubes reinforced with plastic netting, are small and dry until ready to use. They expand to 2 in. when dampened.

Wood or plastic flats or trays are used extensively.

since their root systems do not take well to transplanting. Also use this method to grow the bigger vegetables, such as tomatoes, eggplant, and peppers. The individual pots will allow your seedlings to become larger and more vigorous than they would if grown together in a flat or similar container.

Several kinds of containers can be used for transplanting (see Figure 2–2). *Jiffy-7 pellets* are compressed, sterile sphagnum peat, soil, and fertilizer enclosed in a plastic net. When placed in water, the pellets expand to form small containers. *Jiffy-7 trays,* prepackaged pellets in plastic trays, are convenient because you simply add water to the tray and the pellets expand to full size, ready to plant. The pellets can also be watered directly in the tray without danger of spillage.

Jiffy-9 pellets are held together with a binder instead of a net. When planted in the garden, they will disintegrate faster than Jiffy-7 pellets. *Jiffy-7 special pellets* come with preformed ¼-inch holes and are useful for starting cuttings of tomatoes.

BR 8 Blocks and *Ky Kubes* are fiber blocks or cubes containing fertilizer. *Fertil-cubes* are made from a blend of mosses, plant food, and vermiculite (mineral mica expanded by high heat). Each cube has a depression for planting the seed. Also available is a do-it-yourself kit that allows you to make your own compressed-peat containers.

Peat pots are hollow containers made of compressed fiber. These should be filled with synthetic soil and the seeds planted directly into that soil. Pots are square or round; the square ones come in multiple break-apart strips.

Cell pots or *Cell-Paks* are light plastic pots that you fill with synthetic soil for growing individual pop-out transplants. These pots are often used with a plastic tray and come as single cells or in units of 2, 3, 4, 6, or 12 cells. Large sizes are also offered.

All of the above planting containers are satisfactory for use in Big Yield/Small Space gardens. The soil mix (synthetic soil) you use in them, however, makes a tremendous difference in seedling development. A recent study using tomato plants showed that seedlings planted in ordinary potting mix grew 1 inch in six weeks, while plants grown in Cornell or University of California mix grew 6 inches in six weeks. The recipe for the Cornell mix appears in Table 2–2.

Here are instructions for the one-step method of planting:

1   Choose any of the above containers that appeals to you. (I find the cubes and pellets easiest to work with.) Fill the cubes, biodegradable pots, or plastic cell pots with synthetic soil, which you can mix yourself or purchase at any nursery.

2   Dampen the cubes or synthetic soil (Jiffy-7 cubes need to be thoroughly watered or placed in water so they will expand).

3   Sow the seeds directly into your cubes, peat pots, or cell pots.

4   Place the containers on a tray and put the tray and containers inside a clear plastic bag. Blow up the bag like a balloon and secure the end with a plant tie.

5   Keep the bag at room temperature in a bright area but out of direct sunlight. Keep the containers damp but not soaked.

6   When the plants are 4 to 7 inches high, they are ready to be hardened off and planted in your garden. *Hardening off* means getting an indoor-grown seedling used to outdoor weather by gradual exposure to the outdoor garden environment.

Fig. 2–2 *(continued)*

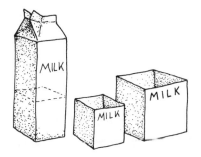

Quart or half-gallon milk cartons cut about 3 in. high make excellent seed starters. Tear carton from soil ball when transplanting to avoid disturbing the roots.

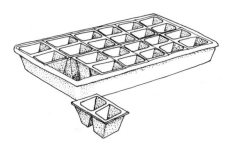

Handi-Paks and Cell-Paks, commercial devices ideal for seed germination, hold Jiffy pellets.

TABLE 2–2. CORNELL–UNIVERSITY OF CALIFORNIA MIX

The two most popular of the many synthetic commercial potting mixes were perfected at Cornell University and the University of California. You can buy modified versions of the Cornell mix under the names Pro Mix, Jiffy Mix, and Redi-Earth. The University of California mix is sold as First Step and Supersoil.

If you'd like to try your hand at playing creator, here's a home gardener's version of the Cornell mix:

Vermiculite	8 quarts
Shredded peat moss	8 quarts
Superphosphate	2 level tablespoons
Limestone	2 tablespoons
Dried cow manure or steamed bone meal	8 tablespoons

Measure and place all ingredients in a plastic garbage-can liner. Shake vigorously.

Fig. 2–3   The Two-Step Method

Step One

Fill container with soil and level off
with knife or stick.

Make furrows with pencil and plant
your seeds. Be sure the medium is
thoroughly damp before planting.

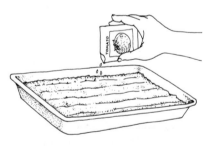

Slip the flat into a plastic bag and keep
at about 75 degrees F. No water is necessary until after seedlings appear.
Then keep damp, not soaked.

The Two-Step Method

For the two-step method, first sow the seeds in plastic flats or half flats, aluminum cake or meat-loaf pans, milk cartons, large frozen-food containers, cutoff gallon bleach jugs, or any similar containers. After leaves have begun to show, gently pick the seedlings out and place each in its own individual pot (see Figure 2–3).

Use this method when you intend to grow large quantities of small vegetables, such as onions or lettuce. You can also start cabbage, broccoli, cauliflower and brussels sprouts this way. Squash, melons, cucumbers, pumpkins, peas, and beans should not be planted together in large containers, however, because their roots cannot take the shock when they are later transplanted into the garden.

Step One

1   Fill the container with the soil mixture. Level it off with a flat knife or stick, then lightly press down the remaining soil.
2   Make furrows with a pencil or similar small tool.
3   Sow the seeds about an inch apart and water lightly. As I already mentioned, seed tapes automatically provide the desired spacing. Sow more seeds than the number of plants you need, and when they come up, thin out the smaller, less vigorous plants by clipping with a small pair of scissors.
4   Slip the trays into a clear plastic bag and keep as close to 75 degrees F. as possible. Don't water again until after germination, that is, until the little sprouts poke through. After that, add only enough water to keep the soil mix damp. Check by feeling the mix with your fingers; when it starts to dry out, add just enough water to dampen it again.

Step Two

1   When the first true leaves have formed, dig out the seedlings and plant them in individual clay or plastic pots. The first two leaflike growths are not actual leaves; the third and succeeding ones are.
2   Transfer the seedlings into your garden when they are 5 to 6 inches high.

For maximum seed germination, as stated above, soil temperature should be kept at around 75 degrees F. The air temperature for seedling growth should be from 70 to 75 degrees during the day, 60 to 65 degrees during the night. Seedlings need approximately 12 hours of light a day and a relative humidity of about 80 percent for optimum growth.

You can meet these conditions by placing the seedlings in a clear plastic bag and keeping them in a bright spot. Direct sunlight, though, can cause the temperature within the bag to become too high. After the seedlings have become fairly well established, you can remove them from the bag and allow them to grow in a window facing south.

There are also a number of commercial devices on the market designed to help you maintain the optimum conditions for seed germination. Several companies offer vegetable-seed starter kits, which take some of the guesswork out of starting seedlings. These kits vary from containers already planted with vegetable seeds to complete sets with cubes, fertilizer trays, heating cables, and clear plastic tops to keep in moisture. Also available are a number of plastic tabletop greenhouses, trays equipped with soil-heater cables, and combinations of both (see Figure 2–4).

Fig. 2–3 *(continued)*

Step Two

When the first true leaf is formed, move seedlings to 3- or 4-in. peat or plastic pots filled with soil mix.

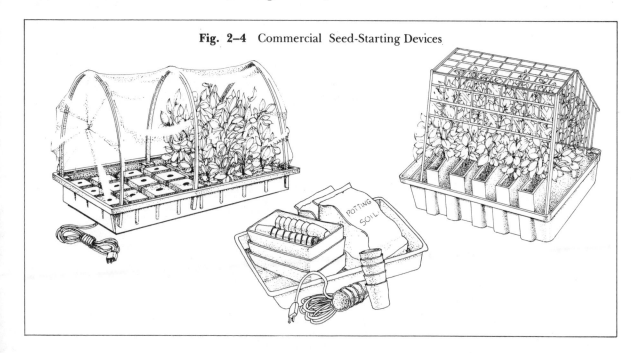

Fig. 2–4 Commercial Seed-Starting Devices

GROWING SEEDLINGS UNDER LIGHTS

One of the best ways to start seedlings is to grow them under fluorescent lights (see Figure 2–5). Because fluorescent lamps provide both heat for sprouting seeds and light for growing seedlings, they give you a high degree of positive control. Generally you can grow seedlings successfully with two 40-watt cool-white fluorescent bulbs. Both bulbs and fixtures are available at most electrical and home-center stores.

The General Electric Bright Stik is the easiest fluorescent to use. Simply plug it in and place in a bookcase, inside a cabinet, or above a shelf. No additional fixtures are needed. You might also want to look into the specially designed fluorescent starting units that can be purchased through catalog seed firms. They can be set up on a table, a desk, a workbench—almost anywhere that's handy.

To sprout seeds, position your seed pans, cubes, or pots 3 to 4 inches below the tubes, then burn the lights constantly until the seedlings emerge. Once they have sprouted, place the seedlings 6 to 12 inches from the tubes. If you move the lights too far from the seedlings, the light intensity will fall off, causing the plants to become spindly.

For maximum production, give your seedlings from 12 to 16 hours of light a day. An inexpensive timer will take

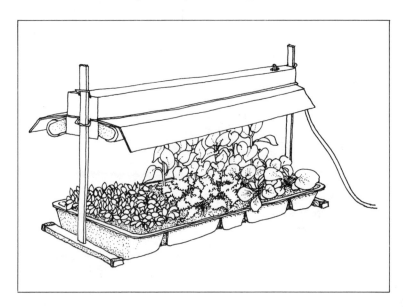

Fig. 2–5 Growing seedlings under light.

the work out of turning the tubes on and off and automatically give your seedlings the correct amount of light every day.

HARDENING OFF YOUR TRANSPLANTS

Whether you purchase plants from a nursery or start them indoors, it takes about a week to get them adjusted to the outdoors. When they are about ready to be transplanted into your garden, slow down their growth by giving them half their normal water supply. Then, for four to five days before planting, take them out during the daytime and bring them back inside at night. You can also harden seedlings outside by placing a plastic cover or a cardboard box over the plants at night.

TRANSPLANTING SEEDLINGS

Dig holes for your transplants in your Big Yield/Small Space garden. Fill the holes with water, letting it soak in. Water the seedlings thoroughly before removing them from their flats. If some of your seedlings are planted in peat pots or cubes, soak these until they are moist and soft.

If you are transplanting from a flat or a container planted with two or more seedlings, carefully separate the root ball of each plant. If plants are in individual pots and are root bound, trim off the long roots and rough up the outer roots of the root ball with your hand. If you have uncovered the roots of any plant and don't intend to transplant it immediately, cover the soil ball with a damp cloth or damp soil to keep from damaging the feeder roots.

Trim off about half the leaves of large transplants, being careful not to trim the central growing tip. Set the plants at the same height in your beds as they were growing in the soil. Planting too deeply can stop the growth of most plants.

Starting vegetables indoors is but one means of extending the growing season. In the next chapter we will explore how to improve the soil environment so that the fruits—or more accurately, the vegetables—of your labor will have maximum opportunity to thrive.

CHAPTER THREE

BIG YIELD/SMALL SPACE SOIL FUNDAMENTALS

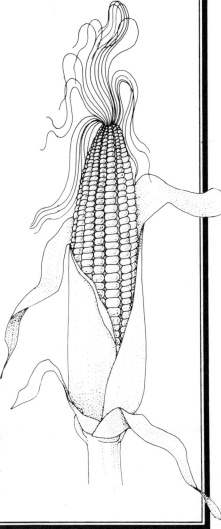

Practically no garden soil is as perfect as it could be, at least not in the beginning. Take a look at a few vegetable gardens. Say the plants in one garden are stunted, the leaves of the vegetables in another have turned partly yellow, and still another produces an extremely small yield for the space used. No matter what problems you encounter, most can be traced to one source: poor soil and lack of proper nutrients.

At this point, the odds are that your soil is far from ideal. Perhaps it's too hard, or it contains too many rocks and pebbles, or it's too sandy. Whatever the condition, however, there's a way to overcome it. In this chapter I'll describe how you can create Big Yield/Small Space supersoil that will give your vegetables the best possible conditions for growth with the least amount of work for you.

THE RAW MATERIAL

The untreated soil in most gardens falls into one or a combination of the following types:

Clay

Clay soil is composed of fine, flat, waferlike particles that fit together tightly and take water in slowly. Chemically, clay is primarily silicon and aluminum along with small amounts of sodium, magnesium, iron, calcium, and potassium.

Once the clay particles absorb moisture, they hold it so tightly that it is almost impossible for vegetables to use it. There is no air space. When clay dries, it is difficult to work, and plant roots have a hard time penetrating it and growing.

Sandy Soil

The particles in sandy soil are at least 25 times larger than those found in clay. Pure sand, while high in mineral content, contains almost no nutrients and has no capacity to store moisture. Air penetrates deeply and water moves through rapidly, dissolving away many of the nutrients. Unless you live in a desert region, you will find sand combined with some clay, gravel, and silt.

Silt

Silt represents an intermediate stage between clay and sand. Silt particles pack down hard, almost like clay. Topsoils of this variety are often not very fertile.

Loam

Loam is a combination of clay, sand, and a generous supply of *humus*, a decomposed organic material. A combination of root growth, worms, and bacteria gives the grains a good structure, which enables the soil to drain well yet retain enough water for good plant growth. Air can circulate freely, and there's plenty of room for roots to grow. If you are lucky enough to have this kind of soil in your garden, your efforts to improve the environment can be minimal.

THE IDEAL SOIL

The best soil for your Big Yield/Small Space garden is crumbly, well-aerated, porous material that holds moisture but drains well and has all the nutrients plants need for growth. It comprises 50 percent soil and 50 percent pore space; moisture should occupy about half the pore space, air the other half. Most of the solid material should be mineral; 5 to 14 percent should be organic. The organic material should be broken down into true humus, a black, sticky substance that holds the soil particles together in crumbs.

This soil should also contain an adequate amount of the three major nutrients—nitrogen (N), phosphorus (P), and potassium (K). It should also include the secondary nutrients calcium, manganese, and sulfur, and the micronutrients zinc, iron, magnesium, copper, molybdenum, boron, and chlorine.

The ideal way to prepare the perfect environment for your Big Yield/Small Space beds is with *compost,* decayed animal and vegetable matter that forms an organic manure. Later in the chapter I'll describe several methods by which you can produce this valuable material. Since, however, it typically takes weeks or months to prepare compost, here are two alternative methods of soil preparation that will allow you to begin immediately and will provide soil environments in which your crops will thrive.

POWER PACKING YOUR SOIL

There are two basic methods of quickly preparing rich, fertile soil for your vegetables. One is organic; the other is not. The major difference lies in the selection of fertilizers: if you create organic soil, all fertilizer ingredients will be of plant or animal origin, whereas with the general, or nonorganic, method, you combine synthetic fertilizers with organic ingredients.

The aim of power packing is to change the physical structure of inadequate soil environments. On the simplest level, this means removing stones and pebbles from gravelly soil. For all types of soil, adding massive amounts of organic matter and the proper nutrients makes it easier to work, improves its drainage, allows air to move through it rapidly, helps it warm up early in the spring, and leads to maximum growth and superior vegetable production. The exact amounts of all materials needed will be discussed in the sections that follow (see Figure 3–1).

The Organic Approach

A number of organic materials can be used to improve your natural soil structure and increase the amount of nutrients in it. The materials listed here are recommended for Big Yield/Small Space gardens because they are easy to obtain and give superior results.

Horse manure and compost upgrade the soil and add nutrients. Rotted horse manure provides the nitrogen

Fig. 3–1 Power Packing: The Organic Approach

1. Spread a layer of rotted horse manure 6 in. deep on top of the soil.

2. Starting at one end of the bed, turn the manure into the soil to a depth of 12 in.

needed in your garden (about 2.5 percent). Nitrogen itself gives your vegetables their dark green color and promotes vigorous leaf growth. The need for nitrogen is indicated by slow growth and pale green to yellow leaf color. Rotted horse manure also contains some phosphorus (0.27 percent) and potassium (0.48 percent).

Always use manure that's rotted, not fresh. The bacteria in your soil will divert some nitrogen from your vegetables for use in breaking down the fresh manure. In addition, the nutrients in rotted manure have already been converted into forms your plants can easily use.

You can often get rotted manure from a riding stable, where it's piled up and stands for months. Many gardeners who live where homeowners keep horses obtain free manure by advertising for it in the classified section of their local newspapers. If you can find only fresh manure, rot it yourself by piling it in a heap, covering it with a thin layer of dirt, and letting it stand for a few months. You can also buy dried horse manure in sacks from your local nursery. Do not buy steer manure, though, because its high salt content will more than offset any benefit.

Bone meal spread on your garden will help your soil meet its phosphorus requirements. Bone meal contains a whopping 20 to 25 percent phosphoric acid as well as 1 to 2 percent nitrogen. Phosphorus itself helps plants develop good roots, gives them a rapid start, and promotes fruit development. You can substitute rock phosphate or superphosphate for bone meal. This is a finely ground rock powder containing up to 30 percent phosphoric acid. Steamed bone meal and rock phosphate are available wherever garden products are sold.

Greensand (glauconite) or **granite dust** supply any needed potassium. This nutrient increases the vigor, the quality, and the disease-resistance of your crop. Both greensand and granite dust contain 5 to 10 percent potassium plus some minor and trace-mineral elements. I recommend them because they can be purchased at many nurseries and garden centers.

Wood ash also contains 7 to 8 percent potassium and can be obtained from wood burned outdoors or in your fireplace. Wood ashes should not be allowed to stand in the rain, as most of the potassium will be leached away.

Fish emulsion can be used during midseason to supply nitrogen to vegetables that are heavy feeders. Most fish emulsions contain 5 to 10 percent nitrogen and sometimes phosphorus and potassium. Many of the major brands are marked on the bottle "5–0–0," which in fertilizer language means 5 percent nitrogen, no phosphorus, no potassium. Just follow the instructions on the bottle.

Liquid compost, if you would wish, can also be added to your garden about every six weeks or at midseason. This will give your vegetables a little extra phosphorus and potassium as well as nitrogen. Make it by mixing a shovelful of compost with a gallon of water in a bucket or garbage can, stirring it up several times. After you've let it sit for about two days, strain out the liquid with a screen, then fertilize your garden with this liquid, using about 2 quarts per square foot of soil.

While there are other good organic fertilizers—blood meal, sewage sludge, cottonseed meal, seaweed, and a variety of animal manures, for example—the ones described above will be all that you really need in your garden. If you want to experiment, however, by all means try some of the others.

Here are the specific steps for creating Big Yield/Small Space beds by the organic approach:

1   Spread a layer of rotted manure 6 inches deep on top of the soil.
2   Starting at one end of the bed, turn the manure into the soil to a depth of 12 inches with either a round-point shovel, a four-pronged spading fork, a Soil Blender, or one of the newer compact tillers. This second step adds massive amounts of organic material to the soil.
3   After the initial digging, take a hand rake or similar tool and break the top 3 or 4 inches of soil into extremely fine particles.
4   Then work a small amount of bone meal or rock phosphate (4 to 5 pounds per 100 square feet) into the top 5 or 6 inches of your bed. You can substitute wood ashes for greensand if you like; use approximately 5 pounds of ashes per 100 square feet.
5   Rake the bed smooth. Now you are ready to plant.

3. With a hand rake or similar tool, break the top 3–4 in. of soil into fine particles.

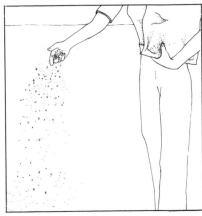

4. Spread and work a small amount of bone meal or rock phosphate and greensand into the top 5–6 in.

5. Rake the bed smooth.

Fig. 3–1 Power Packing: The General Approach

1. Sprinkle time-release fertilizer directly across top of unworked bed.

2. Spread a 6-in. layer of organic soil conditioner on top of the unworked soil.

When you have completely harvested a crop, regenerate the bed by turning a 2- to 3-inch layer of manure and a 2- to 3-inch layer of compost into the soil. Add bone meal and greensand as before, then replant.

Certain tools will simplify your task. The blade of a round-point shovel is attached at a slight angle, which will enable you to dig in medium to heavy soils with a minimum of difficulty. This is the one you'll be shown if you ask at your nursery for a digging shovel. If you have rocky or especially hard soil, use a four-pronged digging fork. There are several grades of shovels and digging forks available, but almost any will serve your purpose. I advise buying a medium-priced tool rather than the cheapest or most expensive.

If you want to dig your garden the easy way, use either a Soil Blender or one of the new compact tillers (see Figure 3–2). A Soil Blender ($100–$150) is a relatively new type of power shovel that uses counter-rotating augers to break up even the hardest soil to a depth of 12 inches. Especially useful in very small beds, it turns on a dime and will cultivate a tiny 2-square-foot area without difficulty. The small 2- to 3-horsepower tillers ($200–$300) are convenient because they fold for carrying. These don't work as well as the Soil Blender in very small beds, however. You can purchase these power tools at many hardware stores and other power-equipment retail outlets.

The General Approach

The nonorganic method produces a superior soil with a minimum of fuss and provides a complete supply of nutrients throughout the growing season. You should begin with a good organic soil conditioner.

Sphagnum peat moss is one of the best and can usually be purchased in bales from a nursery. Be sure to wet it thoroughly before mixing it into your soil.

Nitrogen-treated pulverized bark or sawdust also makes an excellent soil conditioner and costs considerably less than peat moss. This and sphagnum moss are usually available at local garden centers.

Horse manure and compost, as already discussed, make excellent additions to your soil. Compost should always be added to any of the other ingredients as soon as you are able to make your own.

Although I specifically recommend the above soil conditioners, you can use a number of others as well: peanut, rice, or almond hulls; cannery waste; soybean meal; and sewage sludge. Buy them with nitrogen already added or add nitrogen fertilizer yourself.

Time-release fertilizers are especially good for slow-maturing crops, such as melons. There's never any danger of overfertilizing with these substances, and generally one application is enough for all vegetables for an entire season. Manufacturers make entirely different formulations for the same vegetable. A fertilizer rich in nitrogen is especially good for root and leafy crops. This is generally labeled "Vegetable Food" and has a formulation something like 12–6–6, indicating 12 percent nitrogen, 6 percent phosphorus, 6 percent potassium. A fertilizer rich in phosphorus is suitable for most crops that produce fruit, such as tomatoes, peppers, or eggplant. It is typically labeled "Tomato Food" and has a formulation of 6–18–6, or 6 percent nitrogen, 18 percent phosphorus, 6 percent potassium.

While time-release fertilizers are generally too expensive for use in large vegetable gardens, they are almost perfect for Big Yield/Small Space needs and produce maximum results with little work.

Here's the general approach to producing Big Yield/Small Space soil:

1   Sprinkle the time-release fertilizer directly on top of the unworked bed in accordance with the instructions on the container.
2   Spread a 6-inch layer of organic soil conditioner on top of the unworked soil.
3   Starting at one end of the bed, as with the organic method, turn the conditioner and time-release fertilizer into the soil to a depth of 12 inches with either a shovel or one of the power tillers mentioned above. I like to work the soil three times, turning in 2 inches of organic material each time. When you're finished, your soil will be broken into small particles, and the time-release fertilizer will be spread throughout the top 12 inches.

3. Starting at one end of bed, turn materials into soil to a depth of 12 in.

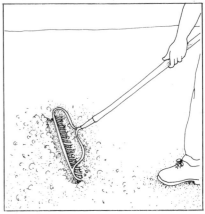

4. After the initial digging, use hand rake or similar tool to break top 3 or 4 in. of soil into fine particles.

5. Rake the bed smooth.

4   After the initial digging, take a hand rake or similar tool and break the top 3 to 4 inches of soil into extremely fine particles.

5   Rake the bed smooth. You are now ready to plant.

When you harvest a crop, regenerate the bed by adding time-release fertilizer in the same proportions as before and turning 2 inches of organic material and 2 to 3 inches of compost into the soil.

Since the time-release fertilizer provides small amounts of nutrients to your plants throughout the growing season, you will not have to give your vegetables supplemental feedings.

Fig. 3–2 Big Yield/Small Space Power Tools

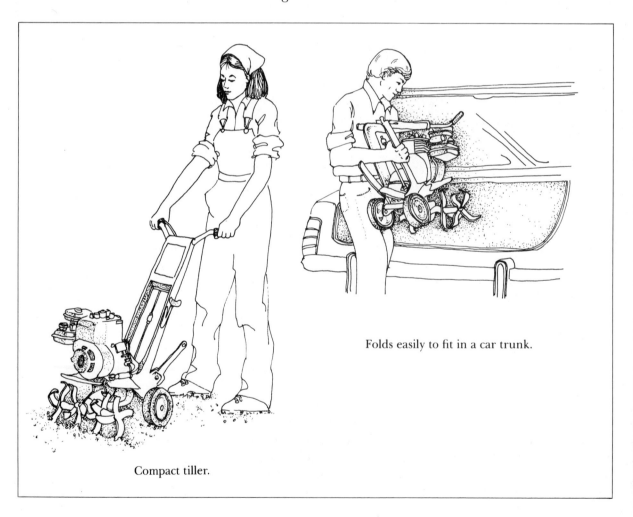

Folds easily to fit in a car trunk.

Compact tiller.

COMPOSTING MAKES A DIFFERENCE

Composting—using waste material to provide organic soil conditioning—is one of the essential steps in Big Yield/Small Space gardening. And contrary to what many gardeners believe, composting doesn't have to be either difficult or messy.

Consider composting as part of a cycle: food scraps from your table and other organic material, such as leaves and grass clippings, are turned back into your garden by way of the compost pile to improve the soil, provide nutrients, and save you money. Some gardeners get fancy and add special ingredients to supply extra nitrogen, phosphorus, or potassium to their compost. Cottonseed meal, feathers, hair, and tankage (slaughterhouse refuse), for instance, are sources of nitrogen. The ashes of lemon skins, apple skins, cucumber skins, and oyster shells contain phosphorus. And potassium can be found in the ashes of banana skins, cantaloupe rinds, and corncobs.

This addition of special ingredients really isn't necessary, however. You'll be giving your vegetables everything they need just by adding to the compost pile all the organic scraps you can get your hands on. Suitable organic materials include lawn clippings, vegetable garbage, meat scraps, fruit skins, hair, feathers, coffee grounds, leather scraps, leaves, shredded newspapers, and similar materials. Cans, foils, and plastics of all types are nonorganic or nonbiodegradable. These should never be added to your compost pile.

Whether you're living in a small lot surrounded on all sides by neighbors or in a suburban home with plenty of outside space, there's a composting method available to meet your needs. Here are several basic ones for you to consider.

The Conventional Pile

Although the traditional method of creating compost requires space, it does produce fairly large quantities. Use it if you have a good-sized suburban lot, don't mind a little smell, and can afford to wait several months for ripe compost. The steps are as follows:

Soil

Fertilizer

Organic
material

Coarse
material

1 Clear off a 5- to 6-foot-square area of ground.

2 Put down a 6-inch layer of fairly coarse material—twigs, brush, cornstalks, or any similar material will do. This provides ventilation underneath the pile.

3 Start building the pile in layers. Put down a 6-inch layer of vegetation, grass clippings, leaves, weeds, vegetable remains, table scraps.

Note that the smaller the particle size, the faster your materials will decompose. The bacteria in the pile can attack more surface area faster if the materials are broken up. Although you may add material to your compost without doing anything to it, you may wish to put it through a shredder-grinder or to break it up with a rotary lawnmower first.

4 Sprinkle this 6-inch layer of organic material with a fertilizer high in nitrogen. Use 2 pounds (1½ pints) of dried blood meal or 1 pound bone meal (1½ cups) for every square foot of surface.

The bacteria in the pile need plenty of nitrogen for proper decomposition. A mixture of about two parts carbonaceous material (leaves, straw, wood chips, meat, food garbage) and one part nitrogenous material (grass clippings, kitchen vegetable waste, weeds, and manure) keeps the action going.

Any compost pile that doesn't heat up indicates a lack of nitrogen. You can correct this by adding large amounts of grass clippings, dried blood meal, or steamed bone meal in the quantities indicated above.

5 Now add about an inch of soil. This soil contains bacteria that will help break down the organic material.

6 Repeat this layering procedure until your pile reaches a height of 5 feet.

A compost pile must heat up to between 140 and 160 degrees F. for good bacterial action to occur. The amount of heat necessary depends on the size of the pile. If it isn't big enough it will lose heat, and the bacterial action will slow down; but if it is too big, the compression of the material will shut off the air supply. Five feet high and 4 to 5 feet wide is generally a good size for a compost pile. As we will see, however, there are ways to compost satisfactorily in much smaller volumes than this.

7   Wet down the pile until it is moist, but not saturated.

Every pile needs moisture for decomposition to take place. A moisture content of 40 to 60 percent should be adequate; more than this can cut down on the oxygen available to the bacteria. The moisture content is about right when the compost feels as wet as a squeezed-out sponge. Put your hand inside the pile and feel—but be careful, because it's hot. If it doesn't seem wet enough, add water until it reaches the right consistency.

It's also a good idea to keep the top of the pile flat or concave so rain will soak into the mixture. In areas of extremely heavy rainfall, you may want to cover it with a sheet of plastic to keep it from becoming saturated.

8   Turn or mix the compost once a month. Using a manure fork or a shovel, move the top and side materials so that they are turned into the center. Most of the bacterial action takes place here because it is the hottest spot in the pile. Material closer to the outside loses heat to the surrounding air. Turning also allows air to penetrate into the interior of the pile.

When finished or ripe, the materials in the compost pile will have converted into a crumbly brown substance smelling like good earth. That's when it's ready to use. As they decompose, most piles shrink to about half their original size; a 5-foot pile will end up hardly more than 2½ feet high. One cubic foot of ripe compost is usually enough to condition 4 square feet of garden soil. The entire process takes three to four months.

The University of California Modified Quick Method

The modified quick method still takes a big outdoor space, but the decomposition is speeded up by the materials being shredded and mixed together so that the bacteria have many surfaces to work on. Use this method if you have a fairly large suburban lot, don't mind a little smell, and need ripe compost quickly. Here are the steps:

1   Mix together one part fresh manure and two parts other compost ingredients (leaves, grass clippings, cut-up cornstalks, table scraps, and the like). You can obtain fresh manure from a local riding stable. It must be fresh, not processed, manure.

2   Using a rotary lawnmower, shred everything completely. (You'll have to catch it in a bag or let it blow onto a large sheet of plastic.) Simply put down a small pile of materials and run the lawnmower over it, then put down another pile and repeat the process. If you own a power shredder, of course, use that. The materials, however, must be shredded into extremely small particles for this method to work well.

3   Mix everything together and form into a 4-foot high, 4-by-6-foot heap.

By the second or third day, the middle of the pile should have begun to heat up to between 130 and 160 degrees F. If it hasn't, add more manure.

Turn the heap on the fourth day. Make sure it's warm and moist by putting your hand inside and feeling around. If it doesn't seem moist to the touch (again, about as wet as a squeezed-out sponge), add some water.

Turn the heap again on the seventh day, and turn it once more on the tenth day. By this point the heap should have started to cool off, for it's almost ready. It is completely ready on the fourteenth day. It won't look like fine humus, but the materials will have broken down into a dark, rich, fairly crumbly substance. If you wish, you can let it rot further, or you can use it right away in your garden.

Composting in a Garbage Can

Use the garbage-can method if you are gardening on a small city lot close to your neighbors, if you want to keep the smell and flies to a minimum, or if you want to keep your compost out of sight. The procedure is outlined below:

1   Buy a 20- or 30-gallon galvanized garbage can and punch several small holes in the bottom. Put the can up on a few bricks and place a pan underneath to catch

any liquids that might drain out from the decaying garbage that you will be adding.

2   Put down a 3-inch layer of soil or peat moss at the bottom of the can.

3   Add 2 to 3 inches of kitchen garbage, then a 2-inch layer of grass clippings and leaves, another layer of kitchen garbage, a layer of grass clippings, and so on until the can is full. The grass clippings help supply needed nitrogen. If you are short on these, sprinkle ½ cup of blood meal on each 2- to 3-inch layer of kitchen garbage.

4   Put the lid on the can.

Grass clippings
or leaves

Kitchen garbage

Grass clippings
or leaves

Kitchen garbage

Soil or peat moss

Ripe compost will be ready in about three to four months, so if you start the can in the fall, the compost will be ready to add to your garden by the spring. You don't need to worry about the moisture content of this pile, nor does it need to be turned. For convenience, keep your compost can in the same area where you keep your other garbage cans, but mark it plainly so the garbage collectors don't dump it.

Composting in a Bin

Many gardeners prefer to put their compost in a bin of some type. There's no doubt that a bin makes composting neater and easier. Use one if you are concerned about the appearance of your yard or want to organize the composting.

A bin in its simplest form is any sort of container that is placed around the compost, such as a chicken-wire structure, a large-construction wire loop, four window screens nailed together, or a wall of rocks or cement blocks (see Figure 3–3). The most elaborate bins have separate compartments for fresh compost, partially decomposed compost, and ripe compost.

Bins generally range in size from about 3 feet square and 3 feet in height to 5 feet in diameter and 3 to 4 feet in height. Whether simple or elaborate, all types should be placed on bare ground.

Build your compost pile within the bin just as you would if there were no enclosure, using either the conventional method or the University of California modified quick method. Some gardeners fill their compost bins and let them sit without turning or additional attention until the compost is ready to use in the garden two to three months later. This is possible because compost in enclosed bins holds moisture better and maintains a more consistent temperature than compost exposed directly to the outside air. Turning the compost, however, is always desirable, as it promotes uniform decomposition of the particles throughout the bin. You will find the smaller amount of compost in a bin easier to turn than the larger amount in a pile.

Fig. 3–3   Types of Compost Bins

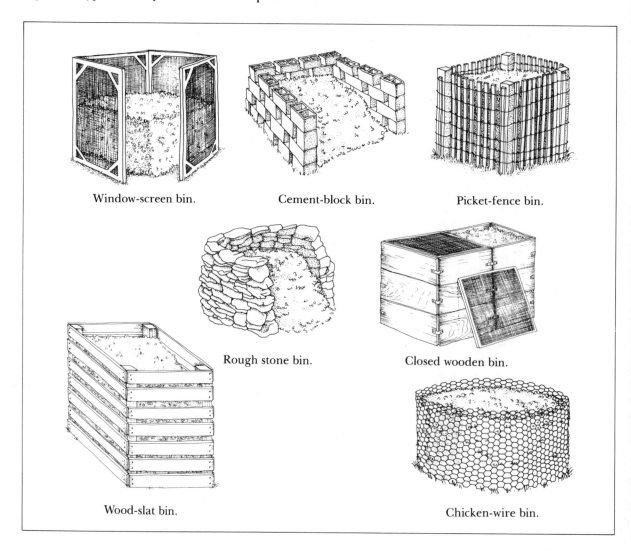

Window-screen bin.

Cement-block bin.

Picket-fence bin.

Rough stone bin.

Closed wooden bin.

Wood-slat bin.

Chicken-wire bin.

Some gardeners like to use one of the three basic types of commercial compost makers that are available today (see Figure 3–4). A *round wire bin* made of plastic or wire fencing can be easily set up almost anywhere. The *upright can type* consists of a heavy plastic container with sliding panels and round ventilation holes. The container is fed from the top; the finished humus is taken from the bottom. Most of these canlike commercial containers work with as little as 12 inches of material. Finally, the *horizontal drum type* is filled with shredded material and turned one to five times a day. The turning and shredding of the material shortens the decomposition period to about 14 days.

Fig. 3–4 Commercial Compost Makers

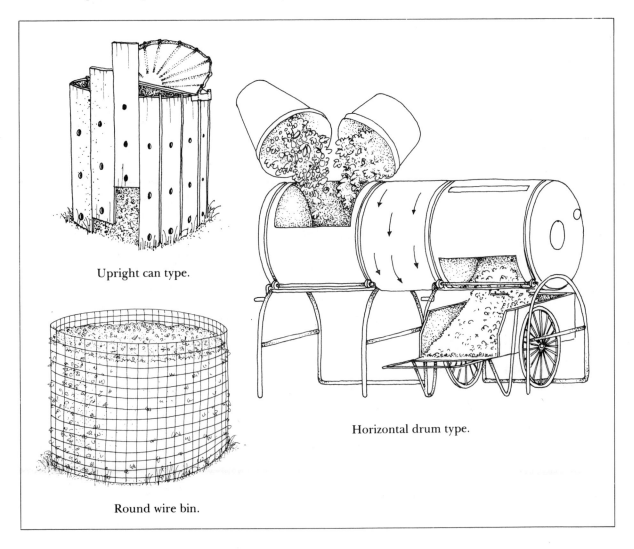

Upright can type.

Round wire bin.

Horizontal drum type.

Also currently on the market is a compost starter material that contains bacteria and fungi to help speed up decomposition. You can purchase starters especially designed to decompose fall leaves, grass clippings, and general compost. Raw, unshredded material treated with a starter takes 60 to 90 days to become ripe humus.

THE RIGHT BALANCE

Soils are frequently *acid* (sour) or *alkaline* (sweet). This is generally expressed in terms of pH (the degree of acidity or alkalinity) on a scale of 1 to 14. Seven is neutral, below 7 is acid, and above 7 is alkaline. You must take this information into consideration, since most vegetables do well in neutral or slightly acid soil.

When the soil is alkaline, your plants will exhibit yellow leaves, stunted growth, and burned leaf margins. In extreme cases, heavy brown or white salt deposits are left on the soil surface. The symptoms of acid soil are more difficult to detect.

The easiest way to determine whether your soil is too acid or alkaline is with a pH test, which you should conduct after the power-packing process. You can take samples of your soil and have them tested by your state's Cooperative Extension Service (see Appendix G), or have your county agent arrange to have this done (usually for free or for a small fee). Alternatively, you can purchase a simple pH test kit from your nursery for about $3 and test the soil yourself. A pH meter is also available from many garden centers; they cost about $20. Insert its prongs in your soil, and the needle will give you the pH reading.

To counteract acid soil, add ground limestone at the rate of 4 pounds per 100 square feet for each unit of pH below 6.5. To correct alkaline soil, add soil sulfur at the rate of 4 pounds per 100 square feet for each unit of pH above 7.

Testing for Toxicity

Recently, because of chemical spills, transformer leaks, and similar causes, toxic substances have been found in the soils of many urban areas. If you have any reason to believe that your garden soil might be contaminated, the Environmental Protection Agency recommends that you take a sample to your county health department, which can send it on to the state toxicology laboratory for analysis.

Now that you've had a chance to test your green thumb (or brown, as the case may be) on the preliminaries of creating the soil environment, let's get to the heart of the Big Yield/Small Space system—planting the wide-row intensive way.

CHAPTER FOUR

AS YE SOW: WIDE-ROW INTENSIVE PLANTING

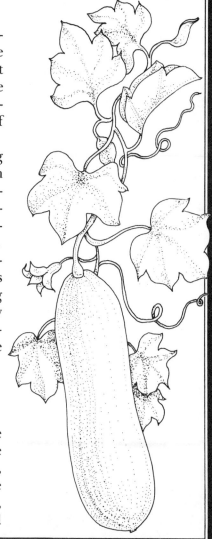

As I stated in the opening of this book, the wide-row intensive planting method alone can double or triple your home vegetable production. For that reason, it's an essential part of the Big Yield/Small Space approach. In this chapter I'll describe this method and provide some general guidelines for timing the planting of your vegetables.

The French intensive method (the broadcast planting of vegetables across a raised bed) was begun in France in 1890. A biodynamic modification of that technique was introduced in this country in 1965 at the University of California, Santa Cruz. The Chinese have long employed a similar procedure, as have thousands of American gardeners.

The wide-row intensive system used as part of our general approach combines the best of these techniques, plus the results of the latest small-garden research. In the Big Yield/Small Space garden, you broadcast plant entirely across the bed instead of placing seeds or seedlings in conventional rows that leave 1 to 3 feet of bare soil between the plants.

HOW TO WIDE-ROW PLANT

The object in wide-row intensive planting is to place the plants in such a way that their outer leaves just touch one another when they are about three-quarters mature. Then, when they are fully mature, the leaves virtually carpet the bed. The plants shade their own root zones at maturity, allowing the bed to retain moisture and preventing weed

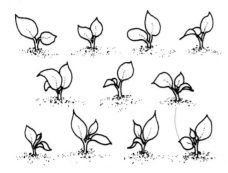

Fig. 4–1 Transplant seedlings in staggered rows.

growth. This means less watering, less weeding, and, because you are gardening in less space, less initial work in preparing the beds.

Sow the seeds of carrots, beets, radishes, and other root crops directly in the garden. Tomatoes, peppers, and eggplant should be started indoors and transplanted into the garden as seedling plants. Cabbage, broccoli, lettuce, onions, peas, beans, corn, cucumbers, and melons can be started either way. Peas, beans, cucumbers, melons, pumpkins, and squash must be started in their own individual pots or cubes because they will not tolerate root disturbance when transplanted to the garden. When planting, space your vegetables just a little closer than suggested on the seed packets.

To transplant seedlings the intensive way, measure the distance between plants with a ruler and stagger your rows as shown in Figure 4–1 instead of placing the seedlings directly across from each other.

Plant large and medium-sized seeds (1/16 inch or more in diameter) of such vegetables as radishes, spinach, beans, beets, and squash in the bed at about the spacing advised on the seed packets. Plant radishes, for instance, 1 inch apart in rows 1 inch wide. A handy device is a grid made of 1- or 2-inch chicken-wire screen: plant the seeds in the middle of the squares on the grid (see Figure 4–2).

Fig. 4–2 Use a 1- or 2-in.-mesh chicken-wire grid to plant large seeds.

Sow fine-seed crops like carrots and turnips (seeds less than 1/16 inch in diameter) completely across the bed. Thin to correct spacing later. You can practice getting an even distribution by "sowing" dried coffee grounds over a piece of clear plastic (see Figure 4–3).

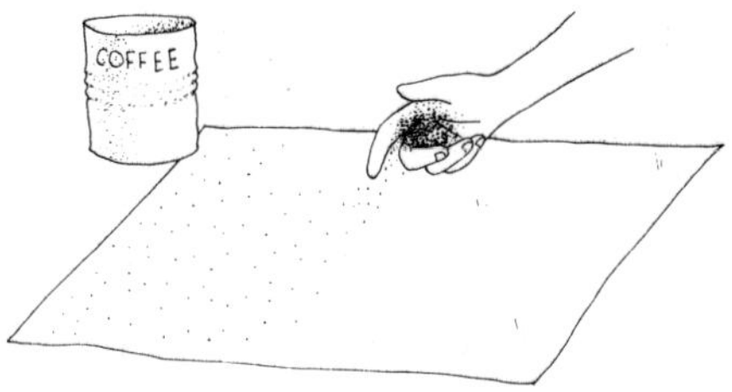

Plant at a depth roughly equal to four times the diameter of the seed. Generally, small seeds (parsnips, carrots, parsley, lettuce) should be planted 1/4 inch deep or less. Plant medium-sized seeds (radishes, rutabaga) 1/2 inch deep. Large seeds (beans, corn, melons, squash) do best planted 1 to 2 inches deep. Climate and soil conditions should also be considered when you're determining seed depth. In wet weather or in heavy soils, plant shallowly; in light, sandy soils or in dry weather, plant more deeply.

Fig. 4–3 Practice sowing dried coffee grounds on plastic before sowing very fine seeds.

GERMINATION KNOW-HOW

All vegetable seeds must be kept moist until they have completely germinated or begun to sprout. In most cases you can accomplish this by watering once a day or by making sure that the soil stays moist at all times.

Seed planted 1/4 inch deep or less, however, often dries out quickly and fails to germinate properly. One way to keep the soil surface moist and increase germination is to cover the planted seed bed with 1/8 to 1/4 inch of compost, rotted horse manure, or organic mulch. You can also cover the seed bed with a piece of black plastic to keep in moisture. When the seedlings poke their heads out of the ground, remove the plastic.

Many gardeners use clear plastic as a mulch (any material that covers the soil to aid cultivation) on hard-to-germinate seeds, such as tomato, pepper, and eggplant, planted directly into the ground. The plastic cover prevents evaporation and raises the temperature of the soil 20 to 30 degrees higher than air temperature. Plant the seed in a shallow trough and cover with clear plastic laid at an angle so water can run off (see Figure 4–4). Remove as soon as the seedlings show.

You can obtain almost perfect results and eliminate the wasteful practice of thinning (pulling up young plants from a group so that the ones that are left in the soil have more room to develop) by presprouting. Place seeds in a

Fig. 4–4 For hard-to-germinate seeds, make a shallow trench, plant seeds at the bottom, and cover with clear plastic at an angle so water can run off.

small plastic bag with moist sphagnum moss and shake. Put the bag in a warm place, such as near a light bulb or sunny window.

Plant when about half the seeds have started roots and shoots by scattering the sprouts across your prepared bed and covering lightly with sifted compost or manure. Water sparingly until the shoots begin to show above the soil. Don't worry about the sprouts being upside down or sideways—they will twist to orient themselves properly.

FURTHER CROP-STRETCHING TACTICS

In addition to broadcast planting your garden, you can employ Mother Nature's own miracle crop stretchers to squeeze every last bit of production out of your garden: interplanting, succession planting, and catch cropping.

Interplanting, or intercropping, means planting quick-maturing crops between slower-maturing ones. Radishes, leaf lettuce, green bunching onions, turnips, mustard greens, and curly cress mature quickly, while tomatoes, corn, squash, cabbage, eggplant, and peppers are planted further apart and take over 60 days to mature. You can plant radishes between rows of broccoli or tomatoes, for example, and harvest them before the larger vegetables become big enough to crowd out the smaller plants.

You can also take advantage of differences in frost hardiness to plant frost-hardy plants in the same bed in which you later intend to plant some of the larger, warm-season crops. For instance, plant carrots, beets, head lettuce, or swiss chard about 20 days before the last killing frost. Then, two weeks after that frost, place tomatoes in the same bed. You will be able to harvest the earlier-planted vegetables before your tomatoes need the additional space. In fact, with a really quickly maturing vegetable like radish, you can often take out two whole crops before the tomatoes begin to spread out.

Succession planting means planting one crop in succession right after another. Let's say you have allotted 3 square feet of garden space to radishes. Divide this space into three sections, and plant the first section. In about ten days, plant the next, and in another ten days, plant the third. When you harvest the first section, immediately replant. This will keep the bed productive the whole season through.

You can also plant cool-season crops several weeks before the last frost, let them reach maturity, harvest, rework the bed, and replant with warm-season vegetables. This system works well for such crops as broccoli, cauliflower, and cabbage.

Another alternative is to plant early, midseason, and later-maturing varieties of the same vegetable. And in mild-winter climates, you can harvest beans and other warm-weather crops, then plant carrots, radishes, turnips, and cole crops (the cabbage family) for fall and winter harvests.

Catch cropping consists of filling the blank space between the rows of slower-growing vegetables whenever these vegetables are harvested. You can, for instance, harvest a couple of broccoli plants in late summer, then grow radishes or green onions in that same space.

To use these last three techniques successfully, it is helpful to know which vegetables like to bask in the summer sun and which ones thrive in cooler temperatures.

VEGETABLES IN SEASON

Vegetables can be classified as either warm-season or cool-season crops (see Table 4–1). Generally, plants we harvest for their fruit—the part in which seeds are produced—need heat (65 to 80 degrees F.) and long days to grow well. Tomatoes, squash, peppers, and beans are examples.

Tomatoes, for instance, may sit and sulk when the daily temperatures average about 70 degrees, but grow mightily when the average daily temperature rises above 80 degrees. As a result, different tomato vines planted a month or even more apart will often start producing fruit at about the same time.

Cool-season plants, on the other hand, do well when the weather is about 55 to 70 degrees F. Such vegetables as carrots, beets, spinach, cabbage, and lettuce put all their efforts into forming leaf and root materials within this temperature range. When the days warm up, however, they start to go to seed. Therefore, you should plant cool-season vegetables at such a time that they reach maturity before the weather becomes too hot.

Within the general categories of warm- and cool-season crops, each vegetable also has its own individual temperature growth requirements; see Appendix D for these figures.

To be a really successful vegetable gardener, you need to plant at the right time or times for your particular area. I know a gardener who rushed out the first balmy spring day and planted her entire garden. A month later, she had to replace most of her tomatoes, eggplant, and other warm-season vegetables because they had been killed off by one or two nights of heavy frost. That's one extreme. I also have a neighbor who doesn't plant anything until late spring, when all chance of frost has passed. Her tomatoes and other warm-season vegetables do well, but by then the days have become so hot that her lettuce immediately bolts to seed (undergoes premature seeding and becomes useless as a vegetable), and many of her other cool-season vegetables simply don't grow well at all.

Some vegetables, such as broccoli, cabbage, onions, peas, radishes, rutabagas, spinach, and turnips, will tolerate freezing temperatures and may be planted in the spring as soon as the soil can be worked (usually four to six weeks before the last frost). Others, such as beets, carrots, cauli-

TABLE 4–1. COOL- AND WARM-SEASON CROPS

COOL-SEASON CROPS*		WARM-SEASON CROPS†	
Very hardy (Plant 4–6 Weeks Before Last Frost-free Date)	**Hardy** (Plant 2–4 Weeks Before Frost-free Date)	**Not Cold Hardy** (Plant on Frost-free Date)	**Needs Hot Weather** (Plant 1 Week or More After Frost-free Date)
Asparagus	Beets	Beans, Snap	Beans, Lima
Broccoli	Carrots	Corn, Sweet	Cucumbers
Cabbage	Chard	Okra	Eggplant
Lettuce	Mustard	Pumpkins	Melons
Onions	Parsnips	Soybeans	Peppers
Peas	Potatoes	Spinach, New Zealand	Sweet Potatoes
Radishes		Squash	
Rhubarb		Tomatoes	
Rutabagas			
Spinach			
Turnips			

*Cold-hardy plants, adapted to 55–70 degrees F., for early-spring planting.
†Cold-tender or heat-hardy plants for late-spring or early-summer planting; require 65–80 degrees F. day and night.

flower, lettuce, parsnips, potatoes, and swiss chard, will tolerate light frosts and can be planted two to four weeks before the last frost. Beans, cantaloupes, cucumbers, eggplant, peppers, pumpkins, squash, tomatoes, and watermelons are damaged by frost and should be planted or transplanted on or after the average date of the last frost. How to determine the planting dates for individual vegetables in your locale will be discussed in Chapter 8.

If you plant at the appropriate times and use the wide-row intensive techniques, you can grow as many carrots in 1 square foot of a Big Yield/Small Space garden as you can in a 12-foot row in a conventional garden. You can also grow eight times as many radishes, five times as many onions, two and a half times as much cabbage, twice as many peppers, and so on, ad infinitum. Just look upon it as your own personal vegetable population explosion. To guarantee this bounty, keep every square inch of garden planted from four to six weeks before the last frost to a month or two after the first killing frost in the fall. In the next chapter, I'll describe some climate modifiers that will help you to stretch the season.

CHAPTER FIVE

SEASON STRETCHERS FOR SUPERPRODUCTION

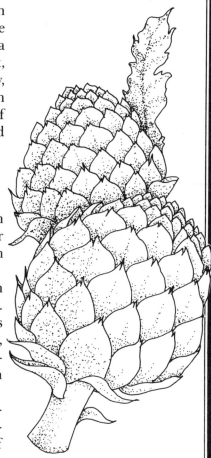

A major part of the Big Yield/Small Space approach consists of modifying planting beds to improve growing conditions. This may mean putting up a simple windscreen, adding a reflector to supply more light, heating the soil to speed up germination, or, most typically, using any of a wide variety of devices to protect plants from frost, thus extending the growing season. What you do, of course, depends on the conditions in your own garden and on your personal preferences.

THE GREENHOUSE EFFECT

Protecting your plants and extending the growing season at its simplest level means placing some sort of a cover over individual plants, a row, or an entire seed bed to keep them from being damaged by the elements, insects, or birds.

Protective devices make it possible to raise the garden temperature under the device 5 to 15 degrees F. or more. This temperature increase is especially useful in areas where the weather warms up, then is hit by a quick frost, then warms up again, or where the first frost of fall is followed by a stretch of balmy weather. Protective devices can be used to grow warm-season crops in cool weather.

Using such devices, you can set out seeds and transplants before the outside temperature would normally support growth. You can also extend the production of tomatoes, peppers, and other frost-sensitive plants by an extra two to four weeks; and in some cases, as described in the previous chapter, you can take two, three, and four successive crops from the same space.

THE SIMPLEST PROTECTORS

The most inexpensive protective devices are constructed from materials that you probably already own. Paper bags with the bottoms cut out, small cardboard boxes turned upside down, do-it-yourself paper "hats" made from large Dixie cups, cutoff milk cartons, newspapers, plastic jugs and buckets, and upside-down coffee cans are all effective (see Figure 5–1). You will have to punch air-circulation holes in some of these protectors, such as the milk cartons, plastic jugs and buckets, and coffee cans.

Similar to these homemade devices are the wax-reinforced paper coverings that are marketed commercially under such names as Hotkap and Hotent (see Figure 5–2). Designed to be placed over individual plants, they come in several heights and diameters to accommodate a variety of transplant and seedling sizes.

ALL KINDS OF CLOCHES

A cloche is anything that allows in the sunlight and is placed over seeds or plants for protection. Therefore, most of the covering devices and contraptions described in this chapter are, technically, cloches. Cloches can be simple or elaborate in design and can be made at home or purchased commercially. Most include a clear or translucent plastic cover or a top layer of glass. Heat trapped beneath this layer raises the temperature of the soil and air under the cover, making them warmer than they would be in an open bed. Even those that are made without such covers, from materials you would typically find around the house, will extend the growing season by at least a few weeks.

Using Plastic to Cover Your Cloches

Plastic covers of all types are extremely useful in the garden. You have a choice of hard plastics—Plexiglass and fiberglass—which come in flat or corrugated rigid sheets, and the soft plastics—polyethylene, mylar, and Lortex (similar to polyethylene)—which are flexible and come in

Fig. 5–1 Simple Protectors

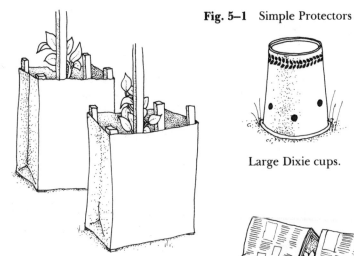

Large Dixie cups.

Upside-down coffee can. Take off on warm, sunny days.

Bottomless paper bags.

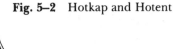

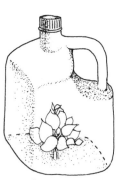

Newspaper tent weighed down with bricks or stones.

Punch holes in the sides of milk cartons to allow air to circulate.

Plastic jug. Remove bottom to convert to a minigreenhouse.

Fig. 5–2 Hotkap and Hotent

Hotkaps, heavy-wax-paper cones, protect your plants against the elements and birds.

Hotents are effective for growing seedlings of large plants, such as squash or tomatoes. Approximate size: 11 in. wide, 14 in. long, 8½ in. high.

rolls. Some gardeners recommend the use of ultraviolet-light-inhibited polyethylene sheets sold as UVI polyethylene. Others use any type available. Use rigid plastic where you want long life—it's more expensive than the soft variety, but it isn't damaged by wind and rain. Soft plastic is the choice (polyethylene is probably best) when you will be moving the devices around frequently, when you want the cover to fit a particular frame easily, or when you want to keep the expense to a minimum.

One word of warning about plastic: on warm, sunny days, the air temperature under the plastic cover can quickly become too hot for your plants. It is therefore essential to provide good ventilation and to check the temperature regularly. The easiest way to do the latter is to place a thermometer inside the device, and when the temperature rises 10 degrees or more above the maximum for the specific vegetable under cover (see Appendix D), remove or open the protective device. Replace or close only on cooler days.

Fig. 5–3   Plastic-Covered Cloches

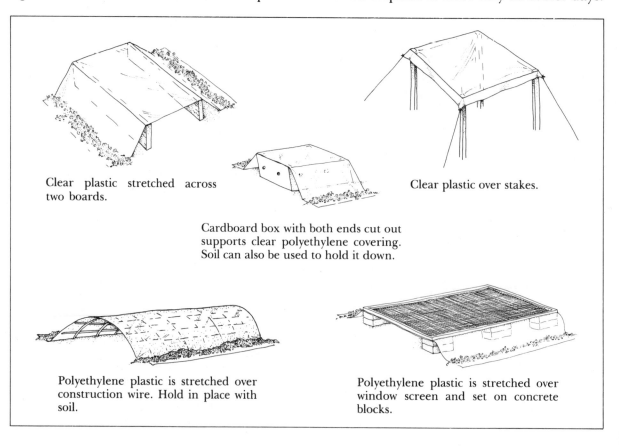

Clear plastic stretched across two boards.

Clear plastic over stakes.

Cardboard box with both ends cut out supports clear polyethylene covering. Soil can also be used to hold it down.

Polyethylene plastic is stretched over construction wire. Hold in place with soil.

Polyethylene plastic is stretched over window screen and set on concrete blocks.

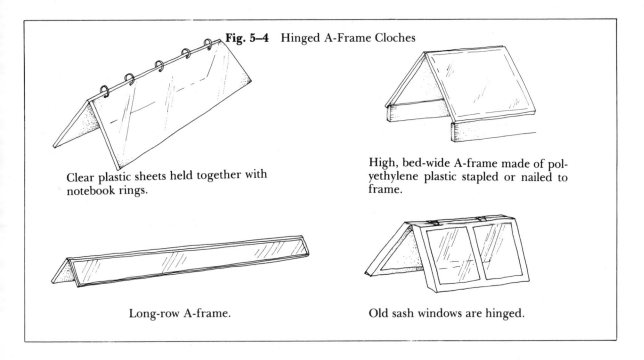

Fig. 5–4   Hinged A-Frame Cloches

Clear plastic sheets held together with notebook rings.

High, bed-wide A-frame made of pol-yethylene plastic stapled or nailed to frame.

Long-row A-frame.

Old sash windows are hinged.

Some Examples of Plastic-Covered Cloches

The simplest plastic-covered cloche consists of a frame over which this material has been stretched. Frames can be fashioned of anything from boards or stakes to cardboard boxes with the tops and bottoms cut out (see Figure 5–3).

These, however, are only the beginning. For those gardeners who want to get fancy, there are many types of more intricate cloches available. Each has its own special features:

Hinged A frames covered with sheets of polyethylene plastic become extremely versatile folding cloches for raising springtime soil temperatures. They can easily be moved indoors during the day and taken back outside at night when temperatures drop too low for optimum growth of temperature-sensitive plants like tomatoes. The open ends provide good air circulation (see Figure 5–4).

Fence- or chicken-wire tunnels make extremely good row- or bed-wide cloches. Arch the wire over the row or bed and cover with clear polyethylene plastic, holding it in place with staples or clothespins. On warm days, if you remove the polyethylene cover, the wire covering becomes a protection from birds (see Figure 5–5).

Fig. 5–5   Tunnel Protectors

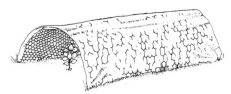

This tunnel cloche is made of chicken wire.

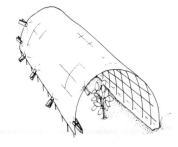

A half cylinder of fence wire. Draped plastic can be held with clothespins, folded back when it's warm.

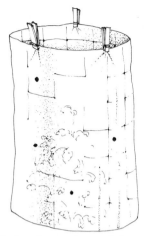

Fig. 5–6 Place a sheet of clear plastic over the top of and around your cage to provide protection against fall frost. Be sure to create vents.

Plastic-covered wooden frames are an easy-to-make variation of the chicken-wire tunnel. Build the frame from scrap lumber and cover with clear plastic. Move around the garden as needed.

Vertical plastic-covered wire cages increase warmth and wind protection for plants normally grown in cages: tomatoes, peppers, zucchini. Wrap a polyethylene sheet around your cage and staple in place (see Figure 5–6).

Arched panels of ribbed translucent fiberglass, typically 4 feet wide by 8 feet long, are staked along the edges and used as cloches. Many gardeners trim two weeks or more off the seed-to-harvest time for cucumbers, squash, pumpkins, and melons by placing the seedlings under a "cucumber incubator," a flexed sheet of translucent fiberglass that traps growth-enhancing heat and carbon dioxide (see Figure 5–7).

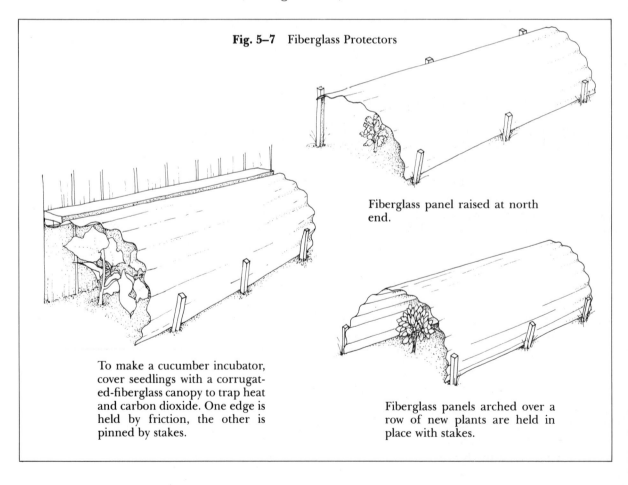

Fig. 5–7 Fiberglass Protectors

Fiberglass panel raised at north end.

To make a cucumber incubator, cover seedlings with a corrugated-fiberglass canopy to trap heat and carbon dioxide. One edge is held by friction, the other is pinned by stakes.

Fiberglass panels arched over a row of new plants are held in place with stakes.

Wicket tunnels can cover an entire bed. Make the wickets or hoops by bending stiff wire or coat hangers into loops, pushing them into the soil 1 to 3 feet apart, and stretching clear polyethylene over them to form a tunnel greenhouse. You can buy clear plastic in 3-foot or wider rolls. Hold the plastic in place with soil (see Figure 5–8).

These tunnels can run as long as 10 to 15 feet or more and therefore will accommodate fairly large vegetables. They generally create their own microclimate by producing heat, relative humidity, and carbon dioxide at levels higher than those of the outside environment.

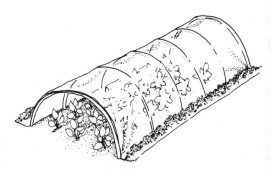

Fig. 5–8 Fashion wickets from coat hangers to construct a tunnel cloche.

Several devices similar to the homemade wicket tunnel are now commercially available. They are usually marketed as portable or roll greenhouses. Also on the market is a three-piece miniature-greenhouse container that allows you to set out tomatoes, peppers, and eggplant at least five weeks early. This device resembles a clear plastic garbage can with a shower-cap-like cover. As the plants grow, you remove the dome, leaving the plastic ring as a support.

COLD FRAMES AND HOTBEDS

Cold frames and hotbeds mark the next step in the Big Yield/Small Space plan to outwit the weather. They can extend the growing season from several months to all year in milder climates. A cold frame consists of a box with a plastic or glass top (see Figure 5–9). It is designed to capture the sun's warming rays and to protect plants from unfavorable weather conditions. Since the cold frame is heated by the sun, its glass or plastic cover must slant toward the winter sun at an angle, typically facing south. Some gardeners give a coat of white paint to the interior of the frame, thereby increasing sunlight reflection. You can purchase these devices or make your own. A hotbed is merely a cold frame with artificial heat added.

Cold frames and hotbeds can cover a portion of a Big Yield/Small Space bed, or several frames can be used together to put an entire garden "under glass." You can plant or transplant your vegetables into the frame and later remove the cover, allowing the plants to mature in place.

To construct a cold frame or hotbed, enclose a portion of your garden with 2-by-8-inch or 2-by-10-inch boards,

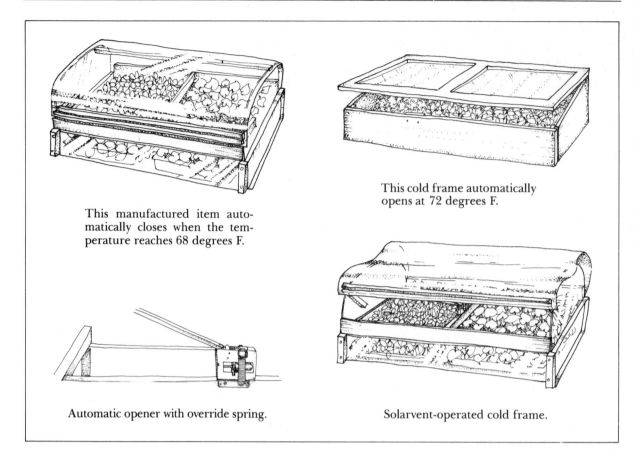

This manufactured item automatically closes when the temperature reaches 68 degrees F.

This cold frame automatically opens at 72 degrees F.

Automatic opener with override spring.

Solarvent-operated cold frame.

Fig. 5–9   Manufactured Cold Frames

forming a box. Make the top of the frame out of 1-by-3-inch boards covered with one or two layers of polyethylene. Place dirt under the northern edge of the frame to make it slant toward the sun and fill in around the sides with more dirt. You can build a better cold frame by adding an additional tier of 2-by-8-inch or 2-by-10-inch boards at the sides and back. Cut the side boards on a diagonal and hinge the top of the frame to the back.

Direct sun can overheat your cold frame, as it does other protective devices. On a warm day, open the top of the frame to allow air to circulate. If overheating is a problem, try placing cheesecloth or burlap over the top. You can also paint the glass or plastic white or build a lath panel with which to cover the top.

In cold weather, insulate the outside of the box with soil or sawdust or protect it with a blanket, tarpaulin, polyethylene plastic, or similar cover.

As mentioned above, a cold frame with heat added becomes a hotbed. To heat the frame naturally, set it on top about 18 inches of green organic material or fresh manure that you have placed in a pit. The bacterial action involved in the rotting of the green material or manure will supply heat to the frame. You can heat the frame artificially by placing one or more light bulbs inside or using soil-heating cables or mats. Most come with a built-in thermostat that enables you to keep the soil at a constant temperature.

By controlling the temperature of the soil in your beds, you can speed up the seed germination of most vegetables. The seed of cool-season crops sprout eagerly at soil temperatures as low as 50 degrees F. Seeds of warm-season crops "sulk" and rot when the soil temperature remains below 65 degrees. Within these two categories, each vegetable has its own temperature requirements for seed germination. Radishes, for example, take 11 days to germinate at 50 degrees but only 4 days at 70 degrees. Appendix D lists seed-germination temperatures for commonly grown vegetables.

BIG YIELD/SMALL SPACE GREENHOUSES

The gardener who really wants to step up vegetable production can turn his or her entire garden into a greenhouse by constructing easy-to-build structures larger than the ones already described. These types of greenhouses add a different dimension to your gardening because their plastic or glass covers allow you to forget frost dates. They also eliminate many insect and animal problems. A Big Yield/Small Space greenhouse is a perfect solution for people who like their gardening neat and orderly. There are three types you might wish to consider (see Figure 5–10).

The cold-frame greenhouse is, in effect, a modified cold frame built large enough to cover your entire garden or a portion of it and high enough (about 4 feet) to allow most vegetables to grow directly in the bed without your having to remove the cover. For vine crops that require greater height, such as tomatoes, remove the frame at the appropriate time and allow the plants to grow to maturity. Smaller varieties of tomatoes that remain under 24 to 30

Fig. 5–10 Greenhouses

A double layer of plastic supported by semicircular PVC pipe creates a portable greenhouse.

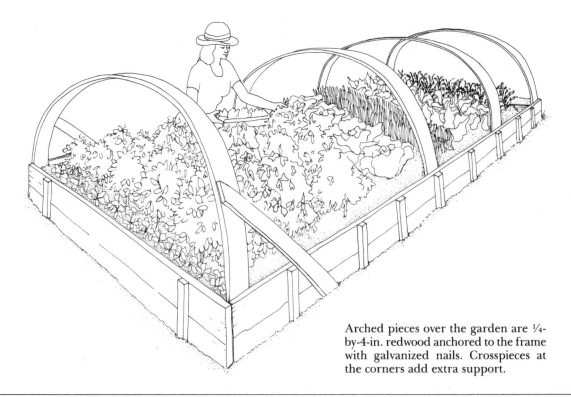

Arched pieces over the garden are ¼-by-4-in. redwood anchored to the frame with galvanized nails. Crosspieces at the corners add extra support.

inches, such as Tiny Tim, Small Fry, Pixie, and Presto, can be grown in this manner without the lid having to be removed, as can the bush varieties of such crops as cucumbers and beans.

The cold-frame greenhouse is ideally suited for use in flower beds or long, narrow vegetable beds located next to a wall or fence. To build one, first enclose your garden with redwood or treated-lumber two-by-fours or two-by-sixes. Use the wall of a building, a fence, or ½-inch plywood supported by 2-by-2-inch posts as the back panel. Cut the sides from pieces of ½-inch plywood. Make the slanting panel frames from one-by-twos or one-by-threes. Cover with clear polyethylene plastic or flat fiberglass. Old windows also make excellent panels. Bolt or nail the greenhouse together. Attach the slanting front panel to the frame with any type of small hinge.

Some gardeners heat their greenhouses with soil cables or soil mats, which can be purchased at garden centers. Others use light bulbs or small electric greenhouse heaters. Another alternative is to solar heat your greenhouse. This requires insulating the sides, adding a heat-storage wall, and weatherproofing the slanting panels. Insulate the side walls by tacking 4 inches of fiberglass insulation on the outside or by building them of double plywood and filling with scrap packing styrofoam, shredded newspaper, or similar insulatory materials.

If you have built your greenhouse against a concrete building foundation, this will make an adequate heat-storage wall. Paint it black to increase its heat-absorption properties. If you do not have a concrete foundation, construct a back heat-storage wall by placing rock, masonry, or adobe blocks against the back wall of the greenhouse. One-gallon bleach bottles painted black and filled with water also make good heat-storage units. Place them the width of the greenhouse on top-to-bottom shelves located on the back wall or stack them in rows on the floor.

Polyethylene plastic on both sides of the frame will help keep the heat inside during cold winter months. The panels should face toward the sun at an angle equal to your latitude plus 20 to 50 degrees. As with regular cold frames, your slanting panels must be open on warm days to allow air to circulate and to keep the temperatures inside the greenhouse within the safe range for your plants. It's wise to hang a small thermometer inside the greenhouse so you can check the temperature regularly.

The freestanding bed greenhouse is a good option if you have beds that aren't built against a fence or wall. This structure should be built high enough to allow most vegetables to grow to maturity without the cover having to be removed, although for taller vegetables and vertical vine crops, you can take off the greenhouse cover when they become big enough and let them grow on to maturity.

The Quonset greenhouse can be built out of 1-inch PVC pipe and polyethylene plastic. Determine the length of pipe needed by arching a length across your bed as shown in Figure 5–10. Your greenhouse should be at least 4 feet high in the middle. Cut all your cross pipes the same length and space at 3- to 4-foot intervals along the bed. To anchor each one, shove both its ends 6 to 8 inches into the ground, cover with polyethylene plastic, and secure to the bed frame with strips of wood. As with the other types of greenhouses, the plastic must be removed or pulled back on warm days.

WHICH ONES WILL WORK FOR YOU?

Now that we have surveyed what is available in the way of Big Yield/Small Space season stretchers, here's some information to assist you in deciding which devices best meet your particular needs.

If you want to plant a week or two earlier than the planting dates recommended for your vegetables or if you wish to protect your plants against an unexpected cold snap, use any one of the simple basic protective devices, including Hotkaps. If you wish to stretch the season four to six weeks or longer on either end yet still want to keep things simple, or if you're gardening in an odd-shaped bed that won't take a greenhouse, use one of the plastic-covered cloches.

Simple cloches such as plastic jugs or buckets are ideal for transplants spaced some distance apart—for example, cabbage, broccoli, or tomatoes. Hinged A frames, chicken-wire tunnels, or plastic-covered wooden frames will provide a warm microclimate for two or three warm-weather plants grown together, such as tomatoes, peppers, and cucumbers. You can also get a jump on the season by using them for spot planting of lettuce, beets, carrots, and other vegetables. Hinged A frames are especially handy for this, since they are lightweight and can be moved and stored easily.

Plastic-covered wire cages are especially appropriate for warm-weather crops—tomatoes, cucumbers, zucchini, and the like. Use a hotbed when you are starting seedlings directly in the ground and want to speed up germination.

If you wish to create a permanent season-stretching environment and have fairly small rectangular beds, consider building one of the Big Yield/Small Space greenhouses. Use a cold-frame greenhouse for beds located against a fence or a wall. A freestanding greenhouse is the choice when you do not have a fence or wall nearby. The Quonset-style greenhouse made with PVC pipe is best if you want to be able to move your greenhouse in and out of the garden easily.

ABOUT PLASTIC AND OTHER MULCHES

Plastic mulches are strips of plastic laid on the ground over a bed. Gardeners have recently begun to use these extensively, and agricultural experiment stations are now working with a number of plastic and other synthetic roll mulches, including polyethylene films, steel and aluminum foils, Kraft papers in various combinations, sky-blue plastics, and biodegradable papers.

Ordinary polyethylene film 1½ mils thick, typically available in rolls 3 to 6 feet wide, makes an excellent Big Yield/Small Space mulch. Clear plastic heats the soil about 10 degrees, black plastic 3 to 6 degrees.

Use clear plastic to promote the early germination of cool-season vegetables and speed up production of warm-season crops. Black plastic is effective for accelerating the growth and increasing the yield of most warm-season crops. Some gardeners also find that a wide strip of black plastic laid directly on the ground will extend the season two to three weeks for such crops as tomatoes, eggplant, and peppers.

Sky-blue plastic can be used in the same way as clear or black polyethylene films to heat the soil in your beds. It has the additional advantage of possessing some insect-repellant properties.

Ordinary kitchen foil cut into strips increases light intensity and can be used effectively to grow vegetables in the shady parts of your garden. Foil also lowers the soil temperature about 10 degrees and helps keep lettuce from going to seed during hot weather. Experiments show that kitchen foil is an effective control against aphids because insects dislike light reflected under leaf surfaces.

Biodegradable plastic films and papers are also now coming on the market. Instead of removing them at the end of each garden season, you work them into the soil.

Fig. 5–11   Planting with a Plastic Mulch

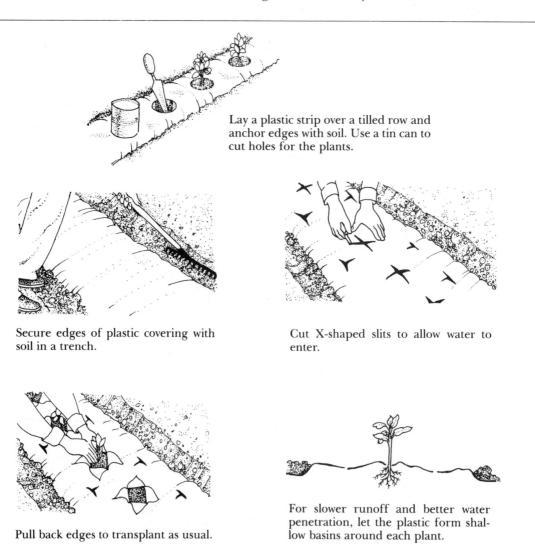

Lay a plastic strip over a tilled row and anchor edges with soil. Use a tin can to cut holes for the plants.

Secure edges of plastic covering with soil in a trench.

Cut X-shaped slits to allow water to enter.

Pull back edges to transplant as usual.

For slower runoff and better water penetration, let the plastic form shallow basins around each plant.

Besides heating your soil, synthetic mulches can help keep weeds down and prevent the rotting of fruits that trail on the ground, such as cantaloupes and tomatoes. To use a plastic mulch in your own garden, soak the soil first, then lay down a plastic strip as wide as the bed, securing it with soil on the ends and sides. Cut out planting holes with a tin can and cut X-shaped slits about 3 inches long for watering with a hose (see Figure 5–11).

MORE WAYS TO REGULATE HEAT AND LIGHT

Technically, vegetables need a minimum of 6 hours of sunlight a day to grow. Unfortunately, however, in small city lots our vegetable-growing space is often jammed between a fence and a wall, sandwiched by two buildings, or crammed into an odd-shaped corner in such a way that the ground is shaded from the sun most of the day.

If this is your problem, don't give up. It is possible to augment your natural light with a reflector panel or wall. Make reflector panels by stapling or gluing kitchen aluminum foil to a large piece of cardboard or plywood. Good sizes are 4 by 4 feet, 4 by 6 feet, and 5 by 8 feet. Panels can be mounted on a 2-by-2-foot frame.

To construct a reflector wall, mount a large piece of cardboard or plywood on a wall facing your garden and cover it with aluminum foil. Make it the same length as the garden.

Since the sun comes up in the east, travels through the southern sky, and sets in the west, light reflectors should be set up on the east, west, or north side of your garden— or all three. You'll have to experiment to determine the size and placement that will work best for you. In some cases one panel or wall will do; in others you will need three to produce adequate light. In difficult-to-light areas, you may have to place your reflector at an angle to direct the light where you want it to go.

Still another way you can raise the temperature in your garden environment is to employ a heat reflector. The easiest methods by which to reflect heat on your vegetables involve painting a wall behind your garden white, setting up white plywood panels behind individual plants, or ar-

Fig. 5–12 Wind Protectors

Half of a milk carton.

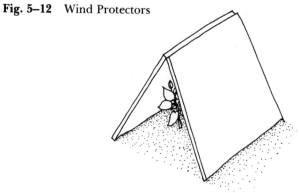

Cardboard tent.

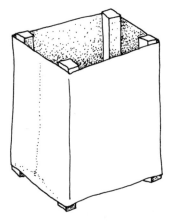

Bottomless sack.

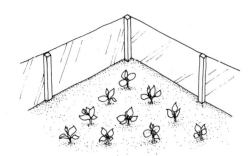

Polyethylene plastic and stakes.

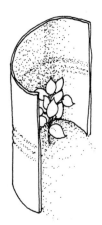

One-quarter open tin can.

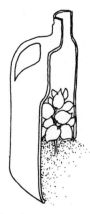

Half of a 2-gal. bleach jug.

ranging sheets of white cardboard on the north side of your wire cages. In some cases, the use of reflected heat will speed the growth of warm-season vegetables by two weeks or more.

In areas where hot summers are the norm, you can sometimes stretch the season for cool-weather crops by planting them early and shielding them during the sunniest part of the day. Shade your garden with a piece of plywood or a lath frame mounted on 2-foot-high posts. Individual heat-sensitive plants can be protected with smaller devices, such as slotted milk cartons or jugs.

PROTECTION FROM THE WIND

If wind blows continually through plants, it will cool their leaves and slow down their development. Wind also places tomatoes and some other plants under stress, causing them to divert the growth process to protection instead of to setting or producing fruit.

You can screen your vegetables from the wind with the same types of devices used for frost protection, although they can be less elaborate if your wind conditions are not severe. Try propping board shingles or half portions of milk cartons in front of individual plants, staking a 2-foot-high plastic wall on the windward side of your beds, or staking bottomless sacks around each plant. A little experimenting will help you determine which devices are best suited to your garden (see Figure 5–12).

You will be amazed at the effectiveness of the various strategies we've listed here for stretching the growing season. Using them has provided me with an increased sense of control and a bountiful harvest. In the next chapter, I discuss yet one more means of maximizing the production of your Big Yield/Small Space garden.

CHAPTER SIX

THE SECRETS OF VERTICAL GARDENING

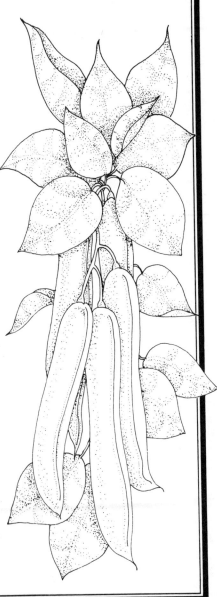

If you're reading this book, obviously you want the biggest possible yield of vegetables from the space you have available. May I suggest vertical gardening as a step beyond—or above—the preceding techniques?

Cucumbers, winter squash, melons, and other vine crops require tremendous amounts of ground space. When they're transferred to the air above the garden, however, huge quantities can be produced in a surprisingly small area. The last 6 inches of a 20-foot flower bed, for instance, can grow all the winter squash a family of four can possibly eat.

To make the most out of your vertical garden, you're going to have to use your imagination. In this chapter, I'll present some basic ideas that work well. Every year, though, inventive gardeners come up with dozens of newer, better, and more clever ways of squeezing even greater production out of their limited space.

MESHING YOUR MANY NEEDS: THE WIRE CAGE

Since its introduction into the garden only a few short years ago, the wire cage has become an invaluable garden organizer, especially in small-space gardens (see Figure 6–1). This device seems to bring out the productive best in such vegetables as tomatoes and cucumbers. It keeps greedy space gobblers like zucchini from crowding out everything within sight and helps squeeze the maximum number of plants into a small patch of ground.

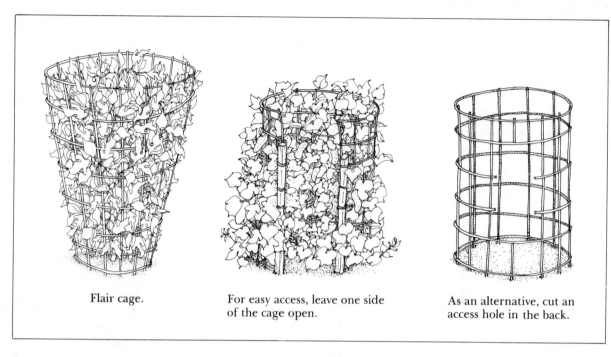

Flair cage.

For easy access, leave one side
of the cage open.

As an alternative, cut an
access hole in the back.

Fig. 6–1 Wire-Cage Basics

Consider this: A tomato plant allowed to go its own
willy-nilly way in a wire cage puts out better foliage cover
to protect its fruit and vines from sun scald and produces
more tomatoes per square foot than it would if grown in
any other way. Cages, in fact, turn a single vine into a production tower. In my own garden I frequently get 150 to
300 tomatoes each season from one vine growing in a 24-
inch-diameter, 6-foot-high cage.

Or how about this: Six cucumber plants grown in a 23-
inch-high, 18-inch-diameter wire cage go wild trying to
outproduce themselves. In several tests, one wire cage with
only six cucumber plants outproduced shoulder-to-shoul-
der cucumber plants sprawled over 15 square feet of
ground space.

Cages vary in size. The ones you select will depend on
the specific variety of the specific vegetable you wish to
grow. Small bush or container types of tomatoes, for example, do best planted in 18-inch-diameter, 2- to 4-foot-
high cages. The cage keeps the fruit and foliage off the
ground and provides support. An ideal cage size for larger,
indeterminate tomato varieties is 18 to 24 inches in diameter by 5 to 6 feet in height. Simply put the cage over individual plants when they are small and let them go. Some

gardeners also like to grow four to six tomato plants in a single 3- or 4-foot-diameter cage, with satisfactory results. Eight plants grown in a single cage, however, don't seem to produce as well as eight plants grown in their own individual cages.

Cucumbers do well in a 4-foot-high, 18-inch-diameter cage. Plant six plants per cage, but don't close the circle: make it horseshoe shape and leave a 10- to 12-inch opening on one side for easy access to the cucumbers.

Summer squash, including zucchini, do well in a 2- to 3-foot-diameter, 2- to 3-foot-high wire cage. If the vine grows out of the mesh, put it back and train it toward the top. If it becomes impossible to keep in check, pick off the fuzzy growing tip.

Some gardeners make their cages of 6-inch-mesh concrete-reinforcing wire because it gives solid support and allows them to reach the fruit easily. In practice, though, I find this wire too stiff and hard to work with and so prefer a lighter galvanized fence wire, which is obtainable at most building-supply stores. This wire comes either welded or woven and in several mesh sizes. You'll need at least a 4-inch mesh to be able to put your hand in comfortably and remove the fruit. You can eliminate this problem altogether by cutting a hole at least 12 inches in diameter on one side of your cage.

To secure a cage, bend 20-inch lengths of standard coat-hanger wire and drive them into the ground around the bottom rim of the cage at 12- to 18-inch intervals. Wooden stakes driven about 6 inches into the ground and wired to the cage also work well.

Recently a number of commercial wire cages have appeared on the market (see Figure 6–2). While most of these are satisfactory, none of them, to this point, work as well as the ones you make yourself.

A-FRAME ABRACADABRA

The A frame, like the wire cage, is creating a gardening revolution. It can easily turn a small garden into a cornucopia for vine crops—cucumbers, winter squash, cantaloupes, watermelon, and pumpkins, for instance—and for other crops that usually waste ground space (see Figure 6–3).

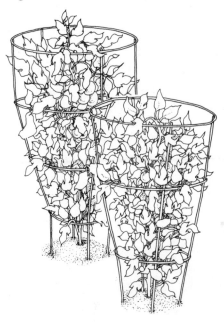

Fig. 6–2 Commercial Cages

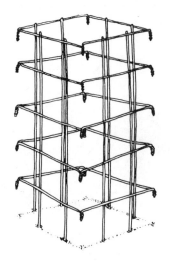

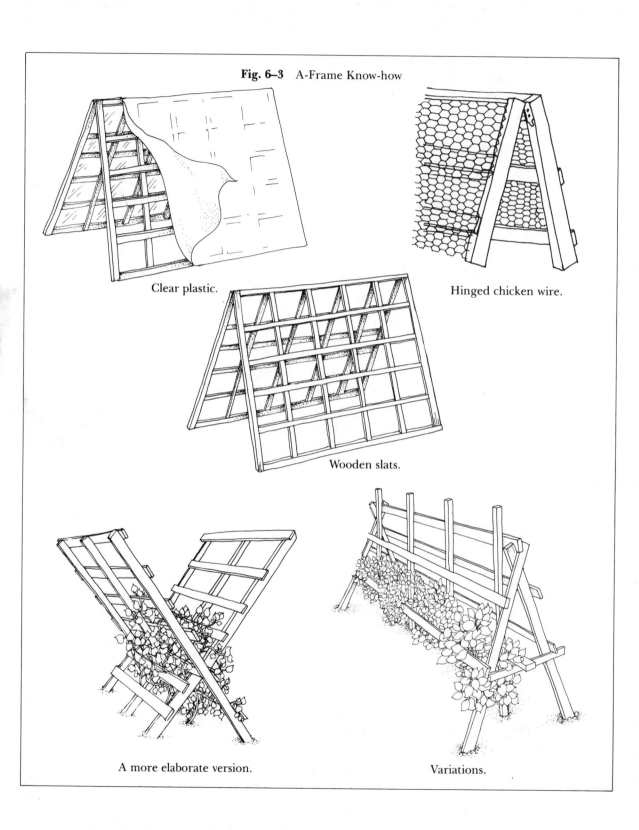

Fig. 6–3 A-Frame Know-how

Clear plastic.

Hinged chicken wire.

Wooden slats.

A more elaborate version.

Variations.

The A frame can be made from 2-by-2-inch and 1-by-2-inch lumber in virtually any size to fit into the space you have available. Even a relatively small A frame tucked away in an odd corner will produce large quantities of vine crops. A 6-by-9-foot structure, for instance, will yield 50 to 60 acorn squash, 100 to 300 cucumbers. This versatile device can be hinged for easy moving and storage, covered with chicken wire or wooden slats to accommodate several different types of vine crops, or covered with clear polyethylene plastic to become a gigantic cloche greenhouse for warm-season plants.

Consider:

Using the A frame at the north end of your garden to grow watermelon or winter squash, instead of putting in a fence.

Making it your only garden. Face it east and west and plant peas on both sides, followed by pole beans on one side, acorn squash on the other, or Armenian Yard Long cucumbers on one side, Italian Romano beans on the other.

Putting five or six A frames of various sizes to work in the same garden. Use small ones for cantaloupes and cucumbers, larger ones for pumpkins, winter squash, and watermelon, and an intermediate size for summer squash.

Intercropping the space underneath the A frame. That is, plant radishes, turnips, leaf lettuce, bunching onions, and other quick-maturing crops in the garden area below the A frame. Harvest before the vines shade out the lower crops. I've sometimes harvested two or three crops of radishes before losing the space. If the A frame faces east and west, you may be able to raise a good crop of leaf lettuce, even when the frame is completely covered with vine crops.

POSTS AND SUCH

The post is another great garden organizer. It takes little space, can be placed anywhere (providing it doesn't shade out other crops), and will produce prodigious quantities of fruit for the amount of space used.

For growing beans, consider an X-frame post, an umbrella post, or a bean-pole garden. Construct all posts as

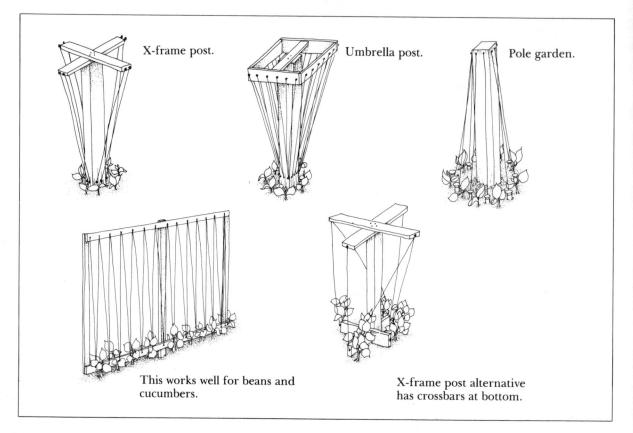

X-frame post.

Umbrella post.

Pole garden.

This works well for beans and cucumbers.

X-frame post alternative has crossbars at bottom.

Fig. 6–4   It's Post Time

shown in Figure 6–4. Drive nails into the post or crossbars at the bottom and into the frame at the top, then run strings between the nails. Plant beans in a 1-foot-diameter circle around the post and train the vines up the strings.

Use these bean posts singly or in groups of twos or threes. Plant other vegetables within 4 or 5 inches of all bean plantings and surround the post with a 1-foot wire cage to keep the plants from crowding each other with their foliage.

For raising cucumbers, consider using a cucumber post or a pickle pole. A cucumber post consists of a 6-foot, 6-by-6-inch or 8-by-8-inch post with 1-foot-long, ½-inch dowels stairstepped around the post 18 inches apart, as shown in Figure 6–5. You can also use large nails. To make a pickle pole, sink a 6-foot-long, 4-by-4-inch post about 12 inches into the soil. Make crossbars from two-by-twos and nail them into the post every 12 inches, as shown in Figure 6–5.

Fig. 6–5 Pickle Poles

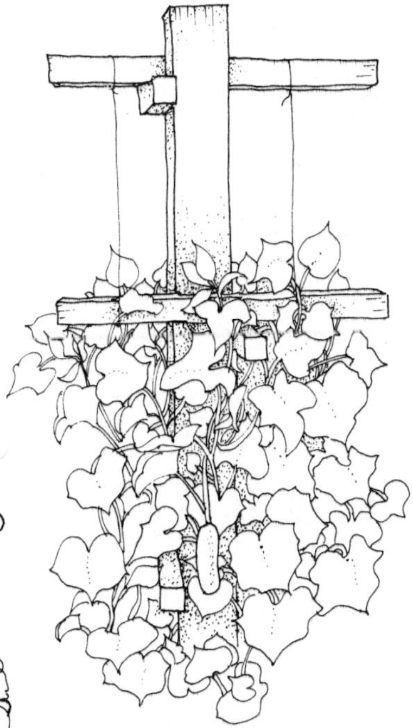

Crossbars on this pickle pole support vines.

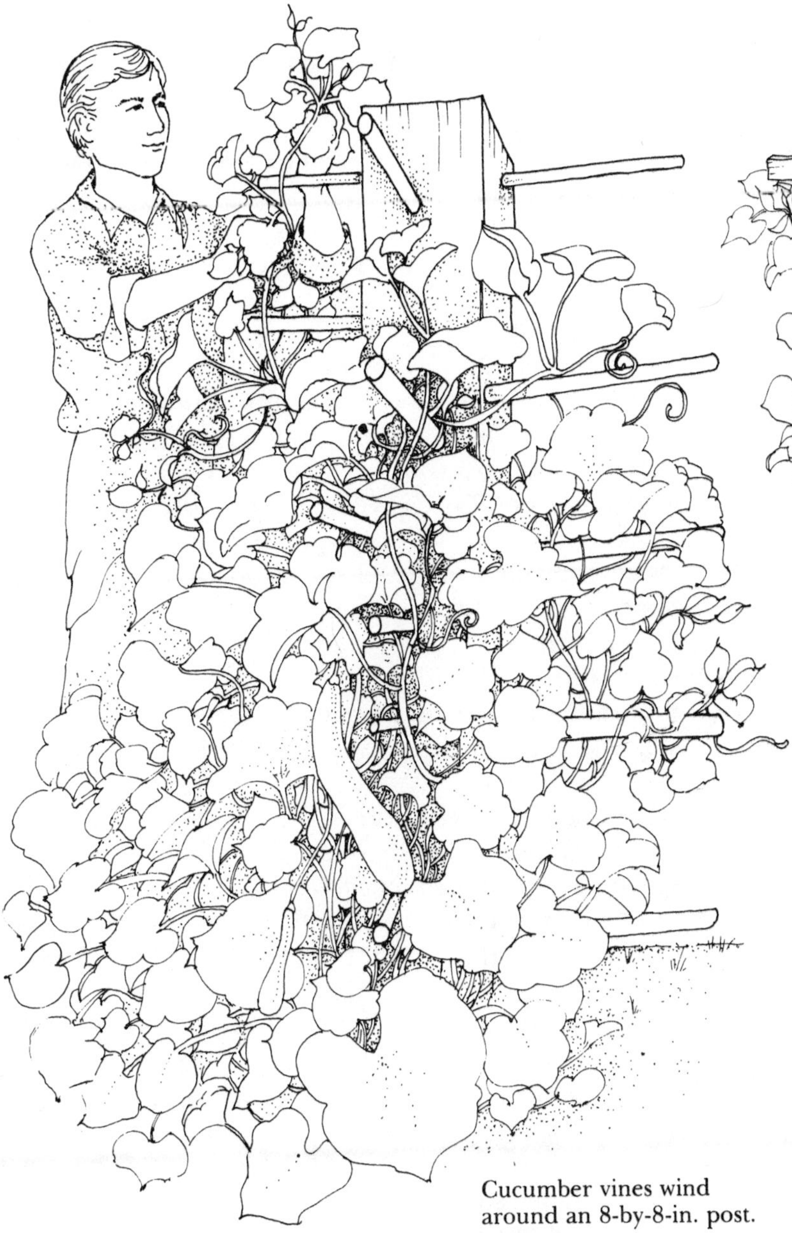

Cucumber vines wind around an 8-by-8-in. post.

Fig. 6–6 Heavy-Fruit Supports

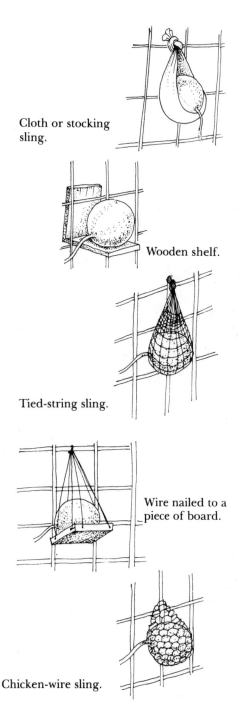

Cloth or stocking sling.

Wooden shelf.

Tied-string sling.

Wire nailed to a piece of board.

Chicken-wire sling.

Plant eight cucumber vines spaced about 4 inches apart around either type of post. To grow summer squash, plant four vines 12 inches apart and tie them to the post. Support the fruit with cloth slings or similar devices (see Figure 6–6).

TRELLISING: THE NEXT STEP UPWARD

After the pole, the trellis is probably the next best method of saving garden space. A trellis, a structure on which vines or other creeping plants are trained, is made of thin strips of wood crossing each other in an open pattern. It is versatile and two dimensional and can take on an infinite variety of forms (see Figure 6–7). Here are some possibilities:

A standard trellis is a frame made of upright pieces and cross members. Use it in place of a fence at the north and/or east side of your garden to support vine crops.

Spot trellises, because of their small size, can be placed in various spots throughout the garden to support the lower vines. A good size is 4 feet long by 4 feet wide. Consider growing cantaloupes or cucumbers on a spot trellis placed along the north edge of a carrot, beet, or spinach bed. Space the cantaloupes 12 inches apart, the cucumbers 4 to 6 inches apart. When the vines start to grow, pinch back their fuzzy growing tips to encourage them to spread out on the trellis. Tie the vines to the trellis with plant ties and support the fruit by one of the methods shown in Figure 6–6.

A ladder trellis consists of two posts placed about 2 feet apart with one-by-ones or similar-sized crosspieces spaced every 4 to 6 inches. Versatile and lightweight, they can be driven into the ground almost anywhere. Use with beans, cucumbers, and tomatoes.

Slanting trellises offer a special advantage, as they enable the fruit of cucumbers to hang down for easy picking. Armenian Yard Long cucumbers look especially attractive growing this way. You can also grow winter squash, beans, and other vine crops on a slanting trellis. You will, however, have to support the larger fruit. Consider using one of these against a wall or porch.

A low horizontal fence trellis (made of wire, netting, or wooden slats) down either side of a row of tomatoes,

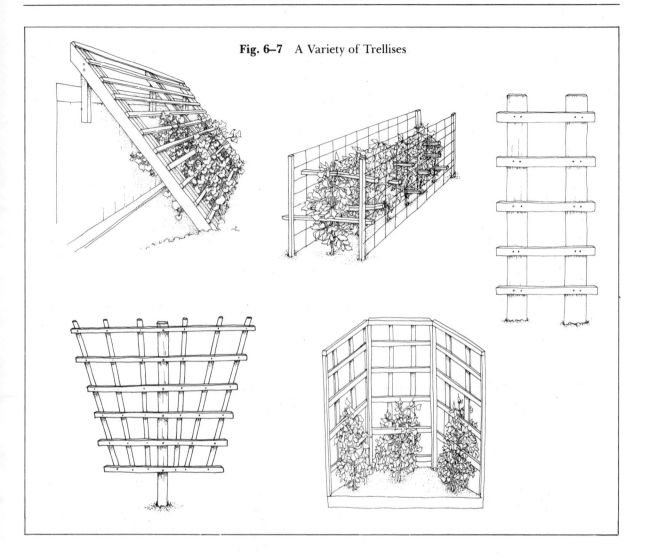

Fig. 6–7   A Variety of Trellises

cucumbers, or summer squash keeps the plants confined in a limited space yet allows them plenty of room to go their own disorderly way. If necessary, support the vines on sticks placed across the sides or tie to either side.

Wire and net trellises are useful for organizing your garden. In any Big Yield/Small Space bed planted with a wide variety of vegetables, some plants will overlap. Zucchini, for instance, will crowd out everything in sight, as will New Zealand spinach. Keep the plants from shading each other and the garden growing mightily by installing a small trellis where the competition gets too fierce.

Fig. 6–8 Wooden-Frame Towers

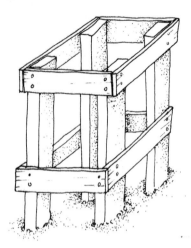

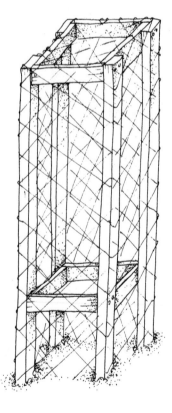

You can also choose from a wide variety of ready-made standard trellises, ladder trellises, and cloth netting that can be stretched between posts. All make highly versatile vertical supports.

TOWER OF POWER: THE WOODEN FRAME

Veteran gardeners have always favored wooden frames for growing large quantities of tomatoes, cucumbers, and other vine crops. Generally they are easy to build and vary from the simple to the complex. You can, for instance, make an effective tomato or cucumber frame using four 2-foot-long two-by-fours as upright posts and six 18-inch-long one-by-threes as horizontal crosspieces. Nail the crosspieces to the posts at the top and 6 inches above the ground, as shown in Figure 6–8. Grow one tomato plant or six to eight cucumber plants spaced 6 inches apart within the structure, letting them spill over the top as they will.

If you prefer a more elaborate tomato or cucumber tower, construct a 2-by-2-foot, 6-foot-high tower from two-by-twos. Cut four 6-foot-long tower supports and nail on eight 2-foot-long cross members 12 inches from the ground and at the top. Drive the structure into the ground over one tomato plant or six to ten cucumber plants spaced 6 inches apart. Cover with 4-inch plastic mesh netting.

Wooden towers can be placed at various spots around the garden or spaced 2 to 3 feet apart in a row. Grow other vegetables around and up to your tower. In the spring and fall, you can turn it into a small greenhouse by covering it with a sheet of polyethylene plastic.

ONWARD AND UPWARD: TIPS FOR GOING VERTICAL

In my years of experimenting with small-space gardens, I've noticed that the more you think "up," the more vegetables you seem to grow. In fact, some of my gardens have resembled gigantic, top-heavy stairsteps, with vegetables growing from a few inches high at the south end to over 10 feet above ground at the north.

Observing a few rules will help you obtain the greatest vertical production possible in your own garden. Whenever you can, locate the north end of your growing space against the south side of a building wall or fence. If you don't have one, construct some type of support at the north end of your garden. A west wall also works well, since it receives the sun's full heat most of the day.

Your vines and fruit can easily be fastened to the wall if you first line the wall with chicken or fence wire. Support the fruit with any of the devices suggested above.

Grow the larger vine crops, such as banana squash and watermelon, on an overhanging roof when possible. Just as having an extra wall is like having a whole extra garden, having a roof to use is like having a supergarden. One California gardener I know grows Bix Max pumpkins up the wall and lets the 30-foot-long vines spill onto his garage roof. In the late fall he usually harvests three or four 80-pound pumpkins. While few gardeners want to bother with a Bix Max, you can raise great quantities of squash simply by letting them climb up a wall and spill onto a roof.

Grow cucumbers and cantaloupes on several trellises or posts or in wire cages in your garden, as these plants do well in small vertical spaces. Save the more extensive wall space for the larger vine crops, like winter squash. You can also save on wall space by raising beans on posts scattered throughout the garden.

Choose long, vining varieties of vegetables for your Big Yield/Small Space garden. Bush varieties are now extremely popular for use in small gardens, but long, vining types grown above the garden on one or more of the structures suggested in this chapter will produce greater volume for the space used.

Vertical gardening, as you have seen, is one step above the traditional growing techniques. Raising crops in containers, our next topic, is the next step beyond.

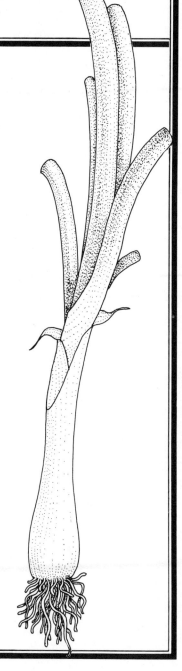

CHAPTER SEVEN

VEGETABLES WITHOUT A GARDEN

Most vegetables feel just as much at home in a 2-foot container on an apartment-house terrace as on a 40-acre farm. In fact, some of the best corn I've ever eaten came from plants growing in a bushel basket on a balcony five stories above the street. Just give your container vegetables good soil and the other conditions they need, and they will add generously to your bounty. This chapter is intended to help you supplement your Big Yield/Small Space production by introducing you to the basics of container gardening.

CONTAINER CREATIVITY

Consider first the possibility of using containers *in* the garden itself. Perch a planter of tomatoes, swiss chard, or eggplant atop a broad-based pickle pole; let a midget cucumber hang down from a bean tower; or suspend wooden boxes or wire baskets of tomatoes, cucumbers, and lettuce from the eaves of your house.

Next, visualize turning nearby soilless areas into productive vegetable patches. Eggplant, peppers, and zucchini can be grouped in large containers on a patio or in a raised bed. Tomatoes do well in paper-pulp pots on porch stairs, and a whole garden of greens can be grown in one long wooden container sitting in front of the house.

Now that you have the general idea, take another look at your available space and see how many places you can find to squeeze in a container or two—or more.

You can garden in almost any type of receptacle, from a plastic garbage can to a wooden box to a wicker basket to a recycled coffee can (see Figure 7–1). I especially recommend containers that hold a minimum of 3½ gallons of

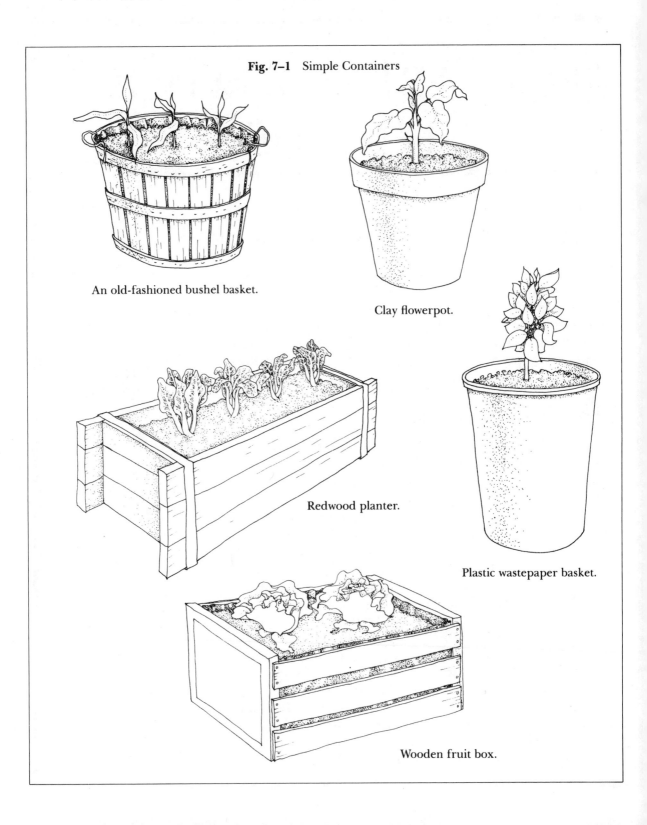

Fig. 7–1 Simple Containers

An old-fashioned bushel basket.

Clay flowerpot.

Redwood planter.

Plastic wastepaper basket.

Wooden fruit box.

soil. That's the amount you would use in a 12-inch clay pot. A cubical planter 1 foot high and 1 foot wide holds 7½ gallons of soil.

You can buy commercial wooden planters in a wide variety of shapes and sizes to fit almost anywhere, or you can construct them yourself. To build a simple cubical planter, purchase five 1-foot squares of 1-inch lumber, 2 feet of 2-by-2-inch stock, and a couple dozen small nails. Nail the four sides to the base, then cut the 2-by-2-inch piece into four equal sections and nail inside the four corners as supports (see Figure 7–2).

Wooden containers made of redwood or cedar resist decay. The interiors of such containers may be lined with black plastic or coated with one of the preservative paints or asphalt compounds that are available at hardware and building-supply stores.

Wooden fruit boxes and old-fashioned bushel baskets are excellent for growing tomatoes, zucchini, and corn. Line them with black plastic and fill with Big Yield/Small Space container soil (see page 98). Plastic pails and plastic wastepaper baskets may not look impressive, but they are relatively inexpensive and will grow almost any kind of vegetable. In addition, some companies, such as Rubbermaid, manufacture attractive plastic planters in many shapes and sizes. Paper-pulp pots are favorites because they are lightweight and therefore easy to move from one spot to another.

Some gardeners favor that old standby, the clay flowerpot. Others use pots made of styrofoam or plastic. Whatever the material, it's best to select pots that are 12 to 18 inches in diameter at the very minimum.

VEGETABLES IN RAISED BEDS

Raised beds are frames made of wood, concrete blocks, railroad ties, or other sturdy material that are placed directly on the ground and filled with soil. They raise the planting surface 8 to 12 inches or more above the surrounding soil. Because they can be constructed to fit almost any location, raised beds fit the Big Yield/Small Space concept perfectly (see Figure 7–3). They can also be modified easily by any number of the climate-control devices described in Chapter 5.

Fig. 7–2 Do-it-yourself Wooden Containers

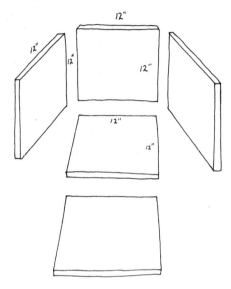

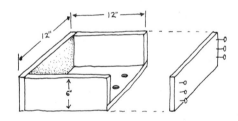

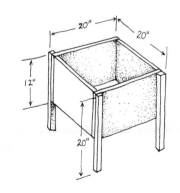

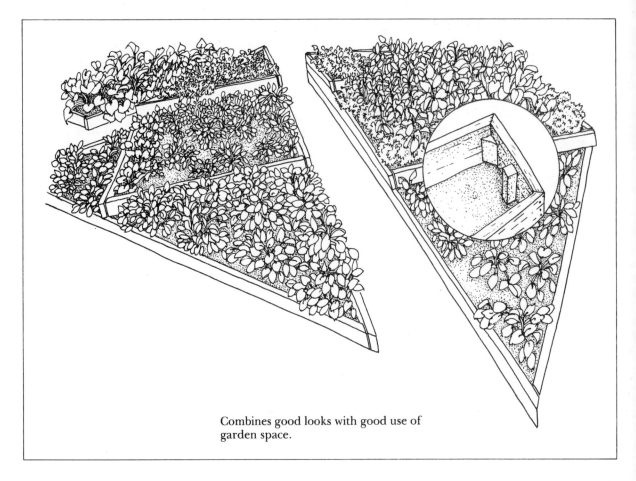

Combines good looks with good use of
garden space.

Fig. 7–3 Raised Beds

Raised beds have several advantages over in-the-ground
planting. They:

1   Speed spring planting. Since the soil in raised beds
    warms up quickly, they can be planted several weeks
    ahead of a ground-level garden.
2   Eliminate the necessity to plant on your hands and
    knees by putting your garden at a more convenient
    height. This height also makes it easier to cultivate and
    harvest your vegetables.
3   Give your garden a neat, organized, permanent ap-
    pearance. In general, raised beds look more attractive
    than flat beds in a landscaped yard.
4   Solve gopher problems easily when 1-inch-mesh
    chicken wire is placed across the bottoms of the
    frames.

Making a Raised Bed

The simplest way to construct a raised bed is to nail together a 2-by-12-inch redwood frame directly in place, reinforcing the corners with 2-by-2-inch redwood posts. If you build your raised beds with 16-inch-wide boards and cap them with 2-by-6-inch boards, you can sit down while you weed. Logs, rocks, railroad ties, and concrete headers are also good materials to use (see Figure 7–4).

A good size for a raised bed is 6 to 10 feet long and just wide enough (4 to 6 feet) that you can comfortably reach the center from the sides. Beds this size can be grouped together, lengthened, or even changed in shape to fit virtually any space. Leave 18- to 24-inch walkways on all sides (unless the beds are built against a wall) so you can plant, water, and harvest easily.

Raised-Bed Soil

Fill your raised beds with a mixture of two parts Big Yield/Small Space soil (made either organically or by the general method) and one part peat moss purchased from a nursery or other gardening-supply source. This soil will be extremely fertile, light, and easy to work.

CONSIDER VERTICAL CONTAINERS

The Bookshelf

One clever way to combine the container and vertical approaches to gardening is to use bookshelf planters (see Figure 7–5). Bookshelf planters can be placed in the garden or on a patio and will produce an abundant harvest of lettuce, spinach, and other leafy vegetables. To construct your own, build top and bottom frames of two-by-twos and connect them with two-by-twelves. Close the open sides with 4-by-4-inch wire mesh. Your planter can be virtually any size, but a width and height of 4 by 5 feet generally allows you to plant and harvest without much difficulty.

Line the planter with black plastic, fill with soil mix (described below), and cut slits in the plastic, centering them in the mesh squares. Leave the top open and water

Fig. 7–4 Raised-Bed Construction

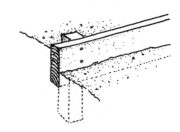

Construction is simple for raised beds of just a few inches.

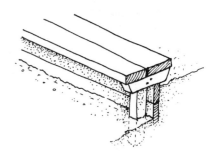

Deeper raised bed with a cap or seat cap has landscape functions.

Railroad ties make ideal raised beds. They can be used singly or up to three deep.

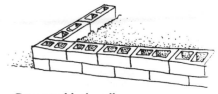

Concrete-block walls.

Fig. 7–5   A Bookshelf Planter

from there and through openings about halfway down. Before planting, wet the mix. Set transplants, not seeds, through the wire mesh and insert individual peat pots firmly into the planting mix. Feed every two weeks with liquid fertilizer containing at least 10 percent nitrogen.

Hang Those Containers

Hanging containers allow you to use space that would otherwise be wasted. You can hang clay pots, wooden boxes, and similar receptacles under the eaves, at the edge of a covered patio, and along the overhang of a porch or balcony. To put your containers in place, use eye hooks and coat hangers or choose from among the several commercial products available for this purpose.

To prepare a wire basket for planting, first stuff the open frame with sphagnum moss, place an aluminum pie pan or piece of black plastic in the bottom to keep the soil from washing out, and fill the basket with container soil mixture. Hanging baskets dry out quickly, so you should water yours daily by immersing them in a pail or sink full of water.

SOIL FUNDAMENTALS

Although it's possible to grow container vegetables in a commercial potting mix as you would indoor plants, I find they do better grown in a mixture containing equal parts of Big Yield/Small Space soil, commercial potting mix, and compost or vermiculite in the following combination:

One part each of: commercial potting mix
compost or vermiculite
Small Space/Big Yield soil

Garden stores sell potting mixes or synthetic soil under a variety of trade names: Jiffy Mix, Metro Mix, Pro Mix, and Supersoil. Most contain a balance of nutrients, although the formulas vary for different types of plants.

If you want to use Big Yield/Small Space soil in your containers, it can be sterilized to kill disease organisms, pests, and weed seed. It's easiest to do this by spreading the soil out in a shallow pan and baking for one hour at 275 degrees F. To overcome any odor problem, soak the soil thoroughly before putting it in the oven. Some gardeners won't sterilize their soil because it destroys microorganisms. Personally, I dislike all the muss and fuss that go with the sterilization process and prefer to take my chances that there's nothing in the soil to harm my vegetables.

MIDGET MAGIC: SELECTING VEGETABLES FOR CONTAINERS

Although you can grow regular full-sized vegetables in receptacles, the midget varieties are especially well suited to container gardening. Some of my favorites are listed in Table 7–1.

TABLE 7–1. MIDGET VARIETIES FOR CONTAINERS

VARIETIES	DAYS TO MATURITY	REMARKS	CATALOG SEED SOURCES
CABBAGE			
Baby Head	72	Miniature head, 2½ inches across, Danish Ballhead type	14, 60
Morden Dwarf	65	Novel midget cabbage, 4-inch-round head, crisp	7, 16
CANTALOUPES			
Early Sugar Midget	60	Medium-sized vines, golden yellow	14
Midget Muskmelon	60	Three-foot vines produce many melons	54
Minnesota Midget	63	Small, 4-inch melons, 3-foot vines	16, 22, 46, 50
Short 'n Sweet	62	Bushy growth, sugary fruit, resistant to powdery mildew	46
CARROTS			
Bunny Bite	65	1½ inches long, ¾ inch in diameter, tapering Chantenay type	52
Little Finger	65	Cylindrical with small core, smooth skin, Nantes type	6, 67
Short 'n Sweet	68	Bright orange, 3½–4 inches long, tapering	6
Tiny Sweet	65	Bright golden orange, 3 inches long	5, 16, 22, 46, 54

TABLE 7–1. MIDGET VARIETIES FOR CONTAINERS *(continued)*

VARIETIES	DAYS TO MATURITY	REMARKS	CATALOG SEED SOURCES
CORN			
Faribo Golden Midget	60	Novel, 30-inch plants, sweet, tender, flavorful	16
Golden Midget	60	Sweet, tender kernels, 2- to 3-foot stalks, 4- to 4½-inch ears	6, 14, 17, 22, 24, 31, 37, 44, 46, 50
Golden Miniature	54	Dwarf plant, 5-inch ears	60
CUCUMBER			
Baby Cucumber	52	Bushy vines, early, productive, 4-inch-cucumbers, pickler	17
Bush Whopper	55	No runners, 6- to 8-inch cucumbers	45, 46
Little Minnie	52	Bushes to 2 feet, 4-inch-long cucumbers, blunt ends	22
Midget	50	Early, 2-foot vines	54
Patio Pik	55	Pickler and slicer, performs well in hanging basket	8, 16, 20, 25, 28, 45, 46, 49, 52, 60, 67
Pot Luck	56	Straight, green, 6½-inch fruit, 18- to 24-inch plants, good in hanging basket	8, 14, 32, 35, 50, 63, 65
EGGPLANT			
Early Black Egg	65	Tender fruit up to 5 inches long	31
Morden Midget	65	Bushy plants, earliest of all, deep purple fruit	16
Nagaoka New Kissin	65	Extra early, dark purple, 4 inches long	36
Ornamental White	Early	Two-and-a-half-inch fruit	Bea's Bric-a-Brac, 15105 Lakeview, Houston, TX 77040
Purple Pickling	75	Bears early masses of tiny eggplant	44
Slim Jim	65	Novel eggplant, grows in 6-inch pots, good for pickling	Ball Seed Company, P.O. Box 335, West Chicago, IL 60185
LETTUCE			
Midget	55	Buttercrunch type, All-America Selection	14, 22
Sweet Midget Cos	60	Upright heads, 5 inches tall	16
Tom Thumb	65	Tennis-ball sized heads, Buttercrunch type	6, 10, 16, 17, 44, 46, 54

TABLE 7–1. MIDGET VARIETIES FOR CONTAINERS (*continued*)

VARIETIES	DAYS TO MATURITY	REMARKS	CATALOG SEED SOURCES
PEAS*			
American Wonder	61	Early, 12-inch plants	16, 17, 48, 54
Greater Progress	62	Dependable and productive, 18-inch vines	23, 52, 65
TOMATOES			
Droplet	65	Determinate, produces 90–120 fruits 1–1½ inches in diameter, sweet	16
Early Salad	45	Compact, 6- to 8-inch plants, produces until frost, 1½- to 1¾-inch fruit	5, 45, 46
German Dwarf Bush	45	Small, rugged plants for pot culture, red, 2-inch fruit	20
Patio	70	Early, determinate, grows 24 to 30 inches, good for tubs	8, 17, 24, 25, 26, 28, 35, 42, 45, 46, 48, 49, 50, 52
Pixie	50	Compact, 15- to 24-inch vine, 1¾-inch fruit	2, 6, 63
Presto	60	Early, suitable for pots or garden, small leaves, bears half-dollar-sized fruit over long season	23
Pretty Patio	70	Upright, 30-inch plants bear abundantly in large pots or tubs, medium-sized fruit	24
Red Cushion	65	Cherry type, can be grown in container, plants spread 18 inches, grow 1 foot tall	50
Salad Top	50	Grows only 18 inches high, fully branched, bright red fruit 1–1½ inches	5
Small Fry	60	Early, heavy cropper, bears large cherry-type fruit in 1-inch-round clusters, All-America Selection	6, 8, 14, 16, 17, 22, 23, 24, 25, 26, 28, 32, 45, 46, 48, 49, 50, 52, 60, 67
Stoke's Alaska	55	Northern garden variety for tubs, 18-inch plant, bushy	60
Tiny Tim	50	Early, 15-inch vine, ideal for hanging basket, scarlet, ¾-inch fruit	2, 6, 8, 14, 16, 17, 24, 25, 32, 33, 35, 39, 43, 44, 45, 46, 50, 54, 60, 67, 68
Toy Boy	60	Early, 2 feet high, fruit size of Ping Pong ball	8, 16, 28, 42, 44, 45, 67
Tumblin' Tom	55	Good for hanging baskets, 20- to 24-inch vines, plum-shaped fruit 1½ to 2 inches	7, 37, 60

*Bush, not midget, varieties.

TABLE 7–1. MIDGET VARIETIES FOR CONTAINERS *(continued)*

VARIETIES	DAYS TO MATURITY	REMARKS	CATALOG SEED SOURCES
WATERMELONS			
Burpee Sugar Bush	80	Needs about 6 square feet growing space per plant, 6- to 8-pound melons	6
Family Fun	88	Dark green, round, slightly oblong, red flesh	65
Golden Midget	65	Red flesh, small and dark seeds, 8 inches, turns golden yellow when ripe	10, 14, 16, 22, 46
Lollipop	70	Yellow and red melons, 3–5 pounds	46
Market Midget	69	Sweet, slightly oval, 3–5 pounds	22, 42, 63
New Hampshire Midget	68	Early, good for short seasons, 7 by 6 inches, striped dark green, All-America Selection	2, 6, 8, 10, 16, 24, 39, 41, 45, 46, 65, 67
Petite Sweet	65	Extra-high sugar content, 8-pound melons	22, 32, 42, 65, 68
Sugar Baby	80	Crisp, sweet, 8 inches in diameter, dark green	5, 6, 7, 8, 10, 17, 22, 23, 24, 26, 30, 32, 34, 35, 38, 41, 45, 46, 49, 50, 52, 54, 60, 61, 65, 67, 68
Sugar Ball	65	Fiery red flesh, many melons on each vine, 12–15 pounds	14, 67
Sugar Doll	72	Sweet, red flesh, 8–10 pounds	25, 42, 46, 50, 65
Sugar Lumps	78	Yellow, white, and red melons, 8–9 inches in diameter	17
You Sweet Thing	70	Round, striped, 12–13 pounds	27, 28, 44, 46, 52, 54

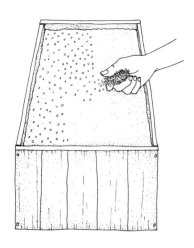

PLANTING CONTAINER VEGETABLES

After you have filled your containers with soil, sow the seed or plant the seedlings directly inside. Before you sow seeds or transplant, though, be sure to soak the soil thoroughly. If the instructions call for seed to be planted ½ inch deep, don't dig holes in the container soil. Instead, broadcast plant the seeds, then cover with a ½-inch layer of soil. Later you can thin them to obtain the required spacing. Transplants should be hardened off in the same way as they are for transplanting outdoors.

The spacing for container vegetables is somewhat different than for those grown directly in the garden. Follow the directions in Table 7–2 for successful cultivation.

TABLE 7–2. SPACING FOR CONTAINER VEGETABLES

VEGETABLE	SPACE BETWEEN PLANTS
Artichokes	Plant singly; 10–15 gallons of soil per plant
Beans	Three to 9 inches apart
Beets	Two to 3 inches apart
Broccoli	Ten inches apart; 5 gallons of soil per plant
Brussels Sprouts	Ten inches apart; 5 gallons of soil per plant
Cabbage	Ten inches apart; 5 gallons of soil per plant
Carrots	One to 2 inches apart
Cauliflower	Twelve inches apart; 5 gallons of soil per plant
Eggplant	Fifteen inches apart; 5 gallons of soil per plant
Kale	Thin to 12–16 inches apart
Lettuce	Four to 10 inches apart
Melon	Twelve inches apart; 5 gallons of soil per plant
Mustard Greens	Thin to 4 inches apart
Okra	Eighteen inches apart; 5–10 gallons of soil per plant
Onions	Two to 3 inches apart
Peas	Two inches apart
Peppers	Eight to 12 inches apart; 2½ gallons of soil per plant
Potatoes	Six to 8 inches apart
Radishes	One to 2 inches apart
Rhubarb	Twelve inches apart; 5 gallons of soil per plant
Rutabagas	Six inches apart
Spinach	Thin to 5 inches apart
Squash	Twelve to 20 inches apart
Swiss Chard	Thin to 8 inches apart
Tomatoes	One-half to 5 gallons of soil per plant
Turnips	Two inches apart

CARE AND FEEDING

Water large containers from above with a watering can or hose. Use a gentle stream or one of the water-breaking nozzles. Drip irrigation systems also make watering a number of containers fairly easy. Spaghetti tubes with drip spitters attached deliver water directly to each container. These more sophisticated systems are described in Chapter 9.

In general, water all vegetables until the soil is completely saturated. Don't water again until the soil is dry to a depth of 1 or 2 inches. To check, poke in your finger to this depth or use a moisture meter.

All containers need outlets or drain holes through which the excess water that percolates through the soil can be released. Otherwise, the soil becomes so saturated that oxygen is cut off from the plant roots.

As a general rule, containers less than 10 inches wide need one hole about ½ inch in diameter. The larger pots need from two to four holes, each just slightly larger than ½ inch. If you have wooden containers, drill holes through their bases. Punch holes in the sides of plastic and metal containers about ½ inch above the base—plastic and metal receptacles are often not strong enough to hold the weight of wet soil when holes are punched in the bottom.

You will have to give these vegetables supplemental feedings of fertilizer because container cultivation requires more water than in-the-ground growing, and this watering leaches out many of the nutrients. Each of the major nutrients affects the health of your plants in a different way. Nitrogen, for instance, is important for the growth of lettuce, chard, kale, and other leafy vegetables. Phosphorus is essential to the production of the fruit of eggplant, peppers, melons, and tomatoes. Potassium promotes strong root growth and is necessary for such crops as carrots, beets, radishes, and turnips.

If you are using the soil formula described in this chapter, add 1 tablespoon of time-release fertilizer for every 5 gallons of soil. If your soil is made up entirely of organic materials, add a liquid fertilizer that contains 4 to 5 percent phosphorus every two or three weeks.

After harvesting a crop and before refilling and replanting, scrub your containers down with a vegetable brush and soapy water, then rinse with boiling water. This prevents disease organisms from being transmitted from one crop to the next.

MOVING YOUR CONTAINERS

If you're not a weight lifter, you will have to make some provision for moving your containers from place to place.

Even a 14-inch clay pot feels as if it weighs a ton if it's filled with soil, and a 1-foot wooden cube may seem nearly impossible to move.

I suggest using a child's wagon or a throw rug to pull those that aren't too heavy. It's also possible to install casters on the heavier wooden containers. As an alternative, consider buying a small dolly from a hardware or building-supply store. Of course, the simplest solution is to put the empty container where you want it, fill it with soil, and leave it there until you harvest the crop. Then empty out the soil and store the container or move it to another location.

Now you know the basic components of the Big Yield/ Small Space system. Since *when* you plant your vegetables is as important as the manner in which it's done, in the next chapter I'll explain how you can fit these components together with a timing that will work for you.

Moving your containers.

CHAPTER EIGHT

TIMING MAKES THE SYSTEM WORK

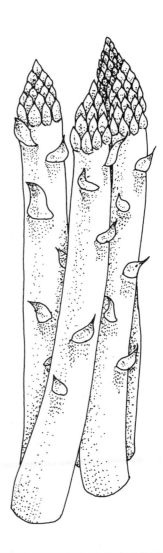

By using intensive planting methods, extending the growing season on either end, and taking advantage of every bit of space around and above your garden, you will increase your harvests substantially. The real key to making your Big Yield/Small Space garden work, though, is the timing.

On the most basic level, it's best to plant your cool-season crops as early in the spring as is feasible, following them with warm-season vegetables, then planting again and extending the fall harvest for as long as possible. In the warmer sun-belt sections of the country, this means you will be able to grow vegetables all year around.

What makes timing such a challenge are the many factors you must take into consideration in order to reach specific decisions about each vegetable. You will, for example, have to determine the best method and time for starting each variety you plan to grow, the average period needed for germination, the time it will take to grow seedlings to transplant size, the average last-in-the-spring and first-in-the-fall freeze dates, the first safe spring planting date and the last safe fall planting date, and the protective season stretchers you intend to use.

At first glance, the process sounds a bit complicated; but all it really involves is simple addition and subtraction, a willingness to invest some planning time, and the use of some basic information that you will find in Appendixes A–D of this book. Whatever your situation, creating a planting timetable in advance will greatly simplify your task.

SPRING/SUMMER PLANTING

Devising Your Timetable

Here are the steps for laying out a spring/summer planting timetable. Follow this general procedure for each type of vegetable you plan to grow in your spring/summer garden.

1   Look up the average date of the last spring frost in your area in Appendix A or call your county extension agent and get an accurate date for your locale.
2   In Appendix B, find the first safe spring date for planting in the open. *This gives you a date for planting or transplanting in the open without protection.*
3   Subtract the number of weeks of protection afforded by each protective device you plan to use. As a rule of thumb, subtract two weeks for simple protective devices, four weeks for plastic tunnels and similar cloches, and four weeks for cold frames and Big Yield/Small Space greenhouses. These are conservative figures and therefore may vary slightly in different climates. *This gives you a date for planting or transplanting outdoors with protection.*
4   Subtract the time needed to germinate seed and grow seedlings to transplant size (see Appendix D). *This gives you a date on which to plant seed for that particular vegetable indoors.*

You will see from the sample plans in Chapter 1 that cool-weather and warm-weather crops generally follow each other in the same bed. When you are ready to plant your warm-weather crops, such as tomatoes, peppers, eggplant, and squash, sow seed or transplant seedlings between the already-growing cool-weather vegetables. When the first crop is harvested, the second will already have a head start.

Sample Planting Scenarios

Now let's go through the process with a few vegetables to see how it works. Say you are gardening in Massachusetts and want to plant pole snap beans early, using cutoff gallon milk cartons as protective devices. You would want to do the following:

1 Look up the average date of the last frost for Massachusetts in Appendix A (*April 25*).
2 Find the first safe spring date for planting pole snap beans in the open (assuming a last spring frost date of April 25) in Appendix B. This date will fall somewhere between the figures given for last spring frost dates of April 20 and April 30. If you estimate, you will find that *you can plant pole snap beans in Massachusetts in the open without protection about May 5.*
3 Subtract two weeks from the May 5 date to account for the protection provided by cutoff milk cartons. By subtracting 2 weeks, *you can plant or transplant pole snap beans in Massachusetts about April 21.*
4 If you are starting your beans indoors, subtract another seven to ten days for bean-seed germination plus the four to six weeks needed for bean seedlings to reach transplant size from the April 21 date above (see Appendix D). I generally average these figures, allowing one week for germination and five weeks for reaching transplant size. After subtracting these six weeks from the April 21 date, you find that *you should plant pole snap bean seed indoors in cubes about March 10.*

Or let's say you're a southern Ohio gardener who wants to start corn early, utilizing plastic-covered wooden frames for protection.

1 Find the average date of the last spring frost for southern Ohio in Appendix A (*April 20*).
2 In Appendix B, look up the first safe date for planting corn in the open (using a last spring frost date of April 20). In this case, *you can plant corn in the open without protection about April 25.*
3 From this date subtract the four weeks you'll gain by protecting your corn with plastic-covered wooden frames. Subtracting four weeks, you find *you can plant or transplant corn in southern Ohio using the protection of plastic-covered wooden frames about March 28.*

4   For indoor planting, subtract from the March 28 date above six to ten days (one week average) for seed germination and the four weeks needed for corn to reach transplant size. *Corn should be planted inside about February 22.*

Corn is usually planted directly in the ground. As with beans, however, you can speed up the harvest by planting first indoors, then transplanting the seedlings into the ground on the desired planting date.

Or you may be a Sierra foothill gardener in northern California who wants to plant tomatoes in a Big Yield/Small Space greenhouse.

1   In Appendix A, look up the average date of the last spring frost for the California mountain areas *(this would be April 20).*

2   Find the first safe date for planting tomatoes in the open (using a last spring frost date of April 20) in Appendix B. *You can plant your tomatoes in the open without protection about May 5.*

3   Subtract four weeks from the May 5 date for the protection afforded by Big Yield/Small Space greenhouses. By subtracting four weeks, you find *you can transplant in this area, using the protection of the Big Yield/Small Space greenhouse, about April 7.*

4   Subtract 5 to 12 days (one and one-half weeks average) for seed germination, plus the five to seven weeks (six weeks average) tomato seedlings need to reach transplant size, from the April 7 date above. *Tomatoes should be started inside from seed about February 15.*

FALL/WINTER PLANTING

Devising Your Timetable

Follow these steps for each vegetable you intend to plant in your fall/winter garden:

1   Look up the average date of the first fall frost in your area in Appendix A or call your county extension agent and get an accurate date for your locale.

2   Find the range of safe fall planting dates in Appendix

C. *This gives you the range of safe fall dates for planting or transplanting in the open without protection.*

   Whenever you create an empty space in your bed by harvesting, fill it immediately with the next crop, within the above range of safe dates.

3   To the last safe date for planting in the open, add the number of weeks of protection afforded by each protective device you plan to use. *This gives you a general last safe planting date with the use of protective devices.*

4   Subtract the time needed to germinate the seed of particular vegetables and to grow the seedlings to transplant size (see Appendix D). *This gives you the date on which to start your plants indoors.*

5   Put your protective devices in place any time the temperature drops below 50 to 60 degrees F. This will keep your vegetables growing at an optimum rate. On sunny days, however, be careful not to burn your plants under plastic.

Crops always take longer to mature at this time of year than they do in the spring and summer, so select the varieties with the shortest maturity dates (see Chapter 11). Plant on or about the last safe planting date directly into the already-growing beds of spring- and summer-planted vegetables. If the growth of such plants as tomatoes and peppers is too thick, take off some of the bottom leaves. When you are ready to harvest your warm-weather vegetables, cut them off; do not dig them out.

Sample Planting Scenarios

   Again, let's go through the steps with a couple of vegetables. Imagine you are gardening in Massachusetts and you want to follow peppers with cabbage and to extend the season with plastic-covered wooden frames.

1   Look up the average date of the first fall frost for Massachusetts in Appendix A (*October 25*).

2   Find the range of safe fall planting dates for cabbage (using a first fall freezing date of October 25) in Appendix C. *Without protection, you can transplant cabbage for fall/winter harvest from about July 20 to August 15.* (You will need to estimate this date from the figures

given for first fall frost dates of October 20 and October 30.)

3   Add four to six weeks from the August 15 date above to allow for the protection of the plastic-covered wooden frames. *Your date for transplanting with protection should be somewhere near September 15.*

4   Subtract four to ten days for cabbage-seed germination (average one week) and five to seven weeks (average six weeks) for cabbage seedlings to grow to transplant size. *Your cabbage should be started inside from seed about July 28.*

5   See Appendix D for minimum and maximum growing temperatures for cabbage. You'll have to put your plastic-covered frames over your cabbage plants when the temperature drops below 50 to 60 degrees F. Although cabbage is frost hardy, it will grow better under protective devices when the temperature drops below this range. Take off the frames when the daytime temperature under the plastic rises above 85 degrees. (It's a good idea to check this with a thermometer.)

Finally, assume you are gardening in southern Ohio and want to follow your tomatoes with spinach, using a Big Yield/Small Space greenhouse to extend the season.

1   In Appendix A, check the average date of the first fall frost for southern Ohio (*September 30*).

2   Look up the range of safe fall planting dates for spinach (using a first fall frost date of September 30) in Appendix C. *You can plant spinach for fall/winter harvest without protection from July 1 to August 15.*

3   Add four weeks to the August 15 date to account for the protection provided by the Big Yield/Small Space greenhouse. Since spinach should be sown directly in the bed rather than transplanted, *your planting date should be approximately September 15.*

4   Find the minimum and maximum growing temperatures for spinach in Appendix D. You'll see that you should put on your Big Yield/Small Space greenhouse cover when the temperature drops below about 50 degrees F.; take it off when the temperature goes above 85 degrees.

Tables 8–1 and 8–2 are sample planting timetables to help you make up your own. For these examples, assume you are going to use plastic-covered wire tunnels to extend the season, the average day of the last spring frost is April 20, and the average date of the first fall frost is October 30. Remember that the figures given in this chapter and in the appendixes should be your starting point; you will need to stretch or shorten these dates according to your own local conditions.

TABLE 8–1. SPRING PLANTING TIMETABLE

VEGETABLE	FIRST SAFE PLANTING DATE*	SUBTRACT 4 WEEKS FOR PROTECTION —ACTUAL PLANTING DATE	SUBTRACT GERMINATION TIME†	SUBTRACT TIME TO GROW TO TRANSPLANT SIZE†	DATE FOR STARTING SEED INSIDE
Beans	April 25	March 25	7–15 days	4–6 weeks	February 8
Beets	March 20	February 20	Plant beets directly in the ground		
Broccoli	March 25	February 25	4–10 days	5–7 weeks	January 8
Carrots	April 1	March 1	Plant carrots directly in the ground		
Cucumbers	May 1	April 1	5–11 days	4–5 weeks	February 26

*See Appendix B.   †See Appendix D.

TABLE 8–2. FALL PLANTING TIMETABLE

VEGETABLE	SAFE-DATE RANGE FOR PLANTING IN OPEN*	ADD 4 WEEKS FOR PROTECTION† —ACTUAL PLANTING DATE	SUBTRACT GERMINATION TIME‡	SUBTRACT TIME TO GROW TO TRANSPLANT SIZE‡	DATE FOR STARTING SEED INSIDE
Broccoli	July 1— August 15	September 15	4–10 days	5–7 weeks	July 28
Cabbage	August 1– September 1	October 1	4–10 days	5–7 weeks	August 13
Cauliflower	July 15– August 15	September 15	4–10 days	5–7 weeks	July 28

*See Appendix C. †Put protective devices in place when temperature drops below 50–60 degrees F.

‡See Appendix D.

You will generally be able to grow many leafy and root crops under protection when the average daytime temperature is in the high 40s, 50s, and 60s and the average nighttime temperature is in the 30s and 40s with some frosts. While some parts of the United States suffer severely low temperatures and frozen ground during the winter months, many areas of the South and along the West Coast have mild winter temperatures in the 30- to 60-degree range. As I suggested, in these areas you could probably garden 9, 10, and even 12 months of the year with protective devices.

You may not get your plantings exactly right the first few times, since you are dealing with factors that will always vary, such as weather, days to maturity, and germination time. This is one situation, though, where practice makes perfect. You'll still get good harvests during the trial years, and within a few seasons you'll be surprised at just how expert a Big Yield/Small Space gardener you have become.

In the next few chapters I will describe how to nourish and protect the vegetables that you have so carefully planted.

CHAPTER NINE

WATERING WISDOM

I f the sun is the heart and power of all vegetable gardens, then certainly water is the soul. Give your vegetables enough liquid refreshment at the right time, and your Big Yield/Small Space garden will look lush and beautiful. Deny your thirsty vegetables the water they need, though, and you're liable to open up a Pandora's box of troubles.

Vegetables, more than any other plants, need to mature rapidly, with no check in growth. Without enough water, they suffer from a stress condition that nearly always sets them back. And once this occurs, they seldom recover—most plants simply wilt. Plants that are consistently overwatered suffer the same sad fate. They often appear weak and spindly.

SOME SIMPLE GUIDELINES

As a general rule, water thoroughly, deeply, and infrequently. The soil in your beds will have roughly 50 percent air space, 50 percent solid material. If you continuously soak the soil to the point where all the air spaces are filled with water (a condition known as *reaching field capacity*), you will stop the exchange of oxygen and carbon dioxide from taking place and quite literally drown your plants. To keep your vegetables growing well, you should water to field capacity, let your beds dry out to the point where the plant roots can no longer take moisture from the soil, then bring the soil back to field capacity again.

In general, your vegetable garden needs the equivalent of 1 inch of rain per week during the growing season. That translates into roughly 15 to 25 gallons for every 25 square feet of garden.

In order for your vegetables to achieve maximum growth, you need to water them in such a way as to make some moisture available at the appropriate root depths for each vegetable. The length of time that this takes will depend on the specific vegetable, for, as you might guess, different vegetables have different root depths. Carrots, broccoli, eggplant, and potatoes, for example, put down roots from 2 to 5 feet deep. Cantaloupes, pumpkins, and tomatoes, on the other hand, seem as if they're trying to reach China, sinking their roots 8 to 10 feet deep or more. Moreover, the type of soil under your bed also affects the watering time. Typically, however, you can count on giving your garden an hour or two of constant soaking.

Whatever the vegetable, a good rule is to water until you can easily sink a stick about 3 feet deep. Then, after watering thoroughly, don't water again until the soil has dried out to a depth of 4 to 8 inches. Check with a trowel or one of the mechanical or electrical moisture meters now on the market. This guideline works well, no matter how dry the season or how much rainfall you have in your area. When it's hot and dry, you may find yourself watering every one to three days. If the weather is cool and damp, this period may stretch to two or three weeks or more.

At the present time in most places, water is relatively inexpensive and available in almost unlimited quantities. In some urban areas, however, the cost of water has risen sharply during the last few years and can be expected to continue to rise in the future. In other areas, water shortages have resulted in cutbacks in use and concern about future availability. Consequently, it is becoming increasingly important to make sure that you are watering in the most effective and efficient manner possible. Now let's look at the three major ways to do this.

WATERING BY SPRINKLER

The easiest way to water is to set up a sprinkler. You can choose from several kinds:

1   A Rainbird type, a pulsating sprinkler that covers 50 to 75 feet in radius
2   Oscillating types that move back and forth over a rectangular area of 50 to 60 square feet
3   Rotating nonmovable sprinklers that water in a 5- to 50-foot circle

4   Spray-head irrigation systems that use plastic pipe and adjustable plastic or brass spray heads to water from a quarter to a full circle

Of these, I favor the pulsating sprinkler because, first, one alone operating in a full circle can completely cover one or more small gardens, and, second, it is a highly flexible device. You can make a pulsating sprinkler part of an underground pipe irrigation system or use it as a single free-standing unit.

Some gardeners prefer the oscillating sprinklers that come equipped with a timing device to allow you to dial the total amount of water you want, up to 1,200 gallons. Overhead-sprinkler watering has a number of advantages, too. It takes little effort, it resembles natural rain more closely than other watering systems do, and the plants benefit from having the dust washed off their leaves.

Unfortunately, however, overhead watering has disadvantages as well. It is wasteful because it indiscriminately covers both garden and nongarden areas. In addition, this watering method can create humid conditions, encouraging mildew, rust, slugs, and snails, especially in foggy areas. As a rule, though, you can compensate for this latter problem by watering in the morning so the plants dry off during the day. Perhaps the most serious drawback is that much of the overhead water supply simply does not reach the root zone because vegetables in Big Yield/Small Space gardens are planted so that their foliage overlaps. Therefore, if you decide to use overhead watering, I advise you to water under the leaves by hand as your garden approaches maturity. Despite these problems, many gardeners favor overhead watering because of its simplicity and use this approach quite successfully.

DRIP-TRICKLE WATERING

Drip-trickle watering is really two different systems that provide small amounts of water to your vegetables along their root zones. The major difference between the two is that trickle systems provide water in a steady, low-volume flow, while drip systems, as the name implies, release water in small droplets. Both are good conservation techniques,

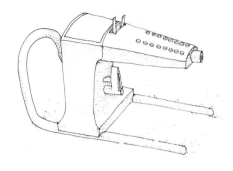

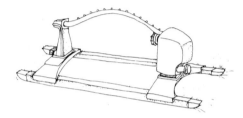

Oscillating sprinklers.

Adjustable rotary sprinkler.

since they cut use by up to 50 percent. They are also equally effective in preventing evaporation problems. If you opt for one of these systems, you will have to lay plastic tubing about ½ inch or less in diameter the length of each row in your garden.

SOAKER SYSTEMS

Water oozes or trickles out of soaker hoses, which are made of perforated or porous plastic tubing, and soaks into the ground along the length of each tube. These tubes are attached to a piece of nonperforated plastic tubing laid across the end of the garden at right angles to the rows or bed. This tubing is in turn connected directly to a garden hose or spigot (see Figure 9–1).

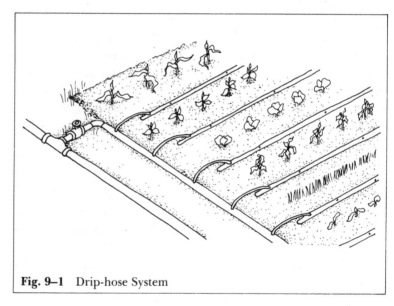

Fig. 9–1   Drip-hose System

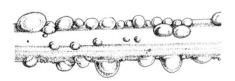

Fig. 9–2   Dupont Viaflo Porous Plastic Tubing

Perforated plastic tubing has small holes punched in its walls. Porous tubing has no holes but has pores that allow the water to seep through the walls. Both types are satisfactory, but Dupont Viaflo porous plastic tubing seems to give the most even distribution (see Figure 9–2). You can buy perforated and porous tubing, as well as the solid connector tubing, at a building-supply store and set up your own system, or you can buy a ready-made drip-trickle soaker hose system in kit form (these start at about $15).

After you prepare the soil in your Big Yield/Small Space bed and before you plant, lay your porous or perforated tubes about 2 feet apart the length of the bed. Since you will want to water your entire bed, you'll need to experiment to get the spacing between the soakers right. Move them closer together or farther apart until you obtain a uniform pattern of water penetration over a period of a few hours. To check, punch holes a foot or two deep in the ground with a stick. When your system is ready to use, water thoroughly to a depth of about 3 feet, then don't water again until the soil has dried out to a depth of 4 to 8 inches.

EMITTER SYSTEMS

An emitter system achieves results similar to those of the soaker hose and is especially useful if you plan to do any planting in conventional rows, which will be the exception rather than the rule in your Big Yield/Small Space garden. This type of system consists of small nozzles, or *emitters,* which drip or trickle and are inserted into plastic tubing wherever you need water. For instance, an emitter can be located at each point where your tubing meets an individual tomato plant to deliver water directly to the plant's root zone.

Home growers have discovered that spaghetti tubes or microtubes, ⅛ inch in diameter or less, are particularly effective for watering vegetables grown in containers (see Figure 9–3). Emitters are inserted in the microtubes at the various containers, and the microtubes are in turn attached to the main tubing, which connects them to a garden hose or water spigot.

Several types of emitters are useful for watering vegetables in containers: spray heads (emitters that spray water like a nozzle), bubblers (devices that let water drip or bubble slowly over the entire surface of the container), and water loops (pieces of perforated tubing that are placed around the perimeter of a round container and water from the outside in). All seem to be equally effective. With any type, water until the soil in the container is saturated, then don't water again until the soil is dry to a depth of 1 to 2 inches.

You can buy individual components for your emitter

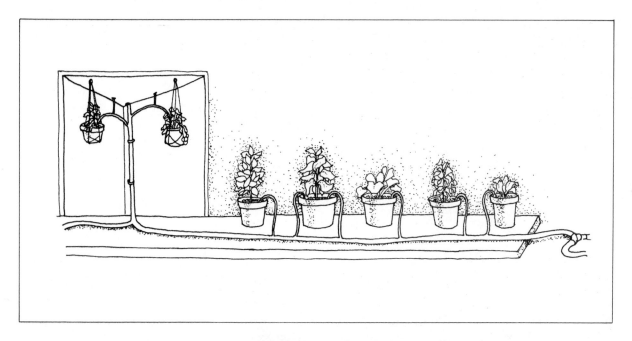

Fig. 9–3 Micro- or spaghetti tubing is ideal for watering plants in containers. Use two tubes to water large plants.

system or obtain a complete system in kit form at a building-supply store. Since most are reasonably priced (starting at about $20), I highly recommend purchasing a kit at the beginning and adding to it as you increase the number of containers in your garden. You should also consider attaching one of several kinds of regulators to your system. A filter-strainer, for example, prevents foreign matter from clogging your hose and emitters, and a ball valve or pressure regulator and gauge control the water flow rate and pressure.

Emitter systems can be simple or sophisticated. All can be connected to one water source or to many, depending on your specific situation. Because they are becoming increasingly popular, you should be able to get any advice you need in the nurseries and building-supply stores in your locale.

ABOUT GOING AUTOMATIC

If you are a lazy gardener like I am, look into automatic watering devices—they'll greatly simplify your work. You can provide your garden with precious nourishment at the same time every day, every third day, or whatever interval is appropriate, whether you're there or not. This is obviously the easiest way to give your vegetables tender, loving care while you're away on vacation.

Automatic sprinkler controls can be used either with overhead systems or with drip-trickle devices. The core of the control is a clock that turns the water on for a preset period of time. The simplest ones use a mechanical device resembling a kitchen timer. You turn it on, and it shuts off the water after a specified duration.

Timers Save You Time

A simple electric timer consists of a clock that can be set to operate a valve and turn on the water for a given number of minutes a day. These start at about $30. Sophisticated timing devices that cost up to several hundred dollars allow you in one step to set different programs for several consecutive days. With these you can also water a number of gardens, lawns, or flower beds at the same time or at different times.

Sensors Make Sense

Just coming on the market too are various moisture sensor systems, most of which sell for under $200. These truly remove all guesswork and solve most of your watering problems. The sensing devices used in all these systems are buried in the garden about 8 to 10 inches deep. With some systems, water is turned on by a controlling device as soon as the sensor dries out. With others, you dial the moisture level you think your plants need, and the sensor activates the control, turning on the water when the moisture content in the soil drops to this preset level. Many building-supply stores, hardware stores, and plumbing outlets sell several types of automatic controls and a variety of sensor systems.

WATERING THE HANDS-ON WAY

Some gardeners insist that Big Yield/Small Space intensive gardens should be watered by hand. Indeed, this approach saves more than overhead techniques do, although it is not as efficient as the drip-trickle methods. If this is how you wish to water, there are many special-purpose nozzles on the market that work nicely. For ground use, the most popular are fan sprays and water bubbles.

You will also find a 24- to 52-inch hand wand especially effective for reaching underneath the leaves to water root zone areas not easily reached by hand nozzles. They come with special seeding nozzles that produce a fine mist for newly planted seed beds or with soft rain irrigation nozzles for general purposes. If you decide to use a wand, I recommend you buy both types of nozzles.

In addition to using the traditional hand methods, some gardeners have invented imaginative water-stretching techniques. Here are several that work well in Big Yield/Small Space gardens (see Figure 9–4).

A plastic or metal pipe, 2 inches in diameter and 18 inches long, driven into the ground near the base of such vegetables as tomatoes, peppers, and eggplant will direct the water to the roots, where it is most needed. This method encourages vigorous growth yet uses almost 50 percent less water than regular overhead methods.

Large clay or plastic flowerpots sunk into the soil within 2 to 6 inches of the base of large plants also direct the water down where the roots are. If possible, fill the pots several times a day during hot weather.

Large metal or plastic funnels sunk into the soil to within an inch of the funnel rim, next to the base of large plants, also put moisture at root-zone depth. Fill the funnel at least three or four times whenever you water.

Perforated half-gallon milk cartons cut off halfway up and set 2 to 3 inches deep in the ground, next to the base of zucchini and other summer squash, perform much the same function as the flowerpots. If you punch only four to five holes per side, you can fill the milk-carton reservoir, and the water will soak into the soil over a prolonged period of time.

Inverted plastic gallon jugs with the bottoms cut off can be sunk into the ground within about 3 inches from the cutoff bottom. Place these 1 to 3 inches from the base of large plants. They make it possible to put large quantities of water at root-zone depth quickly. Leave the cap on and punch four to ten holes on the side of the jug nearest the plant.

Since each of the three primary watering methods described in this chapter is favored by certain gardeners, you

Fig. 9–4 Hand Water-Saving Techniques

Piece of pipe stuck in ground at planting time allows you to direct water to roots of this tomato plant.

Clay pot sunk in soil serves a similar purpose.

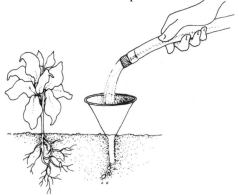

Large metal or plastic funnels put moisture at root zones of large plants.

Perforated milk cartons sunk in ground are an inexpensive means of achieving the same goal.

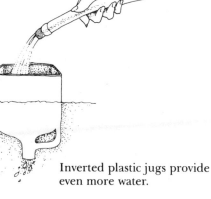

Inverted plastic jugs provide even more water.

will have to experiment to find the one—or the combination—that best suits your particular needs.

One final word of advice: Because Big Yield/Small Space soil contains large amounts of organic material, it can be counted on to go one to three days without watering in the hottest weather and longer than that when the days are cool. If you expect to be gone for a week or more, it's best to ask someone to look in every few days and to give your garden a good soaking whenever it needs a drink. That way you can be sure of coming back to healthy, vigorous crops that will soon be ready to harvest. In the next chapter I'll be describing some other ways you can protect your garden, this time against disease and pests.

CHAPTER TEN

AN OUNCE OF PREVENTION: CONTROLLING PESTS AND DISEASES

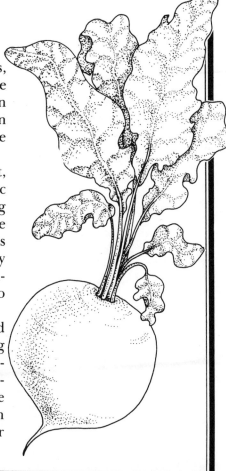

By caring for your garden before any trouble starts, you can often reduce or eliminate many of the problems typically experienced even by veteran growers. I find it invaluable to apply the old adage that an ounce of prevention is worth a pound of cure. Here are some simple rules:

Clean Up That Garden   When you leave rotted fruit, dying plants, scraps of lumber, brush, and other organic material in and around the garden, you're just providing a place for insects and disease to multiply and hibernate during the winter. Get rid of all dead weeds, clean up piles of trash, and remove crop residue. If you have severely diseased plants or rotted fruit, don't put them in the compost, as the problem will eventually find its way back into your garden.

Check Your Garden Carefully   You'll be surprised how effective it is to pay close attention to what's happening in your yard. Often when you find, hand pick, and eliminate insects at an early stage, you will have nipped the problem in the bud. Remove bugs and caterpillars from the leaves and kill by stepping on them or crushing between two boards. Check under the leaves and on the stems for eggs and destroy by crushing.

Watch That Overhead Watering   Mildew and other diseases frequently occur when leaves stay wet over a period of time. You can reduce these problems by watering in the morning so the sun dries the foliage quickly, by hand watering underneath the leaves, or by using an on-the-ground drip irrigation system.

Plant Resistant Varieties   As I'll explain in the chapter to follow, some varieties of vegetables exhibit specific strengths. Certain types of beans, for example, are rust resistant, and several tomato varieties are resistant to nematodes, fusarium, and verticillium wilt. If your area is plagued by particular diseases, your county extension agent can tell you which varieties to plant. In addition, seed catalogs generally list whether a variety has any resistances.

Rotate Your Crops   If some vegetables are grown in the same spot year after year, certain diseases will spread rapidly. Growing cabbage, broccoli, and cauliflower in the same bed repeatedly, for instance, promotes club root. In many situations it will be difficult to move your beds from place to place, but you can rotate the vegetables within the bed. Plant tomatoes where the cabbage was and cabbage in place of the eggplant. This will help keep the problem in check.

Learn to Live with Some Insect Damage   What appears like an all-out invasion one day may well turn out to be nothing the next. Almost any change—the weather, the day's length, an insect's life cycle—can send the bugs out of your garden and off in another direction. In some areas, for example, flea beetles will almost destroy radishes and turnips planted in early summer; but if you hold off and plant a few weeks later, you'd hardly know there were any insects around.

ELIMINATING INSECTS

If neither the preventative nor the do-nothing measures listed above work and you find that insects are still playing havoc with your garden, then you'll have to take stronger action. Here are a few suggestions.

Trap earwigs (they're the bugs with the big pinchers) by placing rolled-up newspapers near the problem plants. They chomp on your plants at night but will hide in the newspapers by day. You can dump them in a pail of water or burn them, newspaper and all.

Pour beer into shallow saucers and set around the garden to get rid of slugs and snails. Despite all the hoopla about high-powered chemical controls, this old-fashioned method still works best. Slugs and snails attracted by the stale beer crawl in the saucer and drown. There are also two recent snail developments on the market you might want to try. Slug-geta from Ortho is a new molluskicide (*mollusk* is a fancy name for animals like snails and oysters) that does a good job of ridding gardens of these pests. And Snail Snare from National Chelating Corporation dehydrates these pests rather than poisoning them.

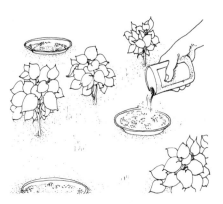

Saucers of beer will keep slugs and snails out of your garden.

Try predator insects, the good guys and gals who will take care of the bad ones for you. There are four main predator insects that will gobble up your garden pests. The larvæ of lacewings go after aphids. Ladybugs have a greedy appetite for aphids, thrips, tree lice, and the eggs and larvæ of other plant-destroying insects. Praying mantis young eat aphids, flies, and small bugs; the larger adults consume quantities of beetles, caterpillars, grasshoppers, and other pests. Trichogramma wasps are especially effective on the larvæ of the cabbage worm. Appendix H lists suppliers of these predator pals.

Use mineral oil to control corn earworm. If these pests are molesting your corn crop, inject half of a medicine dropperful of mineral oil into the end of the ear where the silks are (known as the silk channel) as these begin to dry. This probably works better than anything else.

Sometimes you can spray insects away with water.

Spray small bugs and flying insects with a direct stream of water from a hose. Sometimes they just take off to another part of the garden, but often you can chase them away for good. As an alternative, mix about 20 tablespoons of soap flakes (like Ivory) in 6 gallons of water and spray the mixture directly on the plant leaves. Not only will this give the insects a bath, but it will also help control aphids and other pests. Be sure not to use a detergent.

Make your own spray from plants that have a disagreeable odor: garlic, marigolds, chives, and anything else you think might drive an insect crazy. Put the cloves, petals, leaves, or whatever into a pot, add water to cover, and bring the mixture to the boiling point. Dilute the remaining liquid with four or five parts water, let it sit until cool, then spray it on your plants. Some gardeners swear that—if you can stand the smell—this method works wonders.

Use botanical and biological spray preparations. Surprisingly, these are some of the strongest insecticides around. Perhaps it's not too surprising, for Mother Nature has always been a pretty tough old gal. Pyrethrum, made from the dried and powdered flowers of certain plants of the chrysanthemum genus, is extremely effective against aphids, leafhoppers, thrips, and leaf miners. Rotenone, an insecticide derived from the roots and stems of tropical shrubs and vines, reduces beetles, caterpillars, leaf miners, thrips, and aphids. Ryania, derived from the ground stems of a tropical South American shrub, works well on corn borers. Sabadilla, made from the seeds of a lilylike Mexican plant and sold as a wettable powder, is useful against squash bugs.

Besides using botanical sprays, you can wage germ warfare with Thuricide, a spray preparation that contains the bacterial organism *Bacillus thuringiensis*. It works by paralyzing the digestive systems of caterpillars, cabbage loopers, and tomato hornworms without harming birds, bees, pets, or humans. You will find this and the other preparations mentioned here at most nurseries and in many of the seed catalogs.

As a last resort, use chemical insecticides. The three I recommend for Big Yield/Small Space gardens are carbaryl (Sevin), for chewing insects, such as bean leaf beetles, Mexican bean beetles, cabbage loopers, and cucumber beetles; malathion, for sucking insects, such as aphids; and diazinon, for controlling cutworms, grubs, root maggots, wireworms, and many other insects (see Appendix I).

Since chemical insecticides are extremely toxic and potentially dangerous, it is important that you read the label instructions carefully. Don't use more than the specified dosage, and be sure not to use the insecticide on a crop that is not included on the label. Store carefully to keep out of the reach of children. Finally, don't leave the empty container around; break or puncture it, wrap in a newspaper, and discard in the trash or bury at least 18 inches in the ground.

DEALING WITH DISEASE

The primary methods of controlling disease in your Big Yield/Small Space garden should be prevention and the selection of varieties of vegetables with resistance to diseases prevalent in your area.

Even with the best efforts, though, you may encounter some diseases in your garden. The most common are bacterial wilt (the leaves suddenly start to droop), anthracnose (dark, sunken or oval podlike spots with ooze in the center), mildew (a white, powdery growth on the surfaces of leaves or stems), rust (brown spots, or pustules, on the leaves), scab (appearing as rough, scabby patches), and root rot (decayed roots and wilting leaves).

You can control many of these diseases with foliar fungicides. These are toxic chemicals that are sprayed on the leaves. The right fungicide must be applied early, however, to prevent the rapid spread of the disease.

I suggest that you visit your local nursery, examine the selection of fungicides that are available, read the labels, and ask the people there for advice. See Appendix J for a general guide to disease control, arranged vegetable by vegetable, and Appendix K to help you diagnose and control a number of other garden problems.

KEEPING THE VARMINTS OUT

Dogs, cats, gophers, birds, and people can sometimes be a real nuisance in the city or suburban garden. I usually try to live and let live with dogs and cats. In fact, I cogarden with a cat who occasionally rolls upside down on my young peppers and eggplants. That's okay because they'll snap back, but when an animal rips up a freshly planted bed of carrots, almost any gardener will feel like going on the warpath.

A number of manufacturers offer dog and cat repellents in both stick and aerosol form. The results are mediocre to fair, but if you're desperate, pick up one at the nursery and try it.

Gophers, too, can drive a home grower wild. In one of my gardens, no matter what I tried, my squash plants kept

Gopher traps.

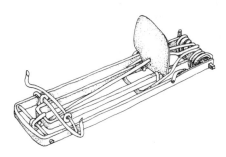

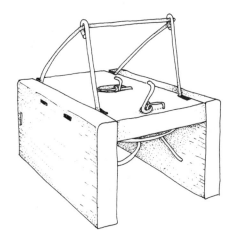

disappearing down gopher holes. Many of the methods for controlling these animals are cumbersome or unappealing, but if it's a choice between your vegetables or the gophers, you may be willing to take extreme action.

Some gardeners favor using two spring-loaded traps. Find a fresh mound of dirt, dig down until you find a run (a tunnel going in both directions 2 to 8 inches below the surface), and place the traps at either side of the run. Lay a board over the hole and cover with dirt. Other growers use box traps, but they have to dig holes large enough to lower the entire traps into the burrows.

Probably the best solution is still the Klipty-Klop, a small windmill mounted on a weather-vane stake driven into the soil. The windmill sets up a vibration that gophers can't seem to stand. Unfortunately, where gophers are concerned, nothing is 100 percent foolproof, so pick your weapons and take your chances, and if one thing doesn't work, try another.

Although birds sometimes help in the garden by ridding it of harmful insects, they can also be destructive. In one of my gardens, the birds kept devouring my baby cucumbers the minute the plants poked their heads above ground level. When they're being selective like this, you can protect the plants with Hotkaps until they get big enough to fend for themselves. If birds are creating a severe problem with the whole garden, cover the entire growing area with netting purchased from a nursery.

Again, when you're dealing with pests and disease, prevention, vigilance, and quick, appropriate responses are your best defenses. Since you will be gardening in small spaces, the amount of time and attention devoted to protecting the growing environment should also be kept within a manageable range.

In the final chapter, everything you have learned about Big Yield/Small Space gardening will be applied to growing those specific vegetables that you and your family most favor.

CHAPTER ELEVEN

GROWING SPECIFIC VEGETABLES THE BIG YIELD/ SMALL SPACE WAY

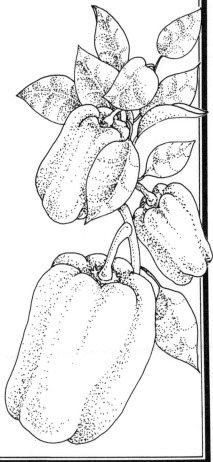

As the preceding chapters illustrate, the Big Yield/ Small Space system is a radical departure from conventional home growing. With the proper location and a yard not much bigger than a bathtub, you can easily raise hubbard and pink banana squash, watermelons, and even a giant Max pumpkin. And with a little more space, you can squeeze in potatoes and other crops that were previously considered impossibilities unless you had spacious grounds. Now what you grow—regular, midget, and exotic vegetable varieties, herbs, marigolds and nasturtiums (for pest control)—depends primarily on your needs and tastes.

In this chapter I provide specific tips on growing most of your personal selections, emphasizing how you can do this in limited space. These tips are meant to assist you in putting all the component parts of your Big Yield/Small Space system together. Vegetables are grouped in categories, such as leafy varieties and root crops, and each grouping has similar production requirements. Accompanying tables give you the number of days to maturity for listed varieties, information about the appearance of each vegetable and its special features, and the numbers of catalog seed sources that can be found in Appendix E. I also recommend that you check Appendix D of this book for even more detailed data than those given here.

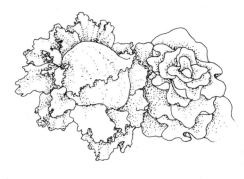

GROWING LEAFY VEGETABLES

Leafy vegetables provide tremendous yields for the amount of space they require. If you use the good, fertile Big Yield/Small Space soil described earlier in this book, you can plant them slightly closer than is generally recommended in planting guides.

Don't get carried away when growing leafy vegetables; a little goes a long way, and you can use the remaining space for other favorites. Many people, for instance, tend to plant large beds of lettuce when, in fact, two to three lettuce plants harvested a few leaves at a time are plenty for one person, and eight lettuce plants are generally enough for a family of four.

If you live in a region of the country where the summers are extremely hot, select leafy-vegetable varieties that are especially heat tolerant. Seed catalogs, as well as the tables below, provide information about these special kinds of tolerances. One more general tip: Plant leafy vegetables that mature in 45 days or less in the same beds with wider-spaced, slower-maturing types, such as cabbage or tomatoes.

Lettuce

Lettuce is by far the most popular of all leafy vegetables and comes in an array of varieties (see Table 11–1).

Planting Lettuce can be planted outside four to six weeks before the last average frost-free date in your area. Sow seed in the bed ¼ inch deep. Thin head lettuce to stand 6 to 12 inches apart, leaf lettuce to stand 4 to 6 inches apart.

You can plant enough leaf lettuce for a family of four in a 1-square-foot area, enough head lettuce in a 2-square-foot section. It's best to divide the space into quarters and plant one of the quarters every two weeks. Whenever you harvest one of the quarters, replant. Since leaf lettuce matures in about 45 days, never plant it separately; always find a place for it in a newly planted or about-to-be-planted bed of larger, slower-maturing vegetables. To get a jump on the season, start lettuce in simple protective devices, cloches, or cold frames.

TABLE 11–1. LETTUCE VARIETIES

VARIETY	DAYS TO MATURITY	REMARKS	CATALOG SEED SOURCE
BUTTERHEAD			
Buttercrunch	68	Smooth, green leaves, heat tolerant, All-America winner	2, 5, 6, 8, 10, 14, 16, 17, 23, 24, 25, 26, 28, 31, 33, 34, 39, 40, 41, 42, 43, 44, 45, 46, 48, 50, 52, 60, 61, 63, 67
Summer Bibb	77	Thick leaves, creamy and firm interior, vigorous, slow to bolt	23, 25, 31, 49, 52
HEAD (CRISPHEAD)			
Great Lakes	85	Large, erect leaves are bright green and fringed, high-quality heads, slow to bolt, All-America winner	2, 5, 6, 10, 14, 15, 16, 17, 22, 24, 25, 28, 30, 31, 41, 44, 45, 46, 47, 48, 49, 54
Ithaca	72	Firm heads, mild heat resistance, does well in midsummer	23, 26, 28, 31, 52, 60, 67
Pennlake	75	Fairly smooth, medium green leaves, early, tolerates tip burn, All-America winner	16, 26, 28, 42, 45, 60, 67
LEAF			
Grand Rapids	45	Early, leaves frilled, deeply cut, and light green, heat resistant	6, 7, 8, 10, 14, 16, 17, 22, 23, 24, 25, 26, 32, 39, 41, 42, 45, 49, 50, 54, 60, 61, 65, 67
Green Ice	45	Dark, glossy green, fringed leaves, heat resistant	6, 39
Oakleaf	45	Leaves resemble oakleaves, tender, long standing	2, 5, 6, 8, 10, 14, 16, 22, 23, 24, 30, 31, 35, 39, 41, 43, 44, 45, 46, 50, 52, 54
Ruby	50	Intense red, frilled leaves, All-America winner	6, 8, 14, 16, 22, 23, 24, 25, 32, 44, 45, 46, 51, 60, 67, 68
Slobolt	45	Crumpled and frilled leaves, good warm-weather lettuce	8, 15, 16, 23, 26, 42, 46, 50
ROMAINE			
Paris Island Cos	76	Large, oval, 8- to 9-inch-long, dark green head, mild flavor	8, 23, 26, 34, 35, 41, 42, 50, 52, 60, 67
Paris White Cos	83	Elongated, 10–12 inches long, light green leaves, crisp, sweet	5, 6, 10, 16, 22, 24, 25, 28, 30, 34, 35, 43, 44, 48, 49, 54, 60, 67

After your lettuce plants have reached 2 or 3 inches in height, a 2-inch mulch of compost or rotted horse manure spread over the beds will keep the soil cool and the plants growing well. In hot-summer areas, you can grow lettuce most of the summer by placing a slat frame or other shading device over the bed.

Harvesting   Start harvesting head lettuce as soon as it is crisp and headed. Stretch your leaf lettuce crop by harvesting a few leaves at a time, as suggested above. With butterhead varieties, cut off the entire plant when it is large enough to use.

Spinach

Spinach, easily the second most popular leafy vegetable, is also the most finicky. This vegetable comes in savoyed (crinkled), semisavoyed, and smooth-leaved varieties. Some types are partially heat tolerant; others have a varietal resistance to disease (see Table 11–2).

Planting   Spinach is a hardy, frost-tolerant vegetable that can be planted outside four to six weeks before the last average frost-free date. It grows best from seed set directly in the ground. Sow the seeds in early spring and again in late summer, planting them about ½ inch deep and 2 inches apart. Thin the seedlings to stand 4 to 6 inches apart.

The biggest problem with spinach is its tendency to flower. You can counteract this to some extent by selecting bolt-resistant varieties. In my own area, where we have cold, early springs but can often expect temperatures in the 80s and 90s in April and May, I have all but given up on spring spinach. Fortunately, it nearly always does well in the fall. If you face similar problems, try a spinach substitute, such as the Malabar and New Zealand varieties.

Five plants are generally enough for one person; multiply according to the number of spinach lovers in your family. Each person's ration will take up roughly 1½ to 2 square feet. Divide that space into quarters and plant one every ten days. Combine your spinach with larger, slower-maturing vegetables. Use cloches or cold frames if you wish to extend the growing season.

Harvesting   It's best to harvest spinach in much the same way you would leafy lettuce, a few leaves at a time to meet your needs. Harvest the outer leaves when they are at least 3 inches long. If you pick just these, the inner leaves will become the next crop.

TABLE 11–2. SPINACH VARIETIES

VARIETY	DAYS TO MATURITY	REMARKS	CATALOG SEED SOURCE
America	50	Glossy, dark green, heavily crumpled leaves, heavy yields, slow bolting, All-America winner	6, 7, 8, 14, 21, 22, 24, 25, 26, 46, 52, 60, 65, 67
Bloomsdale Long Standing	45	Thick, crinkled, dark, glossy leaves, slow to bolt	2, 6, 7, 10, 16, 21, 24, 26, 34, 39, 44, 50, 52, 60, 68
Malabar	70	Large, bright green leaves	6, 20
Melody	42	Large plants, dark green and semi-crinkled leaves, heavy yields, resistant to disease, All-America winner	6, 14, 16, 23, 26, 46, 60, 65, 67
New Zealand	70	Fleshy, brittle leaves, strong heat resistance	14, 16, 17, 22, 23, 24, 25, 26, 28, 30, 32, 35, 39, 41, 42, 43, 44, 45, 51, 52, 54, 60, 61, 67
Nobel Giant	46	Huge, thick, smooth, pointed leaves, enormous yields	7, 10, 16, 24, 34, 45, 49, 51, 52

Swiss Chard

Swiss chard and the other leafy greens described below are especially popular in some regions. If you have never tried them, you are in for a tasty surprise. Swiss chard can't be matched for ease of growth. It matures rapidly in 45 to 60 days, withstands some frost, and even grows well in hot weather (see Table 11–3).

Planting Sow seed ½ inch deep and about 4 inches apart. When the seedlings come up, thin to stand 5 to 8 inches apart. Two to three plants are enough for one person, eight plants plenty for a family of four. New center leaves continually replace the outer leaves as they're harvested, even when you cut off the entire plant to an inch or two above the ground. Don't make solid plantings of chard in your garden; rather, bunch two or three plants together in an odd corner. You can easily squeeze two plants into a 12-inch circle.

Harvesting   Follow the same directions for harvesting chard as you would for spinach or other leafy vegetables. You can also cut off the whole plant a couple of inches above the root crown, and it will produce new leaves.

TABLE 11–3. CHARD VARIETIES

VARIETY	DAYS TO MATURITY	REMARKS	CATALOG SEED SOURCE
Fordhook Giant	60	Crumpled leaves, white stalks	10, 41, 42, 51, 52, 60, 61
Lucullus	60	Yellow green leaves, white stalks	6, 10, 16, 22, 24, 25, 26, 32, 39, 45, 48, 50, 54, 68
Rhubarb	60	Dark green leaves, red stalks	6, 10, 22, 23, 24, 31, 45, 46, 50, 54, 60, 67

Collards

Collards can be grown almost anywhere. The mature plants are frost hardy, yet they can stand summer heat (see Table 11–4).

Planting   Sow seed ½ inch deep, 3 inches apart, then thin to stand 10 to 12 inches apart. Thin collards 5 to 7 inches apart to produce bunchy, dwarfed plants.

Harvesting   I suggest you limit your garden to three or four plants, since you harvest the leaves as needed and the plants keep blooming along. Never harvest the central growing point, or you will delay production until side shoots form.

TABLE 11–4. COLLARD VARIETIES

VARIETY	DAYS TO MATURITY	REMARKS	CATALOG SEED SOURCE
Georgia Green	75	Crumpled, blue green leaves	6, 14, 17, 24, 25, 26, 28, 34, 35, 38, 39, 41, 42, 43, 46, 48, 49, 51, 54, 65, 68
Vates	75	Low-growing, broad-spreading plants	7, 8, 12, 15, 22, 23, 25, 26, 34, 35, 41, 42, 46, 49, 50, 60, 61, 65, 68

Kale

Kale is a cool-weather crop that comes in two basic types: the brœcole, or Scotch types, with blue or dark green leaves, and the Siberian types, with smooth, gray green, frilly-edged leaves and a spreading habit (see Table 11–5).

Planting If your summers are cool, plant in the spring two to four weeks before the last frost; otherwise, plant in the fall. Sow seeds ½ inch deep, 3 to 4 inches apart, and thin to between 8 and 10 inches apart. Kale can be started indoors, then transplanted to the garden. Some gardeners like to grow kale under protective devices about 2 inches apart, then transfer it to open beds two to four weeks before the last frost. Cold weather doesn't seem to bother mature kale plants at all. In fact, it is even crispier and more flavorful after being touched by a light frost.

Two to four plants are enough for one person, eight enough for a family of four. Eight plants would require about 2 square feet of growing space.

Harvesting Harvest the younger, larger leaves individually. After a few weeks, pull up the entire plant—old kale becomes tough and stringy.

TABLE 11–5. KALE VARIETIES

VARIETY	DAYS TO MATURITY	REMARKS	CATALOG SEED SOURCE
Dwarf Blue Curled Vates	55	Finely curled, bluish green leaves, low, compact, short-stemmed plants, withstands below-freezing temperatures	6, 8, 15, 23, 25, 26, 28, 34, 35, 41, 43, 45, 51, 52
Dwarf Siberian Curled	65	Grayish green leaves, 12–16 inches tall, 24- to 36-inch spread, extremely hardy	6, 25, 43, 44

Mustard Greens

Mustard greens, like collards, are a Southern favorite. If you have never tried them, I suggest that you grow a few plants. They can be cooked or used in salads.

Planting   Two to four weeks before the last frost, sow seed ½ inch deep and about 2 inches apart. Thin to stand 3 to 6 inches apart. Since mustard greens take heat well, you can make several plantings throughout the season. Seeds can also be started inside and transplanted to the garden. Mustard greens mature in 35 to 45 days. Plant with larger, slower-maturing crops in sections that are between crops.

Four to 6 plants are enough for an individual, 8 to 14 enough for a family of four (1 to 2 square feet of space).

Harvesting   To harvest, snap off the lower leaves, leaving the growing tip to produce replacements.

TABLE 11–6. MUSTARD VARIETIES

VARIETY	DAYS TO MATURITY	REMARKS	CATALOG SEED SOURCE
Florida Broad Leaf	43	Medium green, broad-leaved, smooth	6, 7, 8, 10, 24, 25, 26, 34, 35, 38, 42, 49, 50, 61, 65, 67, 68
Southern Giant Curled	45	Exceptionally long standing, curled type	6, 7, 8, 10, 16, 17, 22, 25, 35, 36, 39, 41, 45, 46, 49, 50, 54, 62, 67, 68

Special Salad Greens

Here are some special favorites of gourmet cooks: corn salad, cress, dandelion, and endive (see Table 11–7).

Corn Salad

Corn salad, also known as lamb's lettuce, has a bland taste and pale green, spatulate, 3-inch-long leaves.

Planting   Plant corn salad in the fall for a winter crop, ½ inch deep and 4 to 6 inches apart. (It is frost hardy.) Two or three plants provide enough leaves for one person, six to eight plants enough for a family of four (1 square foot or less of area).

Harvesting   All the special salad greens, except endive and escarole, are harvested in the same manner as spinach, chard, and leafy lettuce—a few leaves at a time.

TABLE 11–7. SPECIAL SALAD GREENS VARIETIES

VARIETY	DAYS TO MATURITY	REMARKS	CATALOG SEED SOURCE
Corn Salad	60	Round, large leaves, mild flavor	22, 23, 24, 35, 41, 54
Cress, Garden (peppergrass)	35	Fine, curled, parsleylike leaves, fast-growing annual	6, 8, 10, 11, 22, 23, 24, 26, 30, 32, 39, 43, 44, 45, 46, 52, 54, 60, 68
Cress, Upland	49	Dense growth, 5 to 6 inches high, 10 to 12 inches wide	25, 26, 30, 41, 54, 61
Dandelion	95	Stocky, broad leaves	24, 41, 54, 61
Endive (chicory)	85	Slightly crumpled, dark green leaves, somewhat bitter taste	8, 10, 16, 22, 23, 24, 26, 30, 31, 34, 35, 39, 41, 42, 43, 49
Escarole	90	Finely cut, green, curled leaves, somewhat bitter taste	2, 6, 10, 16, 22, 23, 24, 26, 28, 32, 34, 35, 39, 41, 45, 46, 48, 49, 54, 60

Cress—Garden and Upland

Garden cress, or peppergrass, has fine, curled, parsleylike leaves. It is an annual, reaching maturity in about 35 days. Use it to fill odd spaces between larger plants. This is a cool-season plant that withstands some frost.

Planting Sow seeds of garden cress in the spring or fall across the bed. Cover with a ½-inch layer of compost. Thin plants to stand 2 to 3 inches apart. Start using as soon as the leaves form, in about ten days. Ten plants are probably enough for a family of four.

Upland cress makes a dense growth 5 to 6 inches high, 10 to 12 inches wide. Sow seeds over about a 1-square-foot section, then thin to stand 2 to 4 inches apart. Again, ten plants should be sufficient for four people.

Dandelion

If you've never tried dandelion in your salads, you're in for a treat. This is a hardy plant. Sow seeds in place, thin to about 8 inches apart. Plant at about the same time as lettuce or seed in July or August for a fall crop. You can also start seeds inside four to six weeks before you intend to plant outside and transplant the young seedlings into your garden.

Endive and Escarole

The frilly, somewhat bitter leaf vegetable is called endive (or chicory), the broadleaved, escarole. These are cool-weather, frost-hardy crops.

Planting   They produce best when planted in the fall. Sow seeds ½ inch deep and about 3 inches apart. Thin to stand 8 to 9 inches apart. Or start seeds inside and transfer to the garden. Eight to ten plants (about 2 square feet of space) are enough for a family of four.

Harvesting   Two or three weeks before you intend to harvest, draw the outer leaves over the heart and center leaves. Tie the bunched leaves together with a string.

RAISING ROOT AND TUBER CROPS

Carrots, radishes, beets, onions, garlic, parsnips, horseradish, rutabagas, celeriac, turnips, potatoes, and sweet potatoes can be classified as root or tuber crops. You have to take care not to overplant these crops. The trick, therefore, is to plant small amounts at regular two- or three-week intervals so that you'll have a harvest throughout growing season.

Home growers in most regions of the country have had significant success starting some of these crops as early as January and February, using the more elaborate plastic- or glass-covered protective devices described in Chapter 5.

Carrots

Carrots offer the home gardener many choices. There are fat carrots and long, slender carrots, medium-sized carrots and short-topped carrots, and even midget bite-sized carrots (see Table 11–8).

Planting   You can grow as many as 120 carrots in 1 square foot of space. To enjoy them all season long, plant a square foot approximately every two weeks. Broadcast seed directly in the ground, planting three to four seeds per square inch. Cover with ½ inch of soil. If you have trouble distributing the seed correctly, practice with dry coffee grounds, as described in Chapter 2.

Carrot seeds are sometimes difficult to germinate, especially in hot weather. To reduce loss due to drying out, spread a ¼- to ½-inch layer of compost or rotted manure on top of the bed. Some gardeners also place a black plastic sheet over the mulch to reduce moisture loss even further. When the seedlings start to show, remove the plastic.

Let your carrots grow to about 2 or 3 inches in height, then thin to stand ½ inch apart. When the roots almost touch, thin again to stand 1 to 2 inches apart.

Harvesting Start taking carrots when they reach finger size and continue until they reach about 1½ inches in diameter. Small carrots taste far better than larger ones.

TABLE 11–8. CARROT VARIETIES

VARIETY	DAYS TO MATURITY	REMARKS	CATALOG SEED SOURCE
LONG, SLENDER			
Gold Pak	76	Slender, 8–9 inches long, 1½ inches across	6, 8, 16, 17, 22, 24, 25, 26, 32, 34, 42, 45, 48, 52, 54, 60, 65, 68
Imperator	77	Wide shoulders, 8–9 inches long, deep orange, tender	6, 16, 17, 22, 24, 25, 43, 45, 51, 54, 61, 68
MEDIUM			
Chantenay	70	Medium plump, 5–6 inches long, very sweet	2, 5, 8, 10, 11, 30, 39, 45, 49, 54
Danvers Half Long	78	Medium slender, 5–6 inches long, deep orange, mild flavor	2, 6, 8, 10, 14, 16, 17, 22, 24, 25, 26, 28, 33, 34, 41, 45, 48, 49, 51, 54, 68
Scarlet Nantes	70	Cylindrical, blunt end, 6–8 inches long	16, 17, 23, 24, 26, 28, 31, 33, 34, 40, 45
Spartan Bonus	75	Medium plump, tapering, 5–7 inches long	6, 8, 16, 26, 34, 46, 48, 49
SHORT, FAT			
Ox Heart	75	Short and fat, 4–6 inches long, 4 inches wide, easily dug	10, 11, 22, 26, 41, 44, 49, 51, 54
ROUND			
Golden Ball	58	Round, 2 inches in diameter, golden, early	67
WHITE			
Belgium White	75	White, good for salads	20, 44

Beets

Beets offer a choice of shapes ranging from round to cylindrical and colors ranging from white to red to yellow (see Table 11–9). They are a perfect Big Yield/Small Space vegetable because you can eat both the leaves and the root and they need only a little space to grow like mad.

Planting   Each knobby piece of beet is actually a seed cluster. Sow these seed clusters about an inch apart across the bed, ½ to 1 inch deep. Thin to stand 2 inches apart.

You will need about 40 beets per person. This translates into 160 beets for a family of four, or 40 beets per square foot. Make the first sowing two to four weeks before the last average frost date in your area. Then plant an additional square foot about every two weeks. Growers in many areas like to plant beets in their gardens by February under glass or polyethylene plastic.

Harvesting   Start harvesting your beets when they reach ½ inch in diameter. If allowed to grow larger than about 3 inches, they lose flavor and may develop woody tissue.

TABLE 11–9. BEET VARIETIES

VARIETY	DAYS TO MATURITY	REMARKS	CATALOG SEED SOURCE
CYLINDRICAL			
Cylindra	60	Long, narrow, carrotlike	6, 17, 23, 36, 54, 65
ROUND			
Detroit Dark Red	55	Round, glossy tops, All-America selection	2, 5, 6, 7, 8, 16, 17, 22, 23, 24, 26, 28, 32, 34, 39, 40, 41, 43, 45, 46, 50, 51, 52, 54, 60, 67
SEMIROUND			
Ruby Queen	52	Dark red, short top, All-America selection	5, 11, 16, 22, 23, 25, 26, 28, 34, 42, 45, 46, 52, 60, 63, 67, 68
OTHER			
Baby Canning	54	Golf-ball size	14, 22
Beets for greens	80	Large tops, roots flattened, uneven	3, 29
Golden Beet	55	Golden color	6, 14, 44, 46, 60, 63
Snow White	55	White variety	68

Radishes

There are three main types of radishes: the round to oval types, the long-rooted varieties, and the winter species (see Table 11–10).

Planting   Sow radish seeds about ½ inch deep and ½ inch apart. Radishes start to form bulbs in about two weeks, so before that time, thin to stand 1 to 2 inches apart. It's best to start your plantings four to six weeks before the last frost. Since they mature quickly, in just 21 to 30 days, plant them in the same space as larger, slower-maturing vegetables or squeeze them in wherever you have an odd-shaped space or where you have harvested a crop.

Harvesting   Pick radishes when they're still fairly small and young. Older radishes tend to split or to become pithy or spongy.

TABLE 11–10. RADISH VARIETIES

VARIETY	DAYS TO MATURITY	REMARKS	CATALOG SEED SOURCE
LONG ROOTED			
All Seasons	45	White, 6 inches long, 1 inch in diameter	6, 10, 43
Long Scarlet	30	Deep scarlet, 5–6 inches long	35, 41, 44, 67
ROUND TO OVAL			
Cherry Belle	22	Round, ¾ inch in diameter, resembles red cherry, All-America selection	2, 5, 6, 8, 10, 14, 16, 17, 22, 24, 26, 28, 32, 33, 34, 38, 43, 44, 45, 46, 48, 50, 54, 60, 61, 63, 65
French Breakfast	23	Oblong, 1¾ inches in diameter, upper part red, lower white	2, 6, 8, 10, 16, 17, 22, 24, 28, 32, 41, 44, 45, 46, 48, 50, 51, 52, 54, 60, 67
WINTER			
China Rose	52	Deep rose, 6–7 inches long, 2½ inches in diameter, white flesh	14, 17, 22, 25, 26, 30, 32, 34, 41, 42, 48, 50, 51, 54, 60, 61
Round Black Spanish	55	Large, round, black, white flesh	6, 8, 10, 11, 16, 22, 23, 24, 30, 41, 44, 54, 67
Sakurajima Giant	150	Root grows to 40 pounds or more, vigorous	30, 36, 44, 54
Shogoin	65	Globe shaped, pure white, 5–6 inches	35, 44

Onions

The onion family includes onions, garlic, leeks, and shallots (see Tables 11–11 and 11–12). Varieties of this vegetable are classified as *long day* or *short day*. The former are grown in the north and require 14 to 16 hours of daylight; the latter are designed to grow in areas with warm climates all year around and require about 12 hours of sunlight. Onions give you more eating per square foot than almost any other vegetable.

Planting   Onions can be grown from seeds, seedlings, or sets (small bulbs or roots). Since they are frost hardy, I recommend starting them from seed the wide-row way in your Big Yield/Small Space beds as soon as the soil can be worked (four to six weeks before the average date of last frost); start earlier under glass or polyethylene plastic. Sow seeds across the entire bed and cover with about ½ inch of soil. When seedings first appear, thin until your onions stand about 1 inch apart. About a month later, thin to 2 to 3 inches apart. At this time, dig the soil back to expose the tops and sides of the bulbs. This helps stimulate bulb formation. In areas of mild winters, you can plant onions all year long. Onions need cooler weather for top growth, warmer weather for bulb growth.

Twenty to 50 onions are generally enough for one person, 100 to 200 sufficient for a family of four. This translates into 1 to 1½ square feet of space per person. If you're a real onion lover, plant double this amount.

Be sure to plant extra amounts of regular (dry-bulb) onions to be harvested as green onions. They're ready about 20 to 30 days after planting, so grow them in the same section with larger, slower-maturing vegetables or tuck them into odd spaces.

Harvesting   When the tops of bulb onions begin to turn yellow, bend them over to a nearly horizontal position on the ground. This prevents the flow of sap and diverts all growing energy to the bulbs. When all the tops are dead, dig the bulbs up and let them dry on top of the ground for a few days. Then store them in a dry, frost-free place indefinitely. A warning: Green onions don't remain fresh long after harvesting, even with refrigeration.

TABLE 11–11. ONION VARIETIES

VARIETY	DAYS TO MATURITY	REMARKS	CATALOG SEED SOURCE
FLAT			
Granex White	105–175	Mild flavor, crisp, southern latitudes	35, 48
HALF FLAT			
Red Bermuda	93	Bulbs are early, large, and flat with red skin, short day	10, 26
Burgundy (hamburger onion)	95	Huge bulbs are thick, somewhat flattened	4, 6, 10, 14, 16, 17, 22, 25, 26, 28, 46, 51, 54, 59, 68
ROUND			
Yellow Globe Danvers	110	Globular, heavy producer, long day	2, 10, 16, 24, 39, 41, 43, 44, 45, 54, 61
Yellow Sweet Spanish	105	Globe shaped, large yellow skin	2, 4, 10, 14, 15, 16, 18, 22, 23, 25, 28, 32, 38, 39, 41, 42, 44, 46, 48
White Sweet Spanish	110	Large, white, globe shaped	4, 6, 10, 15, 17, 22, 26, 33, 34
SPINDLE SHAPED			
Italian Red	105	Torpedo shaped, sweet	30
TOP (PEAR) SHAPED			
Texas Early Yellow Grano	168	Soft, mild flesh, short day	15, 25, 26, 34, 35
OTHER			
Egyptian Multiplying	100	Multiplies by forming cluster of bulbs at top of long stem	1, 8, 10, 53
White Nest Egg	100	Multiplies in soil	1

Garlic

Planting and Harvesting It's best to plant garlic in odd spaces or in a short row along one end or a side of your garden. You'll need about 3 to 8 plants for every person in your family. Pull apart a garlic bulb and plant the individual cloves 1 to 1½ inches deep and about 3 inches apart. Mature bulbs should be ready in about three months.

Shallots

Planting and Harvesting Plant shallot cloves 1 inch deep and about 1 inch apart; thin to stand 2 to 4 inches apart. Each planted shallot will multiply and produce four to eight new shallot bulbs. You will need between four and ten shallots per person.

Leeks

Planting and Harvesting Dig several trenches 6 inches deep and 6 inches apart. You can get three trenches 12 inches long into about 1½ square feet, a space in which you can grow about nine leeks. Sow the seed directly in the bed and thin to stand 2 to 6 inches apart, or transplant seedlings to stand 2 to 6 inches apart. (The closer the spacing, the smaller the roots.) Now fill the trench gradually as the leeks develop. Don't brush soil on the leafstalks.

TABLE 11–12. ONION FAMILY MEMBER VARIETIES

VARIETY	DAYS TO MATURITY	REMARKS	CATALOG SEED SOURCE
Garlic			
California White Garlic	110	White, 1½ inches in diameter	17, 32
Elephant Garlic	105	Huge, 4–5 inches in diameter, many 1-pound bulbs	16, 21, 22, 37, 40, 44, 53, 54
Leeks			
American Flag	120–150	Uniform size, 8½–9½ inches long, 1 inch in diameter	10, 15, 26, 30, 41, 42, 44, 49, 50, 61, 63, 67, 68
Broad London (large American Flag)	140	Sweet flavored, 7–9 inches long, 1 inch in diameter	6, 14, 16, 17, 22, 24, 30, 32, 38, 39, 40, 43, 45, 46, 50, 54, 67
Conqueror	125	Hardy strain for winter, blue green	23
Italian Winter Leek	128	Extremely hardy, to 15 inches	10
Shallots			
Dutch Yellow	110	Will keep nearly 12 months	63
Giant Red	105	Mildly spicy yet sweet, stores through winter	63

Potatoes

Potatoes aren't ordinarily considered a good bet for a small-space intensive garden since they generally take up too much room for the quantity produced. Grown right, however, they can give you a tremendous harvest in a very limited space. I suggest giving them their own 2-by-2-foot bed made up with Big Yield/Small Space soil. You can choose red, white, or russet; round, oval, or oblong; early, main crop, or late varieties (see Table 11–13).

Planting   To plant, buy seed potatoes and cut each one into three or four pieces about 1½ inches square. Every piece must have one or two eyes. Set the pieces cut side down 4 inches deep and about 4 inches apart. This spacing is much too close to produce large, mature potatoes, but if you're going for yield you'll do fine. Plant as soon as the ground can be worked or about four to six weeks before the average date of last frost. You can start them sooner in a raised wooden bed covered with polyethylene plastic.

When the tops begin to show, cover the leaves with a mixture of about half soil, half compost to keep them from being damaged by frost. Next time they poke above the ground, let them grow roughly 6 inches high, then place 3 inches of your special soil mixture around the base of the plants. Repeat this procedure several times. Your potatoes will be ready in a couple of months.

Harvesting   Start harvesting about two months after planting. Dig up a small section at a time and take out the potatoes. There will be hundreds of them, ranging from the size of marbles to two to four inches long.

TABLE 11–13. POTATO VARIETIES

VARIETY	DAYS TO MATURITY	REMARKS	CATALOG SEED SOURCE
RED			
Norland	110	Oblong, smooth, extra early	14, 16, 17, 18, 22, 24, 32
Red Pontiac	100	Round, big, heavy yields, main crop	14, 16, 17, 18, 22, 41, 45, 55
Red LaSoda	105	Oval, bright red, heavy yields, medium late	45
RUSSET			
Norgold Russet	105	Oblong, golden netting, early to midseason	16, 17, 18, 22

TABLE 11–13. POTATO VARIETIES *(continued)*

VARIETY	DAYS TO MATURITY	REMARKS	CATALOG SEED SOURCE
Russet Burbank	110	Oblong, netted brown, late	17, 18, 45
WHITE			
Anoka	100	Round to oval, smooth white, extra early	22
Bake King	100	Oval to oblong, good baking, main crop	22
Irish Cobbler	100	Round, white, early	14, 24, 41, 45, 61
OTHER			
All Blue Potato	100	Blue skin and flesh	22

Sweet Potatoes

Sweet potatoes are definitely a crop meant for long, hot summers (see Table 11–14).

Planting Since sweet potato vines tend to go wild and take over everything, grow your plants in a spot separate from the rest of your regular garden, such as a flower bed. Transplants are available from nurseries and seed catalog firms. Set them out after all danger of frost has passed, spacing the plants 16 to 24 inches apart.

If you fertilize with time-release fertilizer (see Chapter 3), don't use regular vegetable or tomato food, as the nitrogen in these causes the plants to put out too much vine. Choose a product low in nitrogen. A fertilizer with the formula 2-10-10 is a good choice; that's 2 percent nitrogen, 10 percent phosphorus, 10 percent potassium.

Harvesting Dig the tubers in the fall before the frost.

TABLE 11–14. SWEET POTATO VARIETIES

VARIETY	DAYS TO MATURITY	REMARKS	CATALOG SEED SOURCE
Centennial	120	Uniform, medium size, deep orange flesh, fine texture	14, 17, 18, 19, 22, 46, 59
New Golden Jewell	110	Highest yielding, deep orange flesh	19, 45, 54, 59

Roots in Brief

You will find that the following more unusual root crops thrive in Big Yield/Small Space plots: celeriac, horseradish, kohlrabi, parsnips, turnips, and rutabagas (see Table 11–15).

TABLE 11–15. ROOT VARIETIES

VARIETY	DAYS TO MATURITY	REMARKS	CATALOG SEED SOURCE
CELERIAC			
Giant Smooth Prague	110	Turnip-shaped root, 4 inches in diameter	8, 10, 11, 26, 32, 41, 45, 50, 60, 61, 67
HORSERADISH			
Bohemian	120	Large roots, snow white flesh	10, 16, 17, 18, 22, 25, 32, 53
KOHLRABI			
Early Purple Vienna	60	Purple skin, green white flesh	6, 8, 10, 14, 16, 23, 24, 26, 28, 42, 45, 54, 60, 67
PARSNIPS			
All American	140	Fine quality, 12 inches long, 3 inches in diameter, white	8, 10, 17, 22, 23, 26, 28, 41, 51, 54, 61
Improved Hollow	110	Good flavor, 10 inches long, 3 inches in diameter, white	41, 60, 61, 63, 67
RUTABAGAS			
American Purple Top	90	Purple tops, buttery yellow globes	2, 14, 17, 22, 24, 26, 30, 34, 35, 41, 43, 44, 45, 46, 47, 48, 49, 60, 61, 65
Laurentian Neckless	90	Purple tops, globe shaped, yellow flesh	16, 31, 32, 42, 45, 60, 67
TURNIPS			
Just Right	40	Globe shaped, white skin	5, 8, 10, 14, 16, 22, 23, 26, 35, 42, 48, 65
Tokyo Cross Hybrid	35	Smooth, semiglobe, pure white, All-America winner	6, 16, 17, 24, 25, 26, 32, 46, 48, 61, 65, 67
Purple Top White Globe	55	Uniform, bright purple tops	Most catalogs

Celeriac

Celeriac is actually a form of celery grown for its swollen root, which may be peeled and used in soups and stews. It is a cool-season, frost-hardy plant.

Planting and Harvesting   Start seed inside four to six weeks before transplanting or sow them in the bed four to six weeks before the average date of last frost. Celeriac grows all season long under glass or polyethylene. Space plants 12 inches apart. Two or three plants are plenty for one person, eight are enough for a family of four. Harvest the whole plant, then remove the leaves and root fibers.

Horseradish

Planting and Harvesting   Horseradish is grown from root cuttings, which can be purchased from a nursery. Cut the carrot-shaped roots to 9-inch lengths. Plant them on a slant, the small end down, the large end about 2 inches below the surface, 6 to 8 inches apart. When the leaves are a foot high, pull back the soil and remove all but one or two of the crown sprouts. Rub off the small roots that have started on the sides. You will need two to three plants per individual. Plant in the spring; harvest the following October or November. Dig out the whole plant and make cuttings from the base for rooting the following spring.

Kohlrabi

Although kohlrabi produces a swollen, edible stem above the ground, it looks and acts much like a turnip. That's why I included it in this section. Many people prize it for its nutty, delicious flavor.

Planting   Plant seed ½ inch deep and about 3 inches apart. Thin to between 4 and 6 inches apart. Plant in succession for a continuous harvest. Kohlrabi can also be started indoors and transplanted to the garden or grown most of the year under glass or polyethylene plastic.

Harvesting   Start harvesting kohlrabi when it gets to be 2½ to 3 inches across.

Parsnips

Planting and Harvesting   Parsnips are a frost-hardy, cool-weather crop. In mild-winter areas, plant in the fall for a spring harvest. If you live in the colder regions of the country, plant in April for an early fall harvest.

Parsnip seeds will germinate faster if you soak them overnight before planting. Sow seeds ½ inch deep in bed, then thin to stand 3 to 4 inches apart. Eight to 20 plants are generally enough for one person, 40 to 50 enough for a family of four. Parsnips should be harvested in the same manner as carrots.

Rutabagas

The rutabaga is a hybrid cousin of the turnip and, like its relative, is ideal for stews. You can time your planting of rutabagas in the same way you would for turnips, but the sowing and spacing instructions are slightly different.

Planting   Sow rutabaga seeds ½ inch deep or cover with ½ inch of soil; they should be spaced 3 inches apart. Thin to stand 8 to 10 inches apart. Each person can easily consume five to ten rutabagas. For a family of four, devote between 2 and 3 square feet to planting.

Harvesting   You should take rutabagas when the roots are about 3 to 5 inches in diameter.

Turnips

The swollen root of the turnip is rich in iron and vitamin C. You can harvest your turnips in both the summer and fall.

Planting   Sow seeds ¼ inch deep and about 1 inch apart. They tend to sprout in clumps that require thinning; complete this process in stages—every few days for the first two to four weeks—so your plants stand 2 or 3 inches apart. If your family loves this vegetable, devote 1 square foot to planting to produce 60 to 120 turnips during the season.

Since this crop is frost hardy, it can be started in the garden four to six weeks before the last average crop (earlier under glass or polyethylene). Plant a second time in late July or August for an early fall harvest. During both plantings, place in the same beds with larger, slower-maturing crops, because turnips mature in 35 to 60 days.

Harvesting   Harvest turnip roots when they are 2 to 4 inches in diameter. For turnip greens, harvest the leaves when they are young and tender.

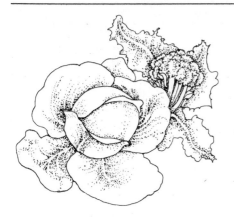

CABBAGE KNOWLEDGE

Cabbage, broccoli, cauliflower, and brussels sprouts are considered part of the cabbage family. They are not especially well suited to Big Yield/Small Space gardens, as they take up too much space for what they give in return; but if they are among your special favorites, try to grow at least some of them. The only saving grace is that you can grow faster-maturing vegetables in the same space while you're waiting for one of these members of the cabbage family to grow to maturity.

All are frost-hardy, cool-weather vegetables. Sow seeds indoors in peat pots or buy seedlings from a nursery and transplant to the garden two to six weeks before the last average frost in the spring. Plant in late summer for a fall crop.

Cabbage

Cabbage offers a delightful number of varieties: red cabbage, which actually ranges from bright red to dark purple in color; savory cabbage, dark green leaves with a bubbly surface; round cabbages, whose forms vary from perfectly globular to slightly flat; flat cabbages, which vary from wide and flat to almost egglike in shape (the drumhead type); and pointed, heart-shaped cabbages (see Table 11–16).

Planting   Start seed indoors or buy transplants from the nursery. Set seedlings in the beds at 12- to 18-inch intervals. You can squeeze cabbage down to about 10 inches, but the heads will be smaller. You can also space your cabbage 6 inches apart and cut the intermediate plants as greens. Plant three to four cabbage plants per person.

Harvesting   Cut heads when firm. Cut the stem off squarely and leave it in the ground so small cabbages will form. Harvest Chinese cabbage as early as possible (the long types should be 15 to 18 inches tall), since the large, compact heads tend to elongate and bolt into flower when hot days arrive. You can harvest cabbage in summer by planting in the spring; in late fall by planting in summer; and all winter long in mild-climate areas. Be sure to trim your planting so that the cabbages reach maturity before or after the hot summer months.

TABLE 11–16. CABBAGE VARIETIES

VARIETY	DAYS TO MATURITY	REMARKS	CATALOG SEED SOURCE
CHINESE CABBAGE			
Michihili	72	Dark green, 8 inches long, 4 inches in diameter, long heading type	5, 6, 7, 8, 10, 17, 23, 24, 25, 35, 36, 39, 41, 42, 45, 46, 48, 49, 50, 52, 60, 63, 67, 68
Wong Bok	70	Solid, dumpy, 10-inch heads, 6–7 pounds, squat heading type	8, 10, 30, 31, 42, 44, 59, 51, 65
FLAT			
Late Dutch Flat	110	Late, bluish green, good winter keeper, up to 15 pounds	4, 10, 22, 59
HEART SHAPED			
Early Jersey Wakefield	65	Dark green, 2–3 pounds, conical, extra early	4, 6, 8, 10, 12, 16, 23, 24, 25, 34, 35, 41, 43, 44, 46, 48, 49, 59, 61, 67, 68
RED			
Red Acre	86	Early to midseason, dark red head, 6–7 inches across, 4–5 pounds	2, 4, 5, 6, 7, 8, 12, 42, 45, 46, 48, 50, 60, 61
Ruby Ball	70	Early, ball shaped, 5 pounds, All-America selection	8, 14, 16, 23, 42, 67
ROUND			
Danish Ballhead	105	Late, large and solid heads, 3–5 pounds	2, 5, 7, 8, 10, 14, 16, 22, 23, 24, 41, 42, 45, 52
Dwarf Morden	53	Early, novel midget cabbage, 4 inches round	7, 16
Golden Acre	63	Early, gray green, round, 6–6½ inches in diameter	2, 4, 5, 6, 7, 8, 10, 11, 14, 16, 17, 22, 24, 32, 34, 38, 41, 42, 43, 45, 46, 47, 54, 59, 67
Penn State Ballhead	110	Late, stands cold weather well, 8 pounds, 7–9 inches across	6, 8, 10, 12, 16, 43, 60, 67
SAVOY			
Chieftain Savoy	85	Blue green, 8 inches across, flattened, 4–5 pounds, All-America selection	4, 11, 12, 24, 25, 35, 41, 42, 45, 50
Savoy King	90	Midseason, dark green, semiflat, 3–5 pounds, extremely hardy	5, 6, 14, 16, 23, 24, 25, 42, 46, 52, 54

Broccoli

Some broccoli varieties put out lots of side branches in addition to a main head; others have a central head but produce few side branches; still others produce side branches but no central head. The best types for small gardens are the varieties that produce good-sized central heads and lots of side branches. With these, you'll get the maximum production for the space used (see Table 11–17).

Planting Broccoli, a cool-weather, frost-hardy vegetable, can be planted in the ground four to six weeks before the average frost-free date in your area. You can also plant in midsummer for a fall crop. Where summers are hot and arrive early, plant in late summer for a fall or winter crop.

Grow the plants indoors from seeds or buy seedlings from a nursery. Transplant them into your garden 12 to 16 inches apart. Be sure to plant a fast-maturing crop in the same space.

You will need about two broccoli plants per person, or eight plants for a family of four.

Harvesting Pick heads before they become discolored or blemished. Heads should be firm and clean white. Softness or yellowing flowers or leaves indicates overmaturity.

TABLE 11–17. BROCCOLI VARIETIES

VARIETY	DAYS TO MATURITY	REMARKS	CATALOG SEED SOURCE
Calabrese	85	Bluish green central head with many side branches	6, 8, 16, 30, 39, 63
Cleopatra Hybrid	75	Central head, vigorous, medium-sized side shoots, All-America selection	25, 45, 46, 50, 60
Green Comet	55	Solid, large central head, red side branches, All-America selection	2, 6, 8, 16, 17, 23, 26, 42, 46, 52, 60, 63
Waltham 29	75	Dark blue green, medium-large heads	2, 7, 23, 26, 31, 34, 35, 41, 42, 60, 61, 65, 67

Cauliflower

Cauliflower is more difficult to grow than other members of the cabbage family. It needs to mature in cool weather and is fairly frost hardy (see Table 11–18).

Planting   Plan your planting so you can harvest in the early summer or in the fall. If summers are very hot in your area, you may want to grow cauliflower in the autumn; set out the plants in July or August. Start seeds inside or buy plants from a nursery, and transplant into your garden 12 to 18 inches apart. When the cauliflower begins to head (to flower by showing buds) you must blanch the head (prevent its turning green) by pulling a few outer leaves over it and tying them loosely with a string or rubber band. You will need 3 plants for an individual, 9 to 12 for a family of four.

Harvesting   Pick heads before they become discolored or blemished. Heads should be firm and clean white. Softness or yellowing flowers or leaves indicates overmaturity.

TABLE 11–18. CAULIFLOWER VARIETIES

VARIETY	DAYS TO MATURITY	REMARKS	CATALOG SEED SOURCE
Purple Head	85	Large purple heads turn green when cooked	6, 17, 22, 24, 43, 60, 67
Snowball Y	68	Medium early, medium-large heads, 6½ inches in diameter	7, 15, 34, 58, 60
Snow Crown	60	Tight, white domes, 5–9 inches across, up to 2 pounds, All-America winner	6, 8, 14, 16, 23, 26, 28, 42, 46, 61, 63, 65
Snow King	55	Flattened head, creamy, 5–9 inches across, heat tolerant, All-America winner	6, 8, 16, 17, 24, 25, 28, 32, 45, 46, 52, 63, 65

Brussels Sprouts

Brussels sprouts are a very winter-hardy vegetable (see Table 11–19).

Planting Grow from seed indoors or buy plants from a nursery. In cool-summer areas, transplant to the garden as soon as the soil can be worked; in other areas, set out in July for a fall harvest. Space 12 to 18 inches apart. You will need one to three plants per individual, five to ten for a family of four.

Harvesting Pick the lowest sprouts when they reach about 1 inch in diameter. Break off any leaves below the sprout, but don't remove the top leaves.

TABLE 11–19. BRUSSELS SPROUTS VARIETIES

VARIETY	DAYS TO MATURITY	REMARKS	CATALOG SEED SOURCE
Jade Cross Hybrid	80	Blue green, oval heads, All-America winner, good freezer	5, 6, 8, 24, 25, 28, 45, 46, 48, 52, 60
Long Island Improved	90	Produces good crop of 1½-inch heads	2, 4, 6, 8, 17, 22, 24, 26, 30, 34, 39, 41, 42, 43, 44, 46, 48, 50, 52, 54, 59, 61, 67, 68

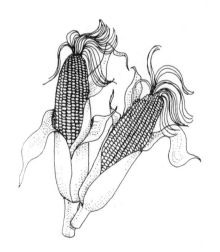

SWEET CORN: KERNELS OF ADVICE

Sweet corn is such a favorite that I include it even though it takes up considerable space. You have a choice of yellow, white, extra-sweet, combination yellow-and-white, popcorn, and ornamental-corn varieties. In areas experiencing cool summers, plant early varieties. If you want corn all summer long, you can plant early, midseason, and late varieties, or you can plant one variety every few weeks until about 85 days before the first fall frost in your area (see Table 11–20).

Planting You will need a minimum of 10 to 15 plants per person. This means you'll need at least a 4-foot-square area in order to raise corn for a family of three or four.

Corn is a wind pollinator. The tassels contain the male

parts of the plant, and the silks that come out of the ears are part of the female flowers. Wind-borne pollen from the tassels of one plant falls on the silks of another plant, and each silk that receives pollen produces a mature kernel. Because the wind can't carry pollen very far, you must group the plants as close together as possible to ensure pollination and completely filled out ears.

Corn should be planted 1 to 2 inches deep and 8 inches apart after the last spring frost. You can also begin corn indoors or directly in the garden before the last frost if you use the season stretchers described in Chapter 5. The most important thing to remember is that corn is a heat lover and thrives on hot summer days.

Harvesting   Pick corn when the silks turn dark and begin to shrivel. The kernels should be plump and milky. To determine if your corn is ready for harvesting, squeeze a kernel with your thumbnail. If it's ready, it'll squirt a milky juice. That means the corn is at its peak of sweetness, a stage at which it will remain for two to five days.

TABLE 11–20. CORN VARIETIES

VARIETY	DAYS TO MATURITY	REMARKS	CATALOG SEED SOURCE
BICOLOR			
Butter and Sugar	80	Yellow and white, extra-sweet, 8-inch ears	2, 8, 16, 23, 24, 25, 40, 41, 52, 60, 65, 67
Honey and Cream	78	Yellow and white, 6½- to 7½-inch ears	2, 6, 8, 14, 24, 26, 33, 37, 39, 44, 52, 63
EXTRA SWEET			
Early Xtra-Sweet	71	Early, holds supersweetness long time, All-America selection	6, 14, 16, 17, 24, 25, 32, 39, 45, 46, 49, 52, 60, 63, 65
ORNAMENTAL			
Indian Ornamental	110	Large, decorative ears, endless array of colors	7, 8, 10, 16, 21, 23, 25, 26, 41, 54, 60, 61, 65, 68
POPCORN			
White Cloud	100	No hulls, pops to large size	7, 23, 26, 45, 60

TABLE 11–20. CORN VARIETIES *(continued)*

VARIETY	DAYS TO MATURITY	REMARKS	CATALOG SEED SOURCE
WHITE			
Country Gentleman	85	Mid- to late season, sweet, white kernels, 8- to 9-inch ears	6, 7, 10, 14, 17, 22, 25, 28, 31, 41, 43, 44, 45, 50, 51, 54, 61, 68
Honey Cream	60	Early, dwarf plant, 6- to 7-inch ears, well suited to small gardens	32
Silver Queen	94	Late, snow white, tender kernels, 8- to 9-inch ears	2, 6, 8, 14, 16, 23, 24, 25, 26, 41, 42, 43, 46, 50, 52, 54, 60, 61, 65, 67
Silver Sweet	65	Early, tender, tasty, 6-inch ears	6
YELLOW			
Earliking	65	Early, bright green husks, 5- to 5½-foot stalks, 8-by-1¾-inch ears	7, 25, 28, 32, 41, 42, 45, 50, 52, 60, 65, 67
Golden Bantam	80	Midseason, one of sweetest yellow corns, 6½-inch ears	7, 8, 14, 16, 22, 24, 30, 31, 32, 34, 45, 49, 51, 67, 68
Golden Beauty	70	Valuable in short-season localities, 7- to 8-inch ears, All-America selection, early	6, 7, 8, 10, 12, 14, 16, 22, 24, 26, 39, 42, 45, 50, 51, 54, 60, 65, 67
Sugar Loaf	83	Late, high sugar content, 8-inch ears	50, 68

BIG-YIELD VINE CROPS

Vine crops give an excellent return in a Big Yield/Small Space garden, provided you make maximum use of the available space above the garden. The vegetables in this category include peas, beans, cucumbers, squash, pumpkins, and melons. Most lend themselves to the season-stretching strategies discussed in Chapter 5.

Peas

Fresh, tender peas are among the oldest of cultivated vegetables. There are a number of varieties you can grow (see Table 11–21), but I especially recommend All-America Sugar Snap developed by the Burpee Seed Company. These are full sized and have edible pods.

Planting Peas pose a problem because you need roughly 90 plants per person per season. You can increase production significantly, however, by employing a few simple strategies.

Start your peas in the spring as soon as the ground can be worked. Plant 2 inches deep and 2 inches apart.

You should also place an inoculant in the soil—an active rhizobia bacteria that improves plant growth through the formation of nitrogen-fixing nodules on the roots—to help them fix nitrogen. Inoculants can be purchased from most nurseries or from catalog seed firms.

To obtain significant production, plant peas across a bed at least 2 feet wide. Train up a wall or fence or place a chicken-wire fence in the middle of the bed and train peas up this. Take them out when the vines dry up and replace with squash, beans, or other vine crops. Follow this with a final crop of peas across the entire 2-foot bed in the fall. Peas planted by this wide-row method do considerably better than peas grown in a single row along a fence. Peas can also be grown spaced 2 inches apart inside a 2-foot-diameter, 4-foot-high wire cage.

TABLE 11–21. PEA VARIETIES

VARIETY	DAYS TO MATURITY	REMARKS	CATALOG SEED SOURCE
Alderman	75	High-quality pea, 4½- to 6-foot vines	6, 8, 16, 23, 34, 41, 51, 60, 61, 66, 67
Freezonian	60	Early, vigorous variety, 2½-foot vines, wilt resistant, All-America selection	2, 5, 6, 7, 8, 10, 16, 17, 23, 24, 26, 39, 41, 44, 46
Improved Tall Telephone	72	Medium late, 4- to 4½-foot vines	2, 24, 25, 49
Mammoth Melting (snow pea)	72	Sweet, tender pods	5, 6, 8, 10, 23, 26, 28, 35, 39, 43, 45, 46, 49, 54, 66, 67
Sugar Snap	70	Edible pods, sweet, heavy producer, 4-foot vines, All-America selection	6, 22, 26, 31, 45, 46, 52, 66
Wando	68	Midseason, 2½-inch, dark green pods, tolerant of hot weather, 2½-foot vines	2, 5, 6, 8, 10, 14, 16, 17, 22, 23, 25, 26, 28, 31, 32, 33, 34, 39, 41, 45, 50, 51, 52, 60, 61, 65, 66, 68

Harvesting Peas are best picked when they are still bright green but the pods are fairly well filled. The flat, dark green pods are immature; the yellowish, hard ones are old. Peas should be very sweet when raw.

Beans

Beans come in such a truly bewildering variety that they create a dilemma for the small-space gardener. Unless you want to turn your entire garden over to beans, you should probably plant just one or two of the more popular types (see Table 11–22).

Planting All except fava beans are warm-weather crops. Plant in the spring after the ground has warmed up.

TABLE 11–22. BEAN VARIETIES

VARIETY	DAYS TO MATURITY	REMARKS	CATALOG SEED SOURCE
BUSH LIMA			
Fordhook 242	75	Large and plump seeds, heavy yielder, All-America selection	Most catalogs
Henderson Bush	75	Baby lima, small seeded	2, 6, 7, 14, 17, 25, 26, 31, 34, 35, 42, 43, 45, 46, 48, 49, 51, 52, 61, 65, 66, 67, 68
BUSH SNAP			
Blue Lake Bush	58	Plump pods, 5½–6½ inches long	2, 7, 8, 46, 48, 51
Green Crop	51	Dark green pods, 6½–7½ inches long, All-America selection	6, 17, 31, 34, 42, 43, 60, 65, 66
FAVA			
Fava Long Podded	85	Pods 7 inches long, very hardy	2, 6, 8, 11, 38, 39, 43, 44, 45, 52, 54, 66
POLE LIMA			
King of the Garden	90	Large, flat beans, 3–5 per pod, climbs 8 feet or more	6, 8, 14, 22, 24, 25, 26, 35, 41, 43, 45, 46, 49, 52, 54, 60, 61, 65, 66
POLE SNAP			
Blue Lake	60	Oval, 5½- to 6-inch-long, dark green pods	6, 17, 23, 24, 25, 26, 28, 32, 43, 44, 45, 46, 48, 49, 50, 51, 54, 60, 61, 66, 68

TABLE 11–22. BEAN VARIETIES *(continued)*

VARIETY	DAYS TO MATURITY	REMARKS	CATALOG SEED SOURCE
Burpee Golden	60	Golden wax, 5½- to 6-inch pods, stringless	6
Kentucky Wonder	65	High quality, flat, oval pods, 6–7 inches long, rust resistant	6, 7, 8, 10, 17, 22, 23, 24, 25, 26, 28, 30, 31, 33, 34, 39, 41, 43
Oregon Giant (Paul Bunyan bean)	65	Giant, foot-long pods	44, 66
Purple Pod	65	Red purple, stringless	17, 22, 49, 67
Romano	65	Flat, wide, Italian bean	6, 8, 10, 17, 23, 24, 26, 33, 44, 45, 48, 50, 52
SHELL			
Pinto	88	Short, broad, oval pod, 5–6 beans per pod	2, 17, 22, 32, 46, 48, 66, 68
Red Kidney	85	Large, pinkish red bean, 20- to 22-inch-tall plant	2, 6, 8, 10, 14, 16, 17, 20, 39, 43, 44, 45, 46
SOY			
Kanrich	93	Heavy yields, 24-inch-high bushes	10, 24, 44, 60

You can start them from two to four weeks before the last frost under glass or polyethylene plastic. Some gardeners also start beans indoors in individual peat pots to get a jump on the season and then transplant to the garden as soon as the soil warms up and all danger of frost has passed.

Plant snap bush beans 1 to 2 inches deep, 3 to 4 inches apart; snap pole beans 1 to 2 inches deep, 6 to 8 inches apart; lima bush beans 1½ to 2 inches deep, 6 to 8 inches apart; lime pole beans 1½ to 2 inches deep, 8 to 10 inches apart; soybeans 1½ to 2 inches deep, 2 to 4 inches apart; shell beans 1 to 2 inches deep, 3 to 4 inches apart. You should anticipate the following number of plants per person: snap bush or dry shell beans, 15 to 45; snap or lima pole beans, 12 to 15 plants; lima bush, 15 to 20; and fava or soybeans, 15 to 30 plants.

Pole beans give the best results when grown on free-standing supports at the north or east end of your garden away from the walls or fence (see Chapter 6). You can also grow pole beans inside a 2-foot-diameter wire cage. Plant 6 inches apart inside the cage. You may have to help them grow up the cage or run a string from the top of the cage to each plant. Drive a small stake into the ground beside each plant and anchor the string to that. Bush beans do not produce a high yield in proportion to the amount of space they require, but they will provide beans earlier than the pole type.

Harvesting   Snap beans are best when the pods snap readily but the tips are still pliable. To keep the beans producing well, pick the pods frequently. Pick lima beans when the pods are well filled but still bright and fresh. The end of the pod should feel spongy when squeezed.

Cucumbers

Cucumbers are a favorite of home gardeners. Like beans, they come in so many different varieties that you could spend forever trying them all (see Table 11–23).

Planting   Cucumbers, another warm-weather crop, should be planted after the last frost, 6 inches apart. You can space them slightly closer around a pickle pole. Start plants inside in individual peat pots or buy your cucumber seedlings from a nursery. You can transplant them outdoors under Hotkaps, glass, or polyethylene plastic several weeks before the last frost. You will need two to three cucumber plants per person, more if you intend to put up pickles.

Grow cucumbers up a fence, on low trellises within the garden, in 2-foot-diameter, 4-foot-high wire cages, or on one of several types of pickle poles. When the plants reach the top of the fence, cage, or pickle pole, pinch out the fuzzy growing tip to make them spread out laterally.

Slicing varieties are generally slender and 6 to 8 inches long, while pickling varieties have shorter, blockier bodies. Frequently you can use one variety for both pickling and slicing.

Harvesting   Cucumbers are best picked when green, firm, and at a moderate size. The spines should just be beginning to soften. They are past prime when dull, puffy, and yellowing. Be sure and pick when they reach usable size so new cucumbers will continue to set.

TABLE 11–23. CUCUMBER VARIETIES

VARIETY	DAYS TO MATURITY	REMARKS	CATALOG SEED SOURCE
NOVELTIES			
Armenian Yard Long	70	Unusual fluting, 1–3 feet long, 3–4 inches around	36, 44, 50, 51
Lemon	64	Round, yellow, 2½–3 inches	8, 10, 23, 31, 32, 43, 44, 48, 50, 52, 60
White Wonder	65	Ivory white when mature, 8–10 inches long	45, 54, 61
PICKLERS			
Gherkin	60	Chunky, covered with tender spines, 2 inches in diameter	14, 22, 41, 43, 44
Pioneer	55	High yielder, all female flowers, useful in northern areas	7, 8, 24, 26, 42, 46, 50, 60, 68
Spartan Dawn	49	Earliest of picklers, high yields, 6 by 2½ inches	5, 10, 23, 26, 45, 46
Wisconsin SMR	58	Medium sized to blocky, best all-purpose, nonhybrid pickling cucumber	2, 5, 6, 22, 24, 31, 32, 43, 45, 52, 60, 65, 67
SLICING			
Burpee Hybrid	60	Somewhat squared, 8 inches long, 2½ inches wide	6, 10, 14, 39, 42, 44, 45, 60
Early Surecrop	58	Holds color well, 8½–9 inches long, All-America selection	7, 8, 10, 17, 22, 24, 32, 33, 46, 48, 49
Marketer	65	Heavy yielder, 10 inches long, All-America selection	6, 7, 8, 10, 16, 17, 22, 24, 25, 26, 34, 38, 39, 42, 43, 49, 50, 60, 61, 68
Spartan Valor	62	Prolific, all female fruit, 8½–9 inches long, All-America selection	5, 8, 16, 24, 25, 33, 42, 46, 60, 68
Triumph	62	Heavy yields, slightly tapered, 7 to 8 inches long, All-America selection	7, 8, 10, 16, 23, 24, 25, 41, 42, 45, 52, 60, 61, 67
Victory	60	Vigorous vines, dark green, straight, All-America selection	6, 7, 14, 16, 22, 23, 24, 25, 26, 28, 34, 41, 42, 45, 46, 48, 49, 50, 52, 60, 61, 65, 67

Squash

Both summer and winter squash produce well in small gardens. The major differences between the two varieties are that winter squash has a thicker skin and can be stored for much longer periods of time than summer squash (see Table 11–24).

Planting Plant seeds of summer squash 1 inch deep and 12 inches apart, seeds of winter squash 1 inch deep and 24 inches apart. Squash can be started in peat pots from seed and transplanted outside after the last frost. You can transplant them into your garden two to four weeks before this if you put them under glass, polyethylene plastic, or Hotkaps.

One to two summer squash plants and the same number of winter squash plants will provide all the squash one person can handle. Four to five zucchini plants will give a family of four plenty to eat; plant more than this, and you'll have to haul it away.

Be sure to give your winter squash plenty of vertical space. It grows well against a wall or, even better, against a wall with a roof beyond. You can also grow squash up a trellis, inside a wire cage, or even on a 7-foot-high pickle pole. Plant four winter squash of the same variety around the base of the pole and support the fruits as described in Chapter 6. For greatest yields, plant the long-vining, not bush, types.

If you plant one type of squash in close proximity to another type, there will be some cross-pollination. Pumpkins or orange squash planted near other winter squash seem to affect the quality adversely.

You will have to do some experimenting to decide which varieties are best for you. After all, there are 40 different varieties of zucchini alone. If you are in a quandary about which winter squash variety to plant, start with acorn squash. It is the most popular and gives about the best yield for the space.

Harvesting Pick summer squash when fruit is a small or moderate size and the rind is easily dented with your thumbnail. Pick winter squash when the rind is thick enough so it is not penetrated by a thumbnail.

TABLE 11–24. SQUASH VARIETIES

VARIETY	DAYS TO MATURITY	REMARKS	CATALOG SEED SOURCE
SUMMER			
Ambassador	53	Dark green zucchini, fantastic early yields	8, 10, 26, 41, 42, 44, 46, 50, 51, 61, 65
Black	55	Bushy-type zucchini plant, greenish white flesh, black outer skin	7, 8, 10, 18, 24, 25, 30, 31, 33, 34, 39, 41, 42, 50, 61
Early Golden Summer Crookneck	48	Yellow, changes to deep golden orange, crookneck	2, 5, 8, 14, 24, 26, 34, 41, 43, 45, 48, 49, 50, 61, 65, 68
Goldbar	50	Heavy yields, compact open bush, straightneck	8, 14, 24, 26, 32, 35, 41, 42, 43, 45, 48, 49, 50, 51, 61, 65
Golden Bush	60	Flat, disk shaped, golden yellow, scallop (patty pan) variety	48
Gold Rush	50	Bright golden skin, All-America selection	26
Green Cocozella	60	Popular Italian zucchini strain, dark green stripes	10, 30, 31, 39, 41, 60
Scallopini	50	Bright green, cross between scallop and zucchini, All-America selection	6, 7, 8, 16, 26
St. Pat Scallop	60	Bell shaped, patty pan, All-America selection	2, 6, 8, 14, 24, 26, 34, 41, 43, 45, 46, 50, 52, 60, 67
WINTER			
Blue Hubbard	120	Bluish gray, olive shaped, keeps well	2, 6, 8, 10, 16, 22, 23, 24, 26, 31, 38, 42, 46, 50, 52, 60, 68
Butternut Waltham	85	Small seed cavity, good keeper, All-America selection, bottle shaped	6, 8, 14, 17, 23, 25, 26, 28, 31, 32, 35, 42, 45, 46, 52, 54, 60, 65, 68
Golden Delicious	103	Bright orange, heart shaped	2, 22, 33, 36, 60, 67, 68
Gold Nugget	85	Bright orange, 1–2 pounds, buttercup variety	2, 8, 10, 16, 22, 23, 24, 25, 45, 46, 52, 54, 60, 65
Pink Banana Jumbo	105	Cylindrical shape, to 30 inches	7, 21, 22, 42, 45, 48, 50, 51
Spaghetti	100	Medium size, yellow, oblong, inside flesh looks like spaghetti	6, 8, 21, 22, 30, 31, 35, 37, 42, 45, 50, 54, 60, 63, 67, 68
Table King	75	Dark, glossy green, acorn-shaped fruits, 5–6 inches long, golden yellow flesh	6, 7, 8, 14, 17, 23, 35, 42, 45, 46, 52, 54, 65, 67

Melons

Melons come in different sizes and shapes and with white, pink, orange, or green flesh (see Table 11–25).

Planting   Grow cantaloupes and similar small melons on 4-foot-high trellises within your garden or in 2-foot-wide, 4-foot-high wire cages. Either of these methods produces a good quantity of fruit. Melons are a warm-weather crop. Plant seeds outdoors about the date of the last frost, 1 inch deep and 6 to 12 inches apart.

Grow watermelons up a wall. If you can let the fruit spill over a roof, so much the better. To make supporting them practical, stay with the smaller fruiting varieties.

Plant watermelon seed outdoors around the date of the last frost, 1 inch deep and 12 inches apart. Melons can be started indoors in individual peat pots and transplanted outdoors about the date of the last frost. They can also be transplanted outdoors earlier than this if you use protective devices; the timing will depend on the device you select. You will need two to four melon plants of each type (except watermelon) per person. One watermelon plant will provide plenty of watermelons for an individual.

Harvesting   Cantaloupes are ready to eat when the stems pull off easily, usually with only a slight touch. The skin also begins to look like a corky net, and the stem cracks all the way around. Smell the blossom end of Persian melons. If it smells fruity and sweet, the melon is probably ripe. Honeydew and casaba melons are ripe when the rinds have turned completely yellow. When watermelons are ripe, they give off a dull-hollow sound when thumped with your knuckle. A sharp sound means they're still green.

TABLE 11–25. MELON VARIETIES

VARIETY	DAYS TO MATURITY	REMARKS	CATALOG SEED SOURCE
CANTALOUPES			
Hales Best Jumbo	80	Well netted, 6–7½ inches long, oval, 4½ pounds	6, 7, 10, 14, 17, 24, 26, 41, 54, 61, 68
Hearts of Gold	90	Deep orange flesh	6, 7, 10, 14, 16, 24, 26, 41, 54, 61, 68
Honey Rock	85	Well netted, 5–6 pounds, heavy, almost round, salmon flesh	6, 16, 22, 24, 25, 26, 32, 39, 41, 42, 45, 52, 60, 65, 67, 68

TABLE 11–25. MELON VARIETIES *(continued)*

VARIETY	DAYS TO MATURITY	REMARKS	CATALOG SEED SOURCE
MUSKMELONS			
Early Hybrid (Crenshaw)	90	Large oval, no netting	5, 6, 39, 65
Golden Beauty Casaba	110	Golden, wrinkled skin, nearly white flesh	6, 7, 30, 42, 48, 50, 73
Honeydew	110	Smooth, ivory skin, emerald green flesh	5, 6, 7, 25, 26, 28, 30, 35, 42, 44, 46, 49, 50, 51, 54, 61, 68
Medium Persian	95	Almost round, heavily netted, 7–8 pounds	30, 44, 48, 50
WATERMELONS			
Crimson Sweet	80	Round, dark red flesh, to 25 pounds	6, 7, 10, 14, 17, 22, 23, 26, 32, 34, 35, 41, 42, 45, 50, 61, 65
Golden Midget	55	Turns golden when ripe, 8 inches in diameter	10, 14, 16, 22, 46
Jubilee	95	Oblong, striped, 25–40 pounds, heavy yielder	7, 10, 25, 33, 34, 35, 42, 43, 45, 48, 49, 50, 51, 61, 65
Sugar Baby	80	Icebox type, round, dark green, to 10 pounds	Most catalogs

Pumpkins

Pumpkins are associated with American traditions of Thanksgiving and Halloween. They can grow to great size, up to 100 pounds. For your Big Yield/Small Space garden, I especially recommend the Small Sugar Pie variety (see Table 11–26).

Planting Pumpkins, like watermelon, do best if grown up a wall, then allowed to spill over onto a roof. Plant pumpkin seed outdoors about the date of the last frost, 1 to 1½ inches deep and 18 inches apart. Or start them indoors in individual peat pots, transplanting outdoors just after the last frost date or earlier if you use protective devices.

Harvesting Allow your pumpkins to ripen fully on the plant but, since they spoil easily, be sure to protect them against frost.

TABLE 11–26. PUMPKIN VARIETIES

VARIETY	DAYS TO MATURITY	REMARKS	CATALOG SEED SOURCE
Small Sugar Pie	100–110	Rich orange, 8–10 inches in diameter	2, 6, 7, 8, 14, 24, 26, 30, 31, 35, 39, 44, 46, 48, 50, 51, 52, 60, 61, 67, 68

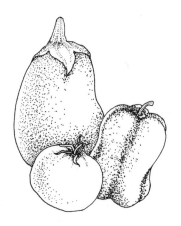

THE TOMATO FAMILY

This family includes four well-known vegetables: tomatoes, peppers, eggplant, and potatoes. All, except potatoes (which are covered in the section on root crops), are warm-weather crops and should be started indoors or purchased as seedlings from a nursery and transplanted to the garden on or about the date of the last frost. You can start them two to four weeks earlier under Hotkaps, glass, or polyethylene plastic.

Tomatoes

Tomatoes are probably the most productive vegetable you can grow in a Big Yield/Small Space garden, and they are certainly the most popular. Over 500 tomato varieties are available for home growing today. As you will see below, I especially recommend the indeterminate varieties for your Big Yield/Small Space garden (see Table 11–27). I've listed some determinate types as well for those of you who wish to experiment.

Planting　Start tomatoes indoors from seed or buy plants from a nursery and transplant 18 to 30 inches apart.

Tomatoes always present a special kind of problem, and even veteran gardeners differ on how to grow them best. Some say they should be allowed to sprawl on the ground, but that increases the chances of the fruit rotting, promotes sun scald on the fruit and vines, and takes up too much space. Others recommend training them up one or two stakes, or growing three or more stems up a wire. Still others think that you should put them in a cage and let them go. What's the right answer for Big Yield/Small Space gardens?

First, you have to understand there are two types of tomato vines, *determinate* and *indeterminate*. I highly recommend that you plant the indeterminate varieties, which outproduce the determinate types hands down. The terminal buds of indeterminate tomato vines set fruit, and the vine grows without stopping until killed by frost. Indeterminate vines must be trained or confined in some way. Examples of this type are Abraham Lincoln, Burpee Big Boy, Super Fantastic, and Beefsteak.

The easiest way to train an indeterminate tomato vine is to put it in a 24-inch-diameter, 5- to 6-foot-high tomato cage and let it go its own way. All evidence shows that tomato plants left alone in this type of structure outproduce pruned vines, sometimes by a ratio of two to one. Some gardeners, however, insist on pinching and poking.

You can train your tomato vines in several ways. For example, grow a plant up a single 4- to 5-foot stake. Tie the vine to the stake and pinch out (and keep pinched) all but one stem. The best way to pinch out unwanted growth is to wait until two leaves develop on a side shoot, then pinch above them. This gives good foliage cover and protects the stems from sun damage.

Since two or more stems produce more tomatoes and give better protection against the sun than a single stem, you can also train these multiple stems up two stakes or up a tomato ladder. Choose the best stems and pinch out all others. For three or four stems, train up a tomato ladder or stretch a taut wire between two 5-foot-high posts. Run three or four strings down to your tomato plant and train the stems up the strings.

The tomato-tower and parallel-horizontal-trellis methods described in Chapter 6 also work well. Other approaches take up too much space to be practical in your Big Yield/Small Space garden.

You can increase the growth of tomatoes by placing a piece of clear plastic over your wire cage early in the season. This increases both the temperature and the amount of carbon dioxide they get, but be careful not to let the temperature become too high under the plastic. See Appendix D for the appropriate temperature range for your tomatoes or check with your nursery.

One or two tomato plants per season are generally enough for one person; four or five will produce enough fruit for a family of four.

Harvesting   Pick when the color is good all over. Size is no indication of maturity. Before frost, cut down the plants and hang them upside down until they ripen. To-matoes should be stored where it is cool and dark. You can also cut the green tomatoes off the plants in fall and place them on a tray or in a shallow pan. Store in the dark at about 50 degrees F. They will ripen over a period of time.

TABLE 11–27. TOMATO VARIETIES

VARIETY	DAYS TO MATURITY	REMARKS	CATALOG SEED SOURCE
CHERRY TO PEAR SHAPED		Size of half dollar, indeterminate	7, 23, 34, 49, 52
Large Red Cherry	72	Paste tomato, pear shaped, indeterminate	5, 6, 24, 26, 30, 34, 42, 43, 44, 45, 48, 50, 51, 54, 60
San Marzano	80		
EARLY			
Earlibell	68	Thick, meaty, heavy producer, indeterminate	22
Early Girl	56	Bears both early and late, indeterminate, 4- to 5-ounce fruits	2, 6, 22, 60
Fireball	64	Compact plant, determinate, fruit 4–5 ounces	2, 8, 16, 23, 24, 26, 39, 42, 52, 60
Spring Giant	68	All-America selection, determinate, VFN (wilt and nematode) resistant	6, 14, 16, 25, 32, 44, 45, 46, 49, 50, 51, 52, 60, 63, 65, 67, 68
LARGE FRUIT			
Abraham Lincoln	70	Sweet, 1¼–3 pounds, indeterminate	54
Beefsteak	90	Large, firm meat, home-garden standard, indeterminate	2, 5, 6, 8, 10, 26, 30, 33, 37, 38, 39, 41, 42, 45, 46, 50, 63, 65, 67
Burgess Colossal	90	Fruit to 2½ pounds, 6 inches across	9
Burpee Big Early	62	Mid-early, fruit to 1 pound, indeterminate	6, 15, 41, 42, 47, 60, 65
MID- TO LATE SEASON			
Ace 55	75	Medium large, meaty, bears heavily, VF resistant	6, 15, 41, 42, 68
Glamour	75	Vigorous plants, grows well in Midwest, Northeast	8, 10, 12, 15, 23, 26, 39, 42, 45, 52, 60, 65

TABLE 11–27. TOMATO VARIETIES (continued)

VARIETY	DAYS TO MATURITY	REMARKS	CATALOG SEED SOURCE
Heinz 1350	75	Flattened, meaty, solid, 6-ounce fruit, VF resistant, determinate	6, 7, 8, 12, 15, 18, 26, 28, 42, 45, 47, 52, 60, 61, 65, 68
Marglobe	75	Smooth, vigorous, long-time favorite, determinate	2, 5, 6, 7, 8, 10, 16, 22, 24, 25, 26, 30, 31, 34, 38, 39, 41
PINK			
Ponderosa	82	Purplish pink, fruit to 2 pounds, indeterminate	6, 8, 10, 14, 16, 22, 23, 24, 25, 26, 30, 39, 42, 44, 46, 48, 50, 54, 60, 65, 68
YELLOW, WHITE			
Jubilee	75	Deep orange to yellow globe	10, 14, 39, 42, 43, 44, 45, 46, 48, 50, 54, 68
White Beauty	84	Ivory skin, large	5, 22, 37, 45, 46
OTHER			
Mr. Stripey	68	Red and yellow stripes, grows well in all states	63

Peppers—Some Hot, Some Not

The big bells are the favorite of most home gardeners, but don't overlook the pimiento peppers, which look much like tomatoes. Some of the cherry types and the long, slender varieties, such as Long Sweet Banana, are also sweet. Several pungent varieties, like Rio Grande 21 and New Mexico Rio Grande, are almost a diet staple in some parts of the country. And if you're a hot-pepper fan, try some of the really pungent types, like Jalapeño, Fresno, and Tabasco (see Table 11–28).

Planting Peppers are a warm-weather crop. Start from seed indoors or purchase plants from a nursery. Set transplants out in the garden about the date of the last frost, 18 to 24 inches apart. They can be put out earlier under Hotkaps, glass, or polyethylene plastic. Wire cages set around pepper plants keep them from being crowded by other vegetables and can also serve as a frame for polyethylene covers. Generally, one plant of each type is enough for each person in the family.

Harvesting   Pick bell peppers when they are firm and crisp. Don't let them turn red. Let hot peppers ripen completely on the vine and pick them when they are firm and crisp as well.

TABLE 11–28. PEPPER VARIETIES

VARIETY	DAYS TO MATURITY	REMARKS	CATALOG SEED SOURCE
BIG BELLS, SWEET			
Bell Boy	70	Glossy, 3 by 3 inches square, All-America selection	6, 14, 17, 18, 24, 25, 26, 28, 41, 42, 46, 48, 50, 52, 60, 61, 65, 67
California Wonder	75	Good stuffing pepper, 4½ by 4½ inches, blocky	2, 5, 7, 10, 12, 14, 15, 16, 17, 18, 24, 25, 26, 30, 39, 41, 42, 45, 47, 48, 49, 51, 54, 60, 65, 68
Emerald Giant	74	Vigorous plants, 3-by-4½ inch fruit	7, 10, 27, 41, 42, 47, 49, 50, 65
Yolo Wonder	76	Thick walls, 4 by 4½ inches	6, 10, 11, 17
HOT			
Anaheim Chili	80	Mildly pungent, tapering pods 6–8 inches long, 1 inch in diameter, plants 2 feet high	7, 8, 9, 42, 46, 48, 49, 50, 51
Fresno	78	Tapers to point, 1½–2½ inches long, 1 inch in diameter, very pungent	7, 48, 50
Jalapeño	78	Tapers to blunt tip, hot, 3½ by 1½ inches, cylindrical	7, 14, 17, 20, 22, 25, 34, 35, 42, 44, 48, 49, 50, 51, 68
Large Red Cherry	75	Medium hot, 1½ inches in diameter, red when mature, round	2, 6, 8, 10, 23, 24, 26, 41, 42, 43, 44, 50, 60
New Mexico Number 6	75	Mildly pungent, tapering pods 6–8 inches long, 2 inches in diameter	48, 49, 50
New Mexico Sandia	76	Tapering pods 6–7 inches long, pungent	21, 48, 50, 51
Santa Fe Grande	75	Hot, yellow wax, 3½ inches long, 1½ inches in diameter, conical	7, 42, 50, 68
LONG, SWEET			
Long Sweet Banana	75	Plants 18–22 inches tall, fruit 6 inches long, 1½ inches in diameter	6, 7, 8, 10,12, 14, 15, 23, 25, 26, 27, 34, 35, 39, 42, 45, 46, 48, 49, 50, 54, 60, 61

Eggplant

Eggplant fruit comes in several shapes, sizes, and colors, ranging from plump to slender and from purple to white (see Table 11–29).

Planting Eggplant is a warm-weather crop. Plant seeds inside or buy seedlings from a nursery. Transplant 24 to 30 inches apart in the garden one week or more after the last frost. You can transplant before this using Big Yield/Small Space season-stretcher methods. Wire cages 1½ feet in diameter and 3 feet high keep other plants from crowding your eggplant. When the plants are 6 inches high, pinch out the growing tip to encourage the formation of side branches.

One or two plants are plenty for each person. Pick when the fruits are half grown, just before the color dulls. Be sure to keep picking the fruits as they become ready so that the plants will continue to bear.

TABLE 11–29. EGGPLANT VARIETIES

VARIETY	DAYS TO MATURITY	REMARKS	CATALOG SEED SOURCE
Black Beauty	78	Globular, dark purple fruit	Most catalogs
Disky	65	Long, cylindrical, early	16, 23, 26, 42, 45
Nagoaka Long Black (Japanese)	65	Glossy black, 8–9 inches long, 2½ inches in diameter	42, 67

STALK TALK

Celery

Planting and Harvesting Celery is a cool-weather, frost-hardy plant (see Table 11–30). Start seed indoors about ten weeks before setting plants outdoors. Transplant two to four weeks before the last frost in the spring (earlier under glass or polyethylene plastic). Space plants 6 to 8 inches apart. Two to three plants are enough for an individual. You can grow either a yellow self-blanching variety or a green type that requires blanching. To blanch, place a 6- to 7-inch-high cardboard collar around the base of each plant.

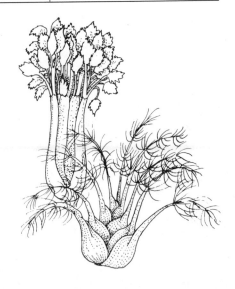

Cardoon

Cardoon, a relative of the artichoke, is raised for its young leafstalks, which are blanched and eaten like celery (see Table 11–30).

Planting and Harvesting   Cardoon is a cool-weather plant. Sow seed in the garden about the date of the last frost or plant seeds in pots and transplant to the garden. Since cardoon takes up considerable space, I advise planting it by itself in a flower bed or with one or two other cardoon plants spaced 18 inches apart.

When the plants become large, typically in September, tie the leaves together, wrap with paper, and mound the soil around them to blanch the leafstalks. To harvest, cut the stalks into sections and boil for an hour to get rid of the natural bitterness.

Florence Fennel

This cool-weather crop is grown for its bulblike base, formed by overlapping leafstalks (see Table 11–30).

TABLE 11–30. STALK VARIETIES

VARIETY	DAYS TO MATURITY	REMARKS	CATALOG SEED SOURCE
CELERY			
Giant Pascal	134	Green, tall, solid stalks	2, 5, 6, 8, 10, 22, 24, 25, 33, 45, 51, 54, 61
Golden Yellow	96	Self-blanching stalks 20–30 inches high	6, 8, 14, 16, 17, 24, 31, 34, 41, 43, 45, 48, 51, 61, 67
CARDOON			
Ivory White	110	Broad, self-blanching, spineless	8, 10, 11, 22, 24, 26, 30
Smooth	110	Fine, smooth stalk	42, 44
Spineless	100	White	54
Tenderheart	105	Large ribs	67
FLORENCE FENNEL	90	Enlarged, flat, oval leaf, grows 2½ feet tall	6, 8, 11, 22, 23, 24, 25, 26, 30, 31, 38, 40, 41, 43, 44, 45, 52, 54, 60, 63, 67

Planting and Harvesting Sow seeds indoors in peat pots and set out 6 to 8 inches apart in very early spring, since cool weather is essential for growth. Where springs and summers are warm, grow as a fall crop. As the plants grow, pull up the soil to cover and blanch the thickened bases. Two or three plants are plenty for a family of four. Pull the Florence fennel plant from the ground when the bulbous base of the stalk measures 3 to 6 inches in length.

PRODUCING PERENNIALS

Artichokes, asparagus, and rhubarb make delicious additions to any garden, but don't try to grow any of these perennials in your regular plots, for they require too much space and can easily overwhelm your other plantings. The virtue is you don't have to replant each year, for these vegetables live on and on.

Artichokes

The globe-shaped flower buds of the artichoke consist of edible "leaves," or sections, on a fleshy base. Varieties with green, not purple, globes are most tender (see Table 11–31).

Planting Artichokes do best in areas that have fairly mild winters and cool summers. The plant is highly decorative and massive (6 feet wide) with silvery green, deeply cut leaves. Give it lots of space in a flower bed.

Buy root divisions in spring. Dig holes 18 inches deep, 4 feet apart. Position the old wood stalk vertically in the hole. Cover the old root with soil and leave the base of the new leafy shoot above the soil line. Water at the time of planting. To start from seed, begin indoors in peat pots four to six weeks before the last heavy frost. Transplant seedlings into your garden 3 to 4 feet apart.

Where winters are severe, cut back the tops in the fall to 8 to 12 inches, tie the old stalks over the root crown, and cover with a mulch or burlap. One plant is enough for one person; two or three are sufficient for a family of four.

Harvesting You can begin to harvest artichokes in the second growing season. Cut the buds, known as *king heads,* while the leaves are still packed and not yet opened for flowering. Leave a 1½-inch stem on each bud.

TABLE 11–31. ARTICHOKE VARIETIES

VARIETY	DAYS TO MATURITY	REMARKS	CATALOG SEED SOURCE
Green Globe	Not applicable	Large flower heads, edible flower buds made up of thick, fleshy scales, solid centers	6, 8, 17, 20, 22, 24, 25, 26, 37, 45, 54, 67

Asparagus

Asparagus takes about 3 years to come into production, so it is a crop that requires patience. Once it's established, though, your plants can be harvested for about 20 years. The time is well worth investing if you love this vegetable, especially given rising supermarket costs. I suggest you give asparagus its own 3-by-3-foot or 4-by-4-foot bed, because otherwise it tends to take over the garden (see Table 11–32).

Planting   Buy one-year-old roots from a nursery or a catalog seed firm and transplant them directly into your bed. Make a hole 5 inches in diameter and 8 inches deep for each plant. Spread out the roots at the bottom of the hole with the crown side up. Cover with 2 inches of power-packed soil. As the plant grows, fill the hole but do not cover the growing tip. The crowns should stand 12 inches apart.

Twenty plants will yield enough asparagus for one individual. Multiply this number to provide for your family's needs.

Harvesting   Don't harvest any spears the first year. When the foliage turns brown in the late fall, cut the stems to the ground. During the spring or early summer of the second year, you can harvest those spears that are 6 to 8 inches high. Cut the spears at ground level or a few inches below the soil, but never closer than 2 inches to the crowns. In the third and following years, you can cut 6- to 8-inch spears for about six weeks.

TABLE 11–32. ASPARAGUS VARIETIES

VARIETY	DAYS TO MATURITY	REMARKS	CATALOG SEED SOURCE
Mary Washington	Not applicable	Medium green with purplish tinge, produces plenty of spears, rust resistant	2, 6, 8, 10, 13, 14, 16, 17, 18, 22, 23, 24, 25, 26, 28, 39, 40, 41, 42, 45, 46, 48, 50, 51, 54, 67, 68

Rhubarb

Rhubarb produces large quantities of stalks in a small space (see Table 11–33). Rhubarb compares favorably with any of the broad-leaved plants grown primarily as ornamentals, so let it play show-off in your flower beds.

Planting   Typically, rhubarb requires about two months of freezing temperatures and a long, cool spring for best taste and yield, though I have seen it do extremely well in mild climates.

Purchase root crowns from your nursery or order from a catalog seed source. Plant them 12 inches apart in spring or fall. This will keep the plants fairly small and squeezed in. To let the plants really spread out and take over, plant 30 to 36 inches apart. Dig the holes and set out the root crowns (the tops of the roots) so that the crowns will be about 2 inches below ground level. Do not allow the crowns to dry out before they are planted.

Harvesting   Wait two years before you begin to harvest the stalks. After that, you can harvest eight weeks or more every year.

TABLE 11–33. RHUBARB VARIETIES

VARIETY	DAYS TO MATURITY	REMARKS	CATALOG SEED SOURCE
Valentine	Not applicable	Red stalks, 18–22 inches long, delicious in pies	6, 14, 18, 22, 29, 33, 52, 55, 58
Victoria	Not applicable	Broad, thick, green stalks, shaded red	6, 16, 17, 18, 26, 33, 40, 51, 55, 68

HERBS IN BRIEF

Every Big Yield/Small Space garden should have a few herbs. Some gardeners grow them because herbs repel certain insects and have a beneficial effect on other plants. Others use them in their cooking. In any event, they make aromatic additions to the garden.

In general, it's best to squeeze herbs in wherever you have a little additional space or plant them to form a narrow border around part of your garden. For the most part, they like to be raised in full sun. You can grow them in the ground or in pots set around your garden. Don't be afraid to pinch the shoots of most herbs regularly, since they just get stronger after each pinching.

Herbs can be annuals, biennials, or perennials. Annuals complete their life cycles in one year, while biennials produce seed the second season (see Table 11–34). Perennials grow year after year without being replanted (see Table 11–35).

A FINAL NOTE

Now you have the complete Big Yield/Small Space approach at your fingertips. Of course, there is no need to do everything at once. Most people consider home growing a long-term process, best eased into over several seasons.

The first season, for example, you might start by planting your vegetables intensively and by growing as much as possible above the garden. The next season you could experiment with a few simple season-extending devices and a bit later try some container gardening. Each season after that, you could add a few Big Yield/Small Space components to your gardening, until finally you are using all the techniques effectively. Or you can simply pick and choose how much or how little you want to do from the start.

Whatever you decide, you will see surprising and pleasing results from the very first harvest. As you begin to experience this satisfaction, you will, I'm sure, be as sold as I am on the Big Yield/Small Space way.

TABLE 11–34. ANNUAL AND BIENNIAL HERBS

Annuals and Biennials: Annuals complete their life cycle in one year. They are killed by frost and must be started from seed each year. Biennials last two years.

HERB	DESCRIPTION	HOW TO GROW	HOW TO HARVEST	USE	CATALOG SEED SOURCE
Anise	Lower leaves oval, serrated edges, small white flowers, low-spreading plant 20–24 inches high	Sow in place, thin to 6–8 inches apart, full sun	Harvest seeds about 1 month after flowers bloom	Use licorice-flavored seeds for cookies, candy, meat, soup; leaves for stews, salads, meats	2, 6, 11, 22, 24, 25, 31, 32, 35, 38, 39, 40, 41, 44, 46, 49, 50, 54, 60, 67
Basil, Sweet	Leafy, light green foliage, spikelets of tiny flowers, 20–24 inches high	Sow seeds in place after last frost or start inside and transplant; space 12 inches apart	Harvest leaves when flowering begins; cut plants 4–6 inches above ground	Use leaves in tomato dishes, spaghetti sauce, soups, vegetables, stews	2, 6, 11, 14, 17, 22, 23, 24, 25, 28, 31, 39, 41, 43, 44, 45, 46, 49, 50, 54, 61, 63
Borage	Coarse, rough, 4- to 6-inch-long, gray green leaves, light blue flowers in clusters, 12–36 inches high	Sow seeds in place, space 12 inches apart	Harvest young leaves before flowers open	Use leaves in salads, flowers in soups, stews	6, 11, 22, 23, 24, 25, 26, 28, 31, 35, 38, 41, 43, 44, 45, 46, 49, 54, 60, 67
Caraway	Carrotlike leaves, creamy white, carrotlike flowers, 12–24 inches high	Biennial; sow seeds in place, space 6 inches apart	Harvest leaves when mature; seeds will form second season	Use seeds to flavor breads, cheese, cakes, salads; leaves for salads	6, 11, 14, 17, 22, 24, 25, 26, 28, 31, 32, 35, 38, 39, 40, 41, 43, 44, 45, 46, 49, 54, 60, 67
Chervil	Fernlike foliage turns pink in fall, small white flowers in clusters, 18 inches high	Sow seeds, keep soil moist, partial shade, space 6 inches apart	Harvest when mature and before flowers open	Use fresh or dried leaves in salads, sauces, soups, poultry dishes	2, 6, 11, 22, 24, 25, 26, 30, 31, 38, 44, 45, 50, 60
Coriander	Large, coarse plant, small flowers in clusters, to 36 inches high	Sow seeds in place in early spring, thin to 6–7 inches apart	Harvest seeds when they begin to turn brown	Use crushed seeds in pastries, sauces, curries, shellfish platters	2, 6, 11, 24, 25, 26, 28, 31, 38, 39, 40, 41, 44, 45, 46, 49, 50, 54, 63, 67

TABLE 11-34. ANNUAL AND BIENNIAL HERBS (*continued*)

HERB	DESCRIPTION	HOW TO GROW	HOW TO HARVEST	USE	CATALOG SEED SOURCE
Dill	Tall plant with light green, feathery foliage, flowers in open heads, 24–40 inches tall	Sow seeds in place in spring, thin to 12 inches	Pick fresh leaves when flowers open, gather seeds when brown	Use slightly bitter seeds in pickles, sauces, meats, salads	2, 5, 6,10, 11, 12, 14, 17, 20, 22, 23, 24, 25, 26, 28, 32, 35, 38, 39, 40, 41, 42, 43, 44, 45, 46, 49, 50, 51, 54, 60, 61, 62, 67
Parsley	Dark green, curled or plain leaves, 5–6 inches high	Biennial; soak seeds in warm water 24 hours before planting, thin to 6–8 inches apart	Pick good-sized, not yellow, leaves when needed	Use as garnish	7, 8, 10, 14, 16, 17, 22, 24, 25, 26, 28, 30, 32, 33, 34, 35, 38, 39, 40, 41, 42, 43, 45, 46, 48, 50, 52, 54, 60, 61, 65, 67
Sweet Marjoram	Small, oval leaves, knotlike clusters of flowers, 12–24 inches high	Sow seeds in place or start inside and transplant when danger of frost is past	Harvest mature leaves before flowers bloom	Leaves complement flavor of salads, eggs, vinegars, pork, veal	2, 6, 11, 14, 22, 23, 24, 25, 26, 28, 31, 32, 35, 38, 39, 41, 43, 44, 45, 46, 49, 50, 52, 54, 60, 63, 67
Summer Savory	Small, gray green leaves with purple and white flowers, 18 inches high	Sow seeds in place after danger of frost is past, space 6–9 inches apart	Gather leaves anytime	Use in salads, soups, dressings, poultry dishes	2, 11, 17, 22, 24, 25, 26, 28, 35, 38, 43, 44, 45, 46, 49, 50, 52, 54, 60

TABLE 11–35. PERENNIAL HERBS

Perennials: Perennials will start from seed the first year and grow year after year. Can be propagated several ways.

HERB	DESCRIPTION	HOW TO GROW	HOW TO HARVEST	USE	CATALOG SEED SOURCE
Chives	Onionlike leaves, lavender flowers, 10 inches high	Grow from seeds or divide the clumps; space 5 inches apart	Clip leaves close to ground	Give an onion/garlic flavor to salads, soups, eggs, sauces	6, 8, 14, 22, 23, 24, 25, 26, 32, 35, 38, 39, 40, 42, 43, 44, 46, 49, 50, 52, 54, 60, 63, 65
Peppermint	Bush-type plant with purple flowers, 18 inches high or more	Start from root divisions or cuttings, space 8–10 inches apart	Cut sprigs or leaves frequently	Leaves in tea, jelly, sauces; sprigs in summer sauces, drinks	14, 22, 26, 31, 35, 38, 39, 43, 46, 61, 63, 67
Spearmint	Reddish stems, crinkled and pointed leaves, lavender flowers in spikes, 12–24 inches high	Start from root divisions or cuttings, space 8–10 inches apart	Cut sprigs or leaves frequently	Use as garnish on fresh fruits, ices, summer drinks	6, 22, 24, 25, 26, 31, 35, 36, 39, 42, 44, 45, 46, 61, 67
Oregano	Shrublike plant with dark leaves, pink flowers, 24 inches high	Start seeds indoors or divide already-established plant	Gather fresh leaves as needed	Use dried or fresh leaves in tomato sauces, beans, soups, roasts	2, 6, 17, 23, 24, 25, 26, 28, 31, 35, 38, 39, 41, 44, 45, 50, 54, 60, 67
Rosemary	Leaves needlelike and glossy green, lavender blue flowers, to 36 inches	Propagate from slips or seed	Gather leaves and sprigs as needed	Use fresh or dried for lamb, pork, veal, sauces, soups	2, 11, 17, 22, 23, 24, 25, 26, 28, 35, 38, 39, 41, 44, 45, 49, 50, 54, 60, 67
Sage	Shrublike plant with gray leaves, purple flowers, 18 inches high or more	Start from seeds or stem cuttings or divide established plants; space 30 inches apart	Harvest leaves before flowering	Use fresh or dried leaves for stuffings, rabbit, chicken, fish, meats	2, 6, 11, 14, 17, 22, 23, 24, 25, 26, 28, 31, 32, 35, 38, 39, 41, 42, 43, 44, 45, 46, 49, 50, 52, 54, 61, 67, 69

TABLE 11–35. PERENNIAL HERBS (*continued*)

HERB	DESCRIPTION	HOW TO GROW	HOW TO HARVEST	USE	CATALOG SEED SOURCE
Tarragon (French)	Dark green leaves, clustered white flowers, 24 inches high	Start from root pieces or seeds, space 12 inches apart	Gather leaves before flower buds show	Use leaves for fish, poultry, eggs, vegetables	2, 24, 26, 28, 38, 39, 44, 50, 54, 63
Thyme	Small gray green leaves, flowers in spikes, 8–12 inches high	Start from seeds indoors or in place, propagate from cuttings, space 10–12 inches apart	Clip off tops of plants in full, leafy growth	Use leaves in soups, salads, omelettes, vegetables	2, 6, 11, 14, 22, 23, 24, 25, 28, 32, 35, 39, 41, 43, 44, 45, 52, 54, 60, 67

APPENDIXES

APPENDIX A

Average Date Last Hard Freeze in Spring, First Hard Freeze in Fall

STATE	LAST SPRING FROST	FIRST FALL FROST	STATE	LAST SPRING FROST	FIRST FALL FROST
Alaska			Iowa		
Interior	June 15	Aug. 15	North	May 1	Oct. 1
Coast	May 30	Sept. 30	South	Apr. 30	Oct. 10
Alabama			Kansas		
North	Mar. 25	Oct. 30	Northwest	Apr. 30	Oct. 10
South	Mar. 8	Nov. 15	Southeast	Apr. 10	Oct. 20
Arizona			Kentucky	Apr. 20	Oct. 20
North	Apr. 23	Oct. 19	Louisiana		
South	Mar. 1	Dec. 1	North	Mar. 20	Nov. 10
Arkansas			South	Feb. 8	Dec. 10
North	Apr. 7	Oct. 23	Maine		
South	Mar. 25	Nov. 3	North	May 30	Sept. 20
California			South	May 10	Oct. 10
Central Valley	Mar. 1	Nov. 15	Maryland	Apr. 20	Oct. 20
Imperial Valley	Jan. 30	Dec. 20	Massachusetts	Apr. 25	Oct. 25
North Coast	Feb. 28	Dec. 1	Michigan		
South Coast	Jan. 30	Dec. 15	Upper Peninsula	May 30	Sept. 20
Mountain	Apr. 20	Sept. 1	North	May 20	Sept. 25
Colorado			South	May 10	Oct. 10
West	May 30	Sept. 15	Minnesota		
Northeast	May 10	Sept. 30	North	May 30	Sept. 10
Southeast	Apr. 30	Oct. 10	South	May 10	Sept. 30
Connecticut	Apr. 28	Oct. 10	Mississippi		
Delaware	Apr. 15	Oct. 20	North	Mar. 30	Oct. 30
Florida			South	Mar. 10	Nov. 10
North	Feb. 20	Nov. 30	Missouri	Apr. 20	Oct. 20
Central	Jan. 30	Dec. 20	Montana	May 20	Sept. 20
South	No Frost		Nebraska		
Hawaii	No Frost		East	Apr. 30	Oct. 10
Georgia			West	May 10	Sept. 30
North	Mar. 30	Nov. 10	Nevada		
South	Mar. 10	Nov. 20	North	May 30	Sept. 5
Idaho	May 30	Sept. 25	South	Apr. 15	Nov. 10
Illinois			New Hampshire	May 20	Sept. 20
North	Apr. 30	Oct. 10	New Jersey	Apr. 20	Oct. 20
South	Apr. 10	Oct. 20	New Mexico		
Indiana			North	Apr. 30	Oct. 10
North	Apr. 30	Oct. 10	South	Apr. 1	Oct. 30
South	Apr. 20	Oct. 20	New York		
			East	May 1	Oct. 10
			West	May 10	Oct. 5

Average Date Last Hard Freeze in Spring, First Hard Freeze in Fall *(continued)*

STATE	LAST SPRING FROST	FIRST FALL FROST	STATE	LAST SPRING FROST	FIRST FALL FROST
New York			Tennessee	Apr. 10	Oct. 30
North	May 20	Sept. 30	Texas		
North Carolina			Northwest	Apr. 20	Oct. 30
Northeast	Apr. 10	Nov. 1	Northeast	Mar. 20	Nov. 20
Southeast	Mar. 30	Nov. 30	South	Feb. 5	Dec. 10
North Dakota	May 20	Sept. 20	Utah		
Ohio			North	May 30	Sept. 30
North	May 10	Sept. 20	South	Apr. 30	Oct. 10
South	Apr. 20	Sept. 30	Vermont	May 20	Sept. 30
Oklahoma	Apr. 1	Oct. 30	Virginia		
Oregon			North	Apr. 20	Oct. 10
West	Apr. 20	Oct. 30	South	Apr. 10	Oct. 20
East	May 30	Sept. 10	Washington		
Pennsylvania			West	Apr. 20	Oct. 30
West	Apr. 20	Oct. 20	East	May 20	Sept. 30
Central	May 20	Oct. 10	West Virginia	May 5	Oct. 10
East	May 10	Sept. 30	Wisconsin		
Rhode Island	Apr. 20	Oct. 20	North	May 20	Sept. 20
South Carolina			South	May 10	Oct. 10
Southeast	Mar. 10	Nov. 10	Wyoming		
Northwest	Mar. 20	Nov. 20	West	June 20	Aug. 25
South Dakota	May 10	Sept. 30	East	May 30	Sept. 30

APPENDIX B

Earliest Dates, and Range of Dates, for Safe Spring Planting of Vegetables in the Open

CROP	PLANTING DATES FOR LOCALITIES IN WHICH AVERAGE DATE OF LAST FREEZE IS—						
	JAN. 30	FEB. 8	FEB. 18	FEB. 28	MAR. 10	MAR. 20	MAR. 30
Asparagus[1]	—	—	—	—	Jan. 1–Mar. 1	Feb. 1–Mar. 10	Feb. 15–Mar. 20
Beans, lima	Feb. 1–Apr. 15	Feb. 10–May 1	Mar. 1–May 1	Mar. 15–June 1	Mar. 20–June 1	Apr. 1–June 15	Apr. 15–June 20
Beans, snap	Feb. 1–Apr. 1	Feb. 1–May 1	Mar. 1–May 1	Mar. 10–May 15	Mar. 15–May 15	Mar. 15–May 25	Apr. 1–June 1
Beet	Jan. 1–Mar. 15	Jan. 10–Mar. 15	Jan. 20–Apr. 1	Feb. 1–Apr. 15	Feb. 15–June 1	Feb. 15–May 15	Mar. 1–June 1
Broccoli, sprouting[1]	Jan. 1–30	Jan. 1–30	Jan 15–Feb. 15	Feb. 1–Mar. 1	Feb. 15–Mar. 15	Feb. 15–Mar. 15	Mar. 1–20
Brussels sprouts[1]	Jan. 1–30	Jan. 1–30	Jan. 15–Feb. 15	Feb. 1–Mar. 1	Feb. 15–Mar. 15	Feb. 15–Mar. 15	Mar. 1–20
Cabbage[1]	Jan. 1–15	Jan. 1–Feb. 10	Jan. 1–Feb. 25	Jan. 15–Feb. 25	Jan. 25–Mar. 1	Feb. 1–Mar. 1	Feb. 15–Mar. 10
Cabbage, Chinese	(2)	(2)	(2)	(2)	(2)	(2)	(2)
Carrot	Jan. 1–Mar. 1	Jan. 1–Mar. 1	Jan. 15–Mar. 1	Feb. 1–Mar. 1	Feb. 10–Mar. 15	Feb. 15–Mar. 20	Mar. 1–Apr. 10
Cauliflower[1]	Jan. 1–Feb. 1	Jan. 1–Feb. 1	Jan. 10–Feb. 10	Jan. 20–Feb. 20	Feb. 1–Mar. 1	Feb. 10–Mar. 10	Feb. 20–Mar. 20
Celery and celeriac	Jan. 1–Feb. 1	Jan. 10–Feb. 10	Jan. 20–Feb. 20	Feb. 1–Mar. 1	Feb. 20–Mar. 20	Mar. 1–Apr. 1	Mar. 15–Apr. 15
Chard	Jan. 1–Apr. 1	Jan. 10–Apr. 1	Jan. 20–Apr. 15	Feb. 1–May 1	Feb. 15–May 15	Feb. 20–May 1	Mar. 1–May 25
Chervil and chives	Jan. 1–Feb. 1	Jan. 1–Feb. 1	Jan. 1–Feb. 1	Jan. 15–Feb. 15	Feb. 1–Mar. 1	Feb. 10–Mar. 10	Feb. 15–Mar. 15
Chicory, witloof	—	—	—	—	June 1–July 1	June 1–July 1	June 1–July 1
Collards[1]	Jan. 1–Feb. 15	Jan. 1–Feb. 15	Jan. 1–Mar. 15	Jan. 15–Mar. 15	Feb. 1–Apr. 1	Feb. 15–May 1	Mar. 1–June 1
Cornsalad	Jan. 1–Feb. 15	Jan. 1–Feb. 15	Jan. 1–Mar. 15	Jan. 1–Mar. 1	Jan. 1–Mar. 15	Jan. 1–May 15	Jan. 15–Mar. 15
Corn, sweet	Feb. 1–Mar. 15	Feb. 1–Apr. 1	Feb. 20–Apr. 15	Mar. 1–Apr. 15	Mar. 10–Apr. 15	Mar. 15–May 1	Mar. 25–May 15
Cress, upland	Jan. 1–Feb. 15	Jan. 1–Feb. 15	Jan. 1–Feb. 15	Feb. 1–Mar. 1	Feb. 10–Mar. 15	Feb. 20–Mar. 15	Mar. 1–Apr. 1
Cucumber	Feb. 15–Apr. 1	Feb. 15–Apr. 1	Feb. 15–Apr. 15	Mar. 1–Apr. 15	Mar. 15–Apr. 15	Apr. 1–May 1	Apr. 10–May 15
Eggplant[1]	Feb. 15–Mar. 1	Feb. 10–Mar. 15	Feb. 20–Apr. 1	Mar. 10–Apr. 15	Mar. 15–Apr. 15	Apr. 1–May 1	Apr. 15–May 15
Endive	Jan. 1–Mar. 1	Jan. 1–Mar. 1	Jan. 1–Mar. 1	Jan. 15–Mar. 1	Feb. 15–Apr. 15	Mar. 1–Apr. 1	Mar. 10–Apr. 10
Fennel, Florence	Jan. 1–Mar. 1	Jan. 1–Mar. 1	Jan. 15–Mar. 1	Feb. 1–Mar. 1	Feb. 15–Mar. 15	Mar. 1–Apr. 1	Mar. 10–Apr. 10
Garlic	(2)	(2)	(2)	(2)	(2)	Feb. 1–Mar. 1	Feb. 10–Mar. 10
Horseradish[1]	—	—	—	—	—	—	—
Kale	Jan. 1–Feb. 1	Jan. 1–Feb. 1	Jan. 20–Feb. 10	Feb. 1–20	Feb. 10–Mar. 1	Feb. 20–Mar. 10	Mar. 1–20
Kohlrabi	Jan. 1–Feb. 1	Jan. 1–Feb. 1	Jan. 20–Feb. 10	Feb. 1–20	Feb. 10–Mar. 1	Feb. 20–Mar. 10	Mar. 1–Apr. 1
Leek	Jan. 1–Feb. 1	Jan. 1–Feb. 1	Jan. 1–Feb. 15	Jan. 15–Feb. 15	Jan. 25–Mar. 1	Feb. 1–Mar. 1	Feb. 15–Mar. 15
Lettuce, head[1]	Jan. 1–Feb. 1	Jan. 1–Feb. 1	Jan. 1–Feb. 1	Jan. 15–Feb. 15	Feb. 1–20	Feb. 15–Mar. 10	Mar. 1–20
Lettuce, leaf	Jan. 1–Feb. 1	Jan. 1–Feb. 1	Jan. 1–Mar. 15	Jan. 1–Mar. 15	Jan. 15–Apr. 1	Feb. 1–Apr. 1	Feb. 15–Apr. 15
Muskmelon	Feb. 15–Mar. 15	Feb. 15–Apr. 15	Feb. 15–Apr. 15	Mar. 1–Apr. 15	Mar. 15–Apr. 15	Apr. 1–May 1	Apr. 10–May 15
Mustard	Jan. 1–Mar. 1	Jan. 1–Mar. 1	Jan. 1–Mar. 1	Feb. 1–Apr. 1	Feb. 10–Apr. 1	Feb. 20–Apr. 1	Mar. 1–Apr. 15
Okra	Feb. 15–Apr. 1	Feb. 15–Apr. 15	Mar. 1–June 1	Mar. 10–June 1	Mar. 20–June 1	Apr. 1–June 15	Apr. 10–June 15
Onion[1]	Jan. 1–15	Jan. 1–15	Jan. 1–15	Jan. 1–Feb. 1	Jan. 15–Feb. 15	Feb. 10–Mar. 10	Feb. 15–Mar. 15
Onion, seed	Jan. 1–15	Jan. 1–15	Jan. 1–15	Jan. 1–Feb. 15	Feb. 1–Mar. 1	Feb. 10–Mar. 10	Feb. 20–Mar. 15
Onion, sets	Jan. 1–15	Jan. 1–15	Jan. 1–15	Jan. 1–Mar. 1	Feb. 1–Mar. 1	Feb. 1–Mar. 20	Feb. 15–Mar. 20
Parsley	Jan. 1–30	Jan. 1–30	Jan. 1–30	Jan. 15–Mar. 1	Jan. 15–Mar. 10	Feb. 15–Mar. 15	Mar. 1–Apr. 1
Parsnip	—	—	Jan. 1–Feb. 1	Jan. 15–Feb. 15	Jan. 15–Mar. 10	Feb. 15–Mar. 15	Mar. 1–Apr. 1
Peas, garden	Jan. 1–Feb. 15	Jan. 1–Feb. 15	Jan. 1–Mar. 1	Jan. 15–Mar. 1	Jan. 15–Mar. 15	Feb. 1–Mar. 15	Feb. 10–Mar. 20
Peas, black-eye	Feb. 15–May 1	Feb. 15–May 15	Mar. 1–June 15	Mar. 10–June 20	Mar. 15–July 1	Apr. 1–July 1	Apr. 15–July 1

[1] Plants.   [2] Generally fall planted.   Source: *Growing Vegetables in Home Gardens, U.S.D.A.*

Earliest Dates, and Range of Dates, for Safe Spring Planting of Vegetables in the Open (continued)

PLANTING DATES FOR LOCALITIES IN WHICH AVERAGE DATE OF LAST FREEZE IS—

CROP	JAN. 30	FEB. 8	FEB. 18	FEB. 28	MAR. 10	MAR. 20	MAR. 30
Pepper[1]	Feb. 1–Apr. 1	Feb. 15–Apr. 15	Mar. 1–May 1	Mar. 15–May 1	Apr. 1–June 1	Apr. 10–June 1	Apr. 15–June 1
Potato	Jan. 1–Feb. 15	Jan. 1–Feb. 15	Jan. 15–Mar. 1	Jan. 15–Mar. 1	Feb. 1–Mar. 1	Feb. 10–Mar. 15	Feb. 20–Mar. 20
Radish	Jan. 1–Apr. 1	Jan. 1–Apr. 1	Jan. 1–Apr. 1	Jan. 1–Apr. 1	Jan. 1–Apr. 15	Jan. 20–May 1	Feb. 15–May 1
Rhubarb[1]	—	—	—	—	—	—	—
Rutabaga	—	Jan. 10–Feb. 10	Jan. 15–Feb. 20	Jan. 1–Feb. 1	Jan. 15–Feb. 15	Jan. 15–Mar. 1	Feb. 1–Mar. 1
Salsify	Jan. 1–Feb. 1	Jan. 1–Feb. 10	Jan. 1–Feb. 20	Jan. 15–Mar. 1	Feb. 1–Mar. 1	Feb. 15–Mar. 1	Mar. 1–15
Shallot	Jan. 1–Feb. 1	Jan. 1–Feb. 10	Jan. 15–Mar. 1	Jan. 15–Mar. 1	Jan. 15–Mar. 1	Feb. 1–Mar. 10	Feb. 15–Mar. 15
Sorrel	Jan. 1–Mar. 1	Jan. 1–Mar. 1	Jan. 1–Mar. 1	Feb. 1–Mar. 10	Feb. 1–Mar. 10	Feb. 10–Mar. 20	Feb. 20–Apr. 1
Soybean	Mar. 1–June 30	Mar. 1–June 30	Mar. 1–June 30	Mar. 20–June 30	Apr. 10–June 30	Apr. 10–June 30	Apr. 20–June 30
Spinach	Jan. 1–Feb. 15	Jan. 1–Feb. 15	Jan. 1–Mar. 1	Jan. 1–Mar. 1	Jan. 15–Mar. 10	Jan. 15–Mar. 15	Feb. 1–Mar. 20
Spinach, New Zealand	Feb. 1–Apr. 15	Feb. 15–Apr. 15	Mar. 1–Apr. 15	Mar. 15–May 15	Mar. 20–May 15	Mar. 20–May 15	Apr. 10–June 1
Squash, summer	Feb. 1–Apr. 15	Feb. 15–Apr. 15	Mar. 1–Apr. 15	Mar. 15–May 15	Mar. 15–May 1	Apr. 1–May 15	Apr. 10–June 1
Sweetpotato	Feb. 15–May 15	Mar. 1–May 15	Mar. 1–June 1	Mar. 20–June 1	Apr. 1–June 1	Apr. 1–June 1	Apr. 20–June 1
Tomato	Feb. 1–Apr. 1	Feb. 20–Apr. 10	Mar. 1–Apr. 20	Mar. 10–May 1	Mar. 20–May 10	Apr. 1–May 20	Apr. 10–June 1
Turnip	Jan. 1–Mar. 1	Jan. 1–Mar. 1	Jan. 10–Mar. 1	Jan. 20–Mar. 1	Feb. 1–Mar. 1	Feb. 10–Mar. 10	Feb. 20–Mar. 20
Watermelon	Feb. 15–Mar. 15	Feb. 15–Apr. 1	Feb. 15–Apr. 15	Mar. 1–Apr. 15	Mar. 15–Apr. 15	Apr. 1–May 1	Apr. 10–May 15

PLANTING DATES FOR LOCALITIES IN WHICH AVERAGE DATE OF LAST FREEZE IS—

CROP	APR. 10	APR. 20	APR. 30	MAY 10	MAY 20	MAY 30	JUNE 10
Asparagus[1]	Mar. 10–Apr. 10	Mar. 15–Apr. 15	Mar. 20–Apr. 15	Mar. 10–Apr. 30	Apr. 20–May 15	May 1–June 1	May 15–June 1
Beans, lima	Apr. 1–June 30	May 1–June 20	May 15–June 15	May 25–June 15	—	—	—
Beans, snap	Apr. 10–June 30	Apr. 25–June 30	May 10–June 30	May 10–June 30	May 15–June 30	May 25–June 15	—
Beet	Mar. 10–June 1	Mar. 20–June 1	Apr. 1–June 15	Apr. 15–June 15	May 1–June 15	May 15–June 15	May 25–June 15
Broccoli, sprouting[1]	Mar. 15–Apr. 15	Mar. 25–Apr. 20	Apr. 1–May 1	Apr. 15–June 1	May 1–June 15	May 10–June 15	May 20–June 10
Brussels sprouts[1]	Mar. 15–Apr. 15	Mar. 25–Apr. 20	Apr. 1–May 1	Apr. 15–June 1	May 1–June 15	May 10–June 15	May 20–June 10
Cabbage[1]	Mar. 1–Apr. 1	Mar. 10–Apr. 1	Mar. 15–Apr. 10	Apr. 1–May 15	May 1–June 15	May 10–June 15	May 20–June 1
Cabbage, Chinese	(2)	(2)	(2)	Apr. 1–May 15	May 1–June 15	May 10–June 15	May 20–June 1
Carrot	Mar. 10–Apr. 20	Apr. 1–May 15	Apr. 10–June 1	Apr. 20–June 15	May 1–June 1	May 20–June 1	—
Cauliflower[1]	Mar. 1–Mar. 20	Mar. 15–Apr. 20	Apr. 10–May 10	May 10–June 15	May 20–June 1	June 1–June 15	—
Celery and celeriac	Apr. 1–Apr. 20	Apr. 10–May 1	Apr. 15–May 1	Apr. 20–June 15	May 10–June 15	June 1–June 15	—
Chard	Mar. 15–June 15	Apr. 1–June 15	Apr. 15–June 15	Apr. 20–June 15	May 20–June 15	June 1–June 15	—
Chervil and chives	Mar. 1–Apr. 1	Mar. 10–Apr. 10	Mar. 20–Apr. 20	Apr. 1–May 1	Apr. 15–May 15	May 1–June 1	May 15–June 15
Chicory, witloof	June 10–July 1	June 15–July 1	June 15–July 1	June 15–July 1	June 1–20	June 1–15	May 15–June 1
Collards[1]	Mar. 1–June 1	Mar. 1–June 1	Apr. 1–June 1	Apr. 15–June 1	May 10–June 1	May 10–June 1	June 1–15
Cornsalad	Feb. 1–Apr. 1	Feb. 15–Apr. 15	Mar. 1–May 1	Apr. 1–June 1	Apr. 15–June 1	May 1–June 1	May 20–June 1
Corn, sweet	Apr. 10–June 1	Apr. 25–June 15	May 10–June 15	May 10–June 1	May 15–June 1	May 20–June 1	May 15–June 15
Cress, upland	Mar. 10–Apr. 15	Mar. 20–May 1	Apr. 10–May 10	Apr. 20–May 20	May 10–June 1	May 15–June 15	—
Cucumber	Apr. 20–June 1	May 1–June 15	May 15–June 15	May 20–June 15	June 1–15	—	May 15–June 15

[1] Plants. [2] Generally fall planted.

Earliest Dates, and Range of Dates, for Safe Spring Planting of Vegetables in the Open (continued)

CROP	PLANTING DATES FOR LOCALITIES IN WHICH AVERAGE DATE OF LAST FREEZE IS—						
	APR. 10	APR. 20	APR. 30	MAY 10	MAY 20	MAY 30	JUNE 10
Eggplant[1]	May 1–June 1	May 10–June 1	May 15–June 10	May 20–June 15	June 1–15	—	
Endive	Mar. 15–Apr. 15	Mar. 25–Apr. 15	Apr. 1–May 1	Apr. 15–May 15	May 1–30	May 1–30	May 15–June 1
Fennel, Florence	Mar. 15–Apr. 15	Mar. 25–Apr. 15	Apr. 1–May 1	Apr. 15–May 15	May 1–30	May 1–30	May 15–June 1
Garlic	Feb. 20–Mar. 20	Mar. 10–Apr. 1	Mar. 15–Apr. 15	Apr. 1–May 1	Apr. 15–May 15	May 1–30	May 15–June 1
Horseradish[1]	Mar. 10–Apr. 10	Mar. 20–Apr. 20	Apr. 1–30	Apr. 15–May 15	Apr. 20–May 20	May 1–30	May 15–June 1
Kale	Mar. 10–Apr. 1	Mar. 20–Apr. 10	Apr. 1–20	Apr. 10–May 1	Apr. 20–May 10	May 1–30	May 15–June 1
Kohlrabi	Mar. 10–Apr. 10	Mar. 20–May 1	Apr. 1–May 10	Apr. 10–May 15	Apr. 20–May 20	May 1–30	May 15–June 1
Leek	Mar. 1–Apr. 1	Mar. 15–Apr. 15	Apr. 1–May 1	Apr. 15–May 15	May 1–May 20	May 1–15	May 1–15
Lettuce, head[1]	Mar. 10–Apr. 1	Mar. 20–Apr. 15	Apr. 1–May 1	Apr. 15–May 15	May 1–June 30	May 10–June 30	May 20–June 30
Lettuce, leaf	Mar. 15–May 15	Mar. 20–May 15	Apr. 1–June 1	Apr. 15–May 15	May 1–June 30	May 10–June 30	May 20–June 30
Muskmelon	Apr. 20–June 1	May 1–June 15	May 15–June 15	June 1–June 15	June 1–15	—	
Mustard	Mar. 10–Apr. 20	Mar. 20–May 1	Apr. 1–May 10	Apr. 15–June 30	May 1–June 30	May 10–June 30	May 20–June 30
Okra	Apr. 20–June 15	May 1–June 1	May 10–June 1	May 20–June 10	June 1–20	—	
Onion[1]	Mar. 1–Apr. 1	Mar. 1–Apr. 10	Apr. 1–May 1	Apr. 10–May 1	Apr. 20–May 15	May 1–30	May 10–June 10
Onion, seed	Mar. 1–Apr. 1	Mar. 15–Apr. 1	Apr. 1–May 1	Apr. 10–May 1	Apr. 20–May 15	May 1–30	May 10–June 10
Onion, sets	Mar. 1–Apr. 1	Mar. 10–Apr. 1	Mar. 10–Apr. 1	Apr. 10–May 1	Apr. 20–May 15	May 1–30	May 10–June 10
Parsley	Mar. 10–Apr. 10	Mar. 20–Apr. 20	Apr. 1–May 1	Apr. 15–May 15	May 1–20	May 10–June 1	May 20–June 10
Parsnip	Mar. 10–Apr. 10	Mar. 20–Apr. 20	Apr. 1–May 1	Apr. 15–May 15	May 1–20	May 10–June 1	May 20–June 10
Peas, garden	Feb. 20–Mar. 20	Mar. 10–Apr. 10	Mar. 20–May 1	Apr. 1–May 15	Apr. 15–June 1	Apr. 15–June 15	May 10–June 15
Peas, black-eye	May 1–July 1	May 10–June 15	May 15–June 15				
Pepper[1]	May 1–June 1	May 10–June 1	May 15–June 10	May 20–June 10	May 25–June 15	June 1–15	
Potato	Mar. 10–Apr. 10	Mar. 15–Apr. 10	Mar. 20–May 10	Apr. 1–June 1	Apr. 15–June 15	Apr. 15–June 15	May 15–June 1
Radish	Mar. 1–May 1	Mar. 15–May 1	Mar. 20–May 10	Apr. 1–June 1	Apr. 15–June 15	Apr. 15–June 15	May 15–June 1
Rhubarb[1]	Mar. 1–Apr. 1	Mar. 10–Apr. 10	Mar. 20–Apr. 15	Apr. 1–May 1	Apr. 15–May 10	May 1–20	May 15–June 1
Rutabaga	—	Mar. 10–Apr. 10	Apr. 1–June 1	May 1–June 1	May 1–20	May 10–20	May 20–June 1
Salsify	Mar. 10–Apr. 15	Mar. 20–May 1	Apr. 1–May 15	Apr. 15–June 1	May 1–June 1	May 10–June 1	May 20–June 1
Shallot	Mar. 1–Apr. 1	Mar. 1–Apr. 15	Apr. 1–May 1	Apr. 10–May 1	Apr. 20–May 10	May 1–June 1	May 20–June 1
Sorrel	Mar. 1–Apr. 15	Mar. 15–May 1	Apr. 1–May 15	Apr. 15–June 1	Apr. 15–June 1	May 10–June 1	May 20–June 10
Soybean	May 1–June 30	May 10–June 20	May 15–June 15	May 25–June 10	May 25–June 10	May 10–June 10	
Spinach	Feb. 15–Apr. 1	Mar. 1–Apr. 15	Mar. 20–Apr. 20	Apr. 1–June 15	Apr. 10–June 15	Apr. 20–June 15	May 1–June 15
Spinach, New Zealand	Apr. 20–June 1	May 1–June 15	May 1–June 15	May 10–June 15	May 20–June 15	June 1–15	
Squash, summer	Apr. 20–June 1	May 1–June 15	May 1–30	May 10–June 10	May 20–June 15	June 1–20	June 10–20
Sweetpotato	May 1–June 1	May 10–June 10	May 20–June 10	—			
Tomato	Apr. 20–June 1	May 5–June 10	May 10–June 15	May 15–June 10	May 25–June 15	June 5–20	June 15–30
Turnip	Mar. 1–Apr. 1	Mar. 10–Apr. 1	Mar. 20–May 1	Apr. 1–June 1	Apr. 15–June 1	May 1–June 1	May 15–June 1
Watermelon	Apr. 20–June 1	May 1–June 15	May 15–June 15	June 1–June 15	June 15–July 1	—	

[1]Plants. [2]Generally fall planted.

APPENDIX C

Latest Dates, and Range of Dates, for Safe Fall Planting of Vegetables in the Open

CROP	PLANTING DATES FOR LOCALITIES IN WHICH AVERAGE DATE OF FIRST FREEZE IS—					
	AUG. 30	SEPT. 10	SEPT. 20	SEPT. 30	OCT. 10	OCT. 20
Asparagus[1]	—	—	—	June 1-15	Oct. 20-Nov. 15	Nov. 1-Dec. 15
Beans, lima	—	—	—	June 1-15	June 1-15	June 15-30
Beans, snap	May 15-June 15	May 15-June 15	June 1-July 1	June 1-July 10	June 15-July 20	July 1-Aug. 1
Beet	May 1-June 15	May 1-June 1	May 1-June 15	June 1-July 10	June 15-July 25	June 15-Aug. 5
Broccoli, sprouting	May 1-June 1	May 1-June 1	May 1-June 15	June 1-30	June 15-July 15	July 1-Aug. 1
Brussels sprouts	May 1-June 1	May 1-June 1	May 1-June 15	June 1-30	June 15-July 15	July 1-Aug. 1
Cabbage[1]	May 1-June 1	May 1-June 1	May 1-July 1	June 1-July 10	June 1-Aug. 1	July 1-20
Cabbage, Chinese	May 15-June 15	May 15-June 15	June 1-July 1	June 1-July 15	June 15-Aug. 1	July 15-Aug. 15
Carrot	May 15-June 15	May 15-June 15	June 1-July 1	June 1-July 10	June 1-July 20	June 15-Aug. 1
Cauliflower[1]	May 1-June 1	May 1-July 1	May 1-July 1	June 1-July 15	June 1-July 25	July 1-Aug. 5
Celery[1] and celeriac	May 1-June 1	May 1-July 1	May 15-July 1	June 1-July 5	June 1-July 15	June 1-Aug. 1
Chard	May 15-June 15	May 15-July 1	June 1-July 1	June 1-July 5	June 1-July 20	June 1-Aug. 1
Chervil and chives	May 10-June 15	May 1-June 15	May 15-June 15	(2)	(2)	(2)
Chicory, witloof	May 15-June 15	May 15-June 15	May 15-June 15	June 1-July 1	June 1-July 1	June 1-July 15
Collards[1]	May 15-June 15	May 15-June 15	May 15-June 15	June 15-July 15	July 1-Aug. 1	July 15-Aug. 15
Cornsalad	May 15-June 15	May 15-July 1	June 15-Aug. 1	July 15-Sept. 1	Aug. 15-Sept. 15	Sept. 1-Oct. 15
Corn, sweet	—	—	June 1-July 1	June 1-July 1	June 1-July 10	June 1-July 20
Cress, upland	May 15-June 15	May 15-July 1	June 15-Aug. 1	July 15-Sept. 1	Aug. 15-Sept. 15	Sept. 1-Oct. 15
Cucumber	—	—	June 1-15	June 1-July 1	June 1-July 1	June 1-July 15
Eggplant[1]	—	—	—	May 20-June 10	May 15-June 15	June 1-July 1
Endive	June 1-July 1	June 1-July 1	June 15-July 15	June 15-Aug. 1	July 1-Aug. 15	July 15-Sept. 1
Fennel, Florence	May 15-June 15	May 15-July 15	June 1-July 1	June 1-July 1	June 15-July 15	June 15-Aug. 1
Garlic	(2)	(2)	(2)	(2)	(2)	(2)
Horseradish[1]	(2)	(2)	(2)	(2)	(2)	(2)
Kale	May 15-June 15	May 15-June 15	June 1-July 1	June 15-July 15	July 1-Aug. 1	July 15-Aug. 15
Kohlrabi	May 15-June 15	June 1-July 1	June 1-July 15	June 15-July 15	July 1-Aug. 1	July 15-Aug. 15
Leek	May 1-June 1	May 1-June 1	(2)	(2)	(2)	(2)
Lettuce, head[1]	May 15-July 1	May 15-July 1	June 1-July 15	June 15-Aug. 1	July 15-Aug. 15	Aug. 1-30
Lettuce, leaf	May 15-July 15	May 15-July 15	June 1-Aug. 1	June 1-Aug. 1	July 15-Sept. 1	July 15-Sept. 1
Muskmelon	—	—	May 1-June 15	May 15-June 1	June 15-July 20	June 15-July 20
Mustard	May 15-July 15	May 15-July 15	June 1-Aug. 1	June 15-Aug. 1	July 15-Aug. 15	Aug. 1-Sept. 1
Okra	—	—	June 1-20	June 1-July 1	June 1-July 15	June 1-Aug. 1
Onion[1]	May 1-June 10	May 1-June 10	(2)	June 1-July 1	June 15-Aug. 1	(2)
Onion, seed	May 1-June 1	May 1-June 10	(2)	(2)	June 1-July 10	(2)
Onion, sets	May 1-June 1	May 1-June 10	(2)	(2)	(2)	(2)
Parsley	May 15-June 15	May 15-June 15	June 1-July 1	June 1-July 15	June 15-Aug. 1	July 15-Aug. 15
Parsnip	May 15-June 1	May 15-June 15	May 15-June 15	June 1-July 1	June 1-July 10	(2)
Peas, garden	May 10-June 15	May 1-July 1	June 1-July 15	June 1-Aug. 1	(2)	July 15-Aug. 15
Peas, black-eye	—	—	—	—	June 1-July 1	June 1-July 1

[1] Plants.   [2] Generally spring planted.

Latest Dates, and Range of Dates, for Safe Fall Planting of Vegetables in the Open (continued)

CROP	PLANTING DATES FOR LOCALITIES IN WHICH AVERAGE DATE OF FIRST FREEZE IS—					
	AUG. 30	SEPT. 10	SEPT. 20	SEPT. 30	OCT. 10	OCT. 20
Pepper[1]	—	—	June 1–June 20	June 1–July 1	June 1–July 1	June 1–July 10
Potato	May 15–June 1	May 1–June 15	May 1–June 15	May 1–June 15	May 1–June 15	June 15–July 15
Radish	May 1–July 15	May 1–Aug. 1	June 1–Aug. 15	July 1–Sept. 1	Aug. 1–Sept. 1	Aug. 1–Oct. 1
Rhubarb[1]	Sept. 1–Oct. 1	Sept. 15–Oct. 15	Sept. 15–Nov. 1	Oct. 1–Nov. 1	Oct. 15–Nov. 15	Oct. 15–Dec. 1
Rutabaga	May 15–June 15	May 1–June 15	June 1–July 1	June 15–July 15	June 15–July 15	July 10–20
Salsify	May 15–June 1	May 10–June 10	May 20–June 20	June 1–20	June 1–July 1	June 1–July 1
Shallot	(2)	(2)	(2)	(2)	(2)	(2)
Sorrel	May 15–June 15	May 1–June 15	June 1–July 1	June 1–July 15	July 1–Aug. 1	July 15–Aug. 15
Soybean	—	—	—	May 25–June 10	June 1–25	June 1–July 5
Spinach	May 15–July 1	June 1–July 15	June 1–Aug. 1	July 1–Aug. 15	Aug. 1–Sept. 1	Aug. 20–Sept. 10
Spinach, New Zealand	—	—	—	May 15–July 1	June 1–Aug. 1	June 1–Aug. 1
Squash, summer	June 10–20	June 1–20	May 15–July 1	June 1–July 1	June 1–July 15	June 1–July 20
Squash, winter	—	—	May 20–June 10	June 1–15	June 1–July 1	June 1–July 1
Sweetpotato	—	—	—	—	May 20–June 10	June 1–15
Tomato	June 20–30	June 10–20	June 1–20	June 1–20	June 1–20	June 1–July 1
Turnip	May 15–June 15	June 1–July 1	June 1–July 15	June 1–Aug. 1	July 1–Aug. 1	July 15–Aug. 15
Watermelon	—	—	May 1–June 15	May 15–June 1	May 15–June 1	June 15–July 20

CROPS	PLANTING DATES FOR LOCALITIES IN WHICH AVERAGE DATE OF FIRST FREEZE IS—					
	OCT. 30	NOV. 10	NOV. 20	NOV. 30	DEC. 10	DEC. 20
Asparagus[1]	Nov. 15–Jan. 1	Dec. 1–Jan. 1	—	—	—	—
Beans, lima	July 1–Aug. 1	July 1–Aug. 15	July 15–Sept. 1	Aug. 1–Sept. 15	Sept. 1–30	Sept. 1–Oct. 1
Beans, snap	July 1–Aug. 15	July 1–Sept. 1	July 1–Sept. 10	Aug. 15–Sept. 20	Sept. 1–30	Sept. 1–Nov. 1
Beet	Aug. 1–Sept. 1	Aug. 1–Oct. 1	Sept. 1–Dec. 1	Sept. 1–Dec. 15	Sept. 1–Dec. 31	Sept. 1–Dec. 31
Broccoli, sprouting	July 1–Aug. 15	Aug. 1–Sept. 1	Aug. 1–Sept. 15	Aug. 1–Oct. 1	Aug. 1–Nov. 1	Sept. 1–Dec. 31
Brussels sprouts	July 1–Aug. 15	Aug. 1–Sept. 1	Aug. 1–Sept. 15	Aug. 1–Oct. 1	Aug. 1–Nov. 1	Sept. 1–Dec. 31
Cabbage[1]	Aug. 1–Sept. 1	Sept. 1–15	Sept. 1–Dec. 1	Sept. 1–Dec. 31	Sept. 1–Dec. 31	Sept. 1–Dec. 31
Cabbage, Chinese	Aug. 1–Sept. 15	Aug. 15–Oct. 1	Sept. 1–Oct. 15	Sept. 1–Nov. 1	Sept. 1–Nov. 15	Sept. 1–Dec. 1
Carrot	July 1–Aug. 15	Aug. 1–Sept. 1	Sept. 1–Nov. 1	Sept. 1–Nov. 1	Sept. 15–Dec. 1	Sept. 15–Dec. 1
Cauliflower[1]	July 15–Aug. 15	Aug. 1–Sept. 1	Aug. 1–Sept. 15	Aug. 15–Oct. 10	Sept. 15–Oct. 20	Sept. 15–Nov. 1
Celery[1] and celeriac	June 15–Aug. 15	July 1–Aug. 15	July 15–Sept. 1	Aug. 1–Dec. 1	Sept. 1–Dec. 31	Oct. 1–Dec. 31
Chard	June 1–Sept. 10	June 1–Sept. 15	June 1–Oct. 1	June 1–Nov. 1	June 1–Dec. 1	June 1–Dec. 31
Chervil and chives	(2)	(2)	Nov. 1–Dec. 31	Nov. 1–Dec. 31	Nov. 1–Dec. 31	Nov. 1–Dec. 31
Chicory, witloof	July 1–Aug. 10	July 10–Aug. 20	July 20–Sept. 1	Aug. 15–Sept. 30	Aug. 15–Oct. 15	Aug. 15–Oct. 15
Collards[1]	Aug. 1–Sept. 15	Aug. 15–Oct. 1	Aug. 25–Nov. 1	Sept. 1–Dec. 1	Sept. 1–Dec. 31	Sept. 1–Dec. 31
Cornsalad	Sept. 15–Nov. 1	Oct. 1–Dec. 1	Oct. 1–Dec. 1	Oct. 1–Dec. 1	Oct. 1–Dec. 31	Oct. 1–Dec. 31
Corn, sweet	June 1–Aug. 1	June 1–Aug. 15	June 1–Sept. 1	June 1–Sept. 1	—	—
Cress, upland	Sept. 15–Nov. 1	Oct. 1–Dec. 1	Oct. 1–Dec. 1	Oct. 1–Dec. 31	Oct. 1–Dec. 31	Oct. 1–Dec. 31
Cucumber	June 1–Aug. 1	June 1–Aug. 15	June 1–Aug. 15	July 15–Sept. 15	Aug. 15–Oct. 1	Aug. 15–Oct. 1
Eggplant[1]	June 1–July 1	June 1–July 15	June 1–Aug. 1	July 1–Sept. 1	Aug. 1–Sept. 30	Aug. 1–Sept. 30
Endive	July 15–Aug. 15	Aug. 1–Sept. 1	Sept. 1–Oct. 1	Sept. 1–Nov. 15	Sept. 1–Dec. 31	Sept. 1–Dec. 31

[1]Plants.   [2]Generally spring planted.

Latest Dates, and Range of Dates, for Safe Fall Planting of Vegetables in the Open (continued)

CROPS	PLANTING DATES FOR LOCALITIES IN WHICH AVERAGE DATE OF FIRST FREEZE IS—					
	OCT. 30	NOV. 10	NOV. 20	NOV. 30	DEC. 10	DEC. 20
Fennel, Florence	July 1–Aug. 1	July 15–Aug. 15	Aug. 15–Sept. 15	Sept. 1–Nov. 15	Sept. 1–Dec. 1	Sept. 1–Dec. 1
Garlic	(2)	Aug. 1–Oct. 1	Aug. 15–Oct. 1	Sept. 1–Nov. 15	Sept. 15–Nov. 15	Sept. 15–Nov. 15
Horseradish[1]	(2)	(2)	(2)	(2)	(2)	(2)
Kale	July 15–Sept. 1	Aug. 1–Sept. 15	Aug. 15–Oct. 15	Sept. 1–Dec. 1	Sept. 1–Dec. 31	Sept. 1–Dec. 31
Kohlrabi	Aug. 1–Sept. 1	Aug. 15–Sept. 15	Sept. 1–Oct. 15	Sept. 1–Dec. 1	Sept. 15–Dec. 31	Sept. 1–Dec. 31
Leek	(2)	(2)	Sept. 1–Nov. 1	Sept. 1–Nov. 1	Sept. 1–Nov. 1	Sept. 15–Nov. 1
Lettuce, head[1]	Aug. 1–Sept. 15	Aug. 15–Oct. 15	Sept. 1–Nov. 1	Sept. 1–Dec. 1	Sept. 15–Dec. 31	Sept. 15–Dec. 31
Lettuce, leaf	Aug. 15–Oct. 1	Aug. 25–Oct. 1	Sept. 1–Nov. 1	Sept. 1–Dec. 1	Sept. 15–Dec. 31	Sept. 15–Dec. 31
Muskmelon	July 1–July 15	July 15–July 30	—	—	—	—
Mustard	Aug. 15–Oct. 15	Aug. 15–Nov. 1	Sept. 1–Dec. 1	Sept. 1–Dec. 1	Sept. 1–Dec. 1	Sept. 15–Dec. 1
Okra	June 1–Aug. 10	June 1–Aug. 20	June 1–Sept. 10	June 1–Sept. 20	Aug. 1–Oct. 1	Aug. 1–Oct. 1
Onion[1]	—	Sept. 1–Oct. 15	Oct. 1–Dec. 31	Oct. 1–Dec. 31	Oct. 1–Dec. 31	Oct. 1–Dec. 31
Onion, seed	—	—	Sept. 1–Nov. 1	Sept. 1–Nov. 1	Sept. 1–Nov. 1	Sept. 15–Nov. 1
Onion, sets	—	Oct. 1–Dec. 1	Nov. 1–Dec. 31	Nov. 1–Dec. 31	Nov. 1–Dec. 31	Nov. 1–Dec. 31
Parsley	Aug. 1–Sept. 15	Sept. 1–Nov. 15	Sept. 1–Dec. 31	Sept. 1–Dec. 31	Sept. 1–Dec. 31	Sept. 1–Dec. 31
Parsnip	(2)	(2)	Aug. 1–Sept. 1	Sept. 1–Dec. 1	Sept. 1–Dec. 1	Sept. 1–Dec. 1
Peas, garden	Aug. 1–Sept. 15	Sept. 1–Nov. 1	Oct. 1–Dec. 1	Oct. 1–Dec. 31	Oct. 1–Dec. 31	Oct. 1–Dec. 31
Peas, black-eye	June 1–Aug. 1	June 15–Aug. 15	July 1–Sept. 1	July 1–Sept. 10	July 1–Sept. 20	July 1–Sept. 20
Pepper[1]	June 1–July 20	June 1–Aug. 1	June 1–Aug. 15	June 15–Sept. 1	Aug. 15–Oct. 1	Aug. 15–Oct. 1
Potato	July 20–Aug. 10	July 25–Aug. 20	Aug. 10–Sept. 15	Aug. 1–Sept. 15	Aug. 1–Sept. 15	Aug. 1–Sept. 15
Radish	Aug. 15–Oct. 15	Sept. 1–Nov. 15	Sept. 1–Dec. 1	Sept. 1–Nov. 15	Sept. 1–Dec. 31	Oct. 1–Dec. 31
Rhubarb[1]	Nov. 1–Dec. 1	—	—	—	—	—
Rutabaga	July 15–Aug. 1	July 15–Aug. 15	Aug. 1–Sept. 1	Sept. 1–Nov. 15	Oct. 1–Nov. 15	Oct. 15–Nov. 15
Salsify	June 1–July 10	June 15–July 20	July 15–Aug. 15	Aug. 15–Sept. 30	Aug. 15–Oct. 15	Sept. 1–Oct. 31
Shallot	(2)	Aug. 1–Oct. 1	Aug. 15–Oct. 1	Aug. 15–Oct. 15	Sept. 15–Nov. 1	Sept. 15–Nov. 1
Sorrel	Aug. 1–Sept. 15	Aug. 15–Oct. 1	Aug. 15–Oct. 15	Sept. 1–Nov. 15	Sept. 1–Dec. 15	Sept. 15–Dec. 31
Soybean	June 1–July 15	June 1–July 25	June 1–July 30	June 1–July 30	June 1–July 30	June 1–July 30
Spinach	Sept. 1–Oct. 1	Sept. 15–Nov. 1	Oct. 1–Dec. 1	Oct. 1–Dec. 31	Oct. 1–Dec. 31	Oct. 1–Dec. 31
Spinach, New Zealand	June 1–Aug. 1	June 1–Aug. 15	June 1–Aug. 15	June 1–Sept. 1	June 1–Sept. 15	June 1–Oct. 1
Squash, summer	June 1–Aug. 1	June 1–Aug. 10	June 1–Aug. 20	June 1–Aug. 20	June 1–Sept. 15	June 1–Oct. 1
Squash, winter	June 10–July 10	June 20–July 20	July 1–Aug. 1	July 1–Aug. 1	Aug. 1–Sept. 1	Aug. 1–Sept. 1
Sweetpotato	June 1–15	June 1–July 1	June 1–July 1	June 1–July 1	June 1–July 1	June 1–July 1
Tomato	June 1–July 1	June 1–July 15	June 1–Aug. 1	Aug. 1–Sept. 1	Aug. 15–Oct. 1	Sept. 1–Nov. 1
Turnip	Aug. 1–Sept. 15	Sept. 1–Oct. 15	Sept. 1–Nov. 15	Sept. 1–Nov. 15	Oct. 1–Dec. 1	Oct. 1–Dec. 31
Watermelon	July 1–July 15	July 15–July 30	—	—	—	—

[1]Plants. [2]Generally spring planted.

APPENDIX D
Vegetable Planting Guide

	Seed germination temperature range, degrees F.	Optimum growing temperature, degrees F.	Max/min growing temperature, degrees F.	Sow seeds or transplant	Number of days for seed to germinate	Days to transplant size	Days to maturity	Plant outside 4 to 6 weeks before last frost	Plant outside 2 to 4 weeks before last frost	Plant outside after last frost	Seed planting depth, inches	Spacing between plants, inches	Plants needed per person	Number of plants per sq. foot, or space needed per plant
Artichoke	50 to 85	65	45 to 75	a	7 to 15	4 to 6 wk.	na	x			½	36 to 48	1	3 to 4 sq. ft. per plant
Asparagus	na	65	30 to 85	b	na	na	3 yr.	see text			1½	12 to 18	20	1 to 2
Beans — Snap Bush	65 to 85	85	60 to 90	c	7 to 15	4 to 6 wk.	45 to 65			x	1 to 2	3 to 4	15 to 45	9 to 12
Beans — Snap Pole	65 to 85	85	60 to 90	c	7 to 15	4 to 6 wk.	60 to 70			x	1 to 2	6 to 8	12 to 15	4
Beans — Lima Bush	65 to 85	85	60 to 90	c	7 to 13	4 to 6 wk.	60 to 80			x	1½ to 2	6 to 8	15	4
Beans — Lima Pole	65 to 85	85	60 to 90	c	7 to 13	4 to 6 wk.	85 to 90			x	1½ to 2	8 to 10	12 to 15	2 to 3
Beans — Fava	50 to 85	65	40 to 75	d	6 to 15	na	80 to 95		x		2½	3 to 5	15 to 30	9 to 12
Beans — Soybean	65 to 85	85	60 to 90	c	6 to 14	4 to 6 wk.	60 to 100			x	1½ to 2	2 to 4	15 to 30	16 to 30
Beans — Dry, Shell	65 to 75	85	60 to 90	c	7 to 15	4 to 6 wk.	60 to 100			x	1 to 2	3 to 4	15 to 45	12 to 16
Beets	50 to 85	65	40 to 75	d	8 to 11	na	50 to 70		x		½ to 1	2	40	36
Broccoli	50 to 85	65	40 to 75	b	4 to 10	5 to 7 wk.	60 to 90	x			½	12 to 16	2	1
Brussels Sprouts	50 to 85	65	40 to 75	b	4 to 10	4 to 6 wk.	70 to 130	x			½	12 to 18	1 to 3	1 to 2
Cabbage	50 to 85	65	40 to 75	b	4 to 10	5 to 7 wk.	65 to 110	x			½	12 to 18	3 to 4	1 to 2
Cabbage, Chinese	50 to 85	65	40 to 75	c	4 to 10	4 to 7 wk.	75 to 90			x	½	8 to 12	3 to 4	1 to 2

aStart from root cuttings, slips, crowns, or tubers.   bTransplant seedlings into the garden   cTransplant or direct seed.   dSow seed directly into the garden

naNot applicable, see text

Vegetable Planting Guide (continued)

	Seed germination temperature range, degrees F.	Optimum growing temperature, degrees F.	Max/min growing temperature, degrees F.	Sow seeds or transplant	Number of days for seed to germinate	Days to transplant size	Days to maturity	Plant outside 4 to 6 weeks before last frost	Plant outside 2 to 4 weeks before last frost	Plant outside after last frost	Seed planting depth, inches	Spacing between plants, inches	Plants needed per person	Number of plants per square foot, or space needed per plant
Cardoon	50 to 85	65	45 to 75	b	7 to 14	7 to 8 wk.	110 to 150		x		1/2	14 to 18	1	1 to 2
Carrot	50 to 85	65	45 to 75	d	12 to 25	na	60 to 80		x		1/4	1 to 2	60 to 90	40 to 144
Cauliflower	50 to 85	65	45 to 75	b	5 to 10	5 to 7 wk.	60 to 75		x		1/2	12 to 18	2 to 3	1 to 2
Celeriac	50 to 65	65	45 to 75	b	10 to 20	10 to 12 wk.	90 to 120	x			1/2	4 to 8	20	4 to 9
Celery	50 to 65	65	45 to 75	b	10 to 20	10 to 12 wk.	90 to 120		x		1/8	6 to 8	2 to 3	4
Chard, Swiss	50 to 85	60	40 to 75	d	8 to 10	na	55 to 70		x		1/2	6	10 to 15	6
Collards	50 to 85	60	40 to 75	c	5 to 10	4 to 6 wk.	70 to 80		x		1/4	12	3 to 5	1
Corn, Salad	50 to 85	65	45 to 75	d	6 to 10	na	45 to 55		x		1/2	4 to 6	2 to 3	5 to 9
Corn, sweet	65 to 85	80	50 to 90	c	6 to 10	4 wk.	60 to 100			x	1 to 2	8	10 to 15	4
Cress, garden	50 to 85	60	45 to 75	d	5 to 10	na	30 to 45		x		1/4	2 to 3	5 to 10	16 to 36
Cucumber	65 to 85	80	60 to 90	c	5 to 11	4 to 5 wk.	50 to 70			x	1	6	2 to 3	4 to 5
Dandelion	50 to 85	60	40 to 75	c	10 to 15	4 to 6 wk.	75 to 90	x			1/2	8	2 to 3	4
Eggplant	65 to 85	80	65 to 95	b	8 to 15	6 to 9 wk.	75 to 85			x	1/4 to 1/2	24 to 30	1 to 2	4
Endive/Escarole	50 to 85	60	45 to 75	c	5 to 9	4 to 6 wk.	60 to 90	x			1/4 to 1/2	8 to 9	4 to 8	2
Florence Fennel	50 to 85	60	45 to 75	b	5 to 16	na	90		x		1/4 to 1/2	6 to 8	1	4
Garlic	50 to 85	70	45 to 85	Sets	6 to 10	na	90	x			1 to 1 1/2	3	5 to 8	16

aStart from root cuttings, slips, crowns, or tubers. bTransplant seedlings into the garden cTransplant or direct seed. dSow seed directly into the garden
naNot applicable, see text

Vegetable Planting Guide (continued)

	Seed germination temperature range, degrees F.	Optimum growing temperature, degrees F.	Max/min growing temperature, degrees F.	Sow seeds or transplant	Number of days for seed to germinate	Days to transplant size	Days to maturity	Plant outside 4 to 6 weeks before last frost	Plant outside 2 to 4 weeks before last frost	Plant outside after last frost	Seed planting depth, inches	Spacing between plants, inches	Plants needed per person	Number of plants per square foot, or space needed per plant
Horseradish	50 to 85	60	40 to 75	roots	na	na	6 to 8 mo.	see text			2	6 to 8	2 to 3	2 to 4
Kale	50 to 85	60	40 to 75	c	3 to 10	4 to 6 wk.	60 to 80	x			½	8 to 10	2 to 4	4
Kohlrabi	50 to 85	60	40 to 75	c	3 to 10	4 to 6 wk.	50 to 70	x			½	4 to 6	5 to 6	6 to 9
Leeks	50 to 85	70	45 to 85	c	5 to 10	10 to 12 wk.	80 to 100	x			½ to 1	2 to 6	6 to 10	4 to 36
Lettuce head	50 to 65	65	45 to 75	c	5 to 8	3 to 4 wk.	60 to 80	x			¼	8 to 12	3 to 4	2 to 4
Lettuce leaf	50 to 65	65	45 to 75	c	5 to 8	3 to 4 wk.	45 to 60	x			¼	4 to 6	2 to 2	4 to 16
Muskmelon	55 to 85	75 to 80	60 to 90	c	3 to 9	3 to 5 wk.	70 to 100			x	1	12	2 to 4	1
Mustard	50 to 75	45 to 55	60	c	4 to 10	3 to 4 wk.	50		x		½	3 to 6	4 to 6	6 to 16
Okra	65 to 85	85	65 to 95	d	8 to 12	na	55 to 70			x	1	15 to 18	1 to 2	1 to 3
Onion seed/sets/plants	50 to 65	65	45 to 85	c	6 to 10	6 to 8 wk.	95 to 150	x			½ / 1 to 2 / 2 to 3	2 to 3	20 to 50	16 to 36
Parsnips	50 to 85	65	40 to 75	d	20	na	100 to 125	x			½	3 to 4	15 to 20	9 to 16
Peas	50 to 65	65	45 to 75	c	5 to 12	3 to 4 wk.	60 to 90	x			2	2 to 3	90	16 to 36
Peppers	65 to 85	75	65 to 80	b	12 to 18	6 to 8 wk.	60 to 80			x	½	18 to 24	1 to 2	1 to 4
Potato	50 to 85	65	45 to 75	a,d	9 to 15	na	100 to 115		x		4 see text	4	10 to 20	9

a Start from root cuttings, slips, crowns, or tubers.
b Transplant seedlings into the garden
c Transplant or direct seed.
d Sow seed directly into the garden
na Not applicable, see text

Vegetable Planting Guide (continued)

Vegetable	Seed germination temperature range, degrees F.	Optimum growing temperature, degrees F.	Max/min growing temperature, degrees F.	Sow seeds or transplant	Number of days for seed to germinate	Days to transplant size	Days to maturity	Plant outside 4 to 6 weeks before last frost	Plant outside 2 to 4 weeks before last frost	Plant outside after last frost	Seed planting depth, inches	Spacing between plants, inches	Plants needed per person	Number of plants per square foot, or space needed per plant
Pumpkin	65 to 85	80	50 to 90	c	6 to 12	6 to 8 wk.	70 to 120			x	1 to 1½	18	1	1 to 4
Radish	50 to 65	60	40 to 75	d	3 to 10	na	20 to 60	x			½	1 to 2	30 to 60	36 to 144
Rhubarb	50 to 85	65	30 to 85	a,b	na	na	2 yr.	see text			3 to 4	12 to 36	1	1 to 8
Rutabaga	50 to 85	60	40 to 75	d	4 to 8	na	80 to 90	x			½	8 to 10	5 to 10	2 to 4
Salsify	50 to 65	65	45 to 85	d	7 to 14	na	115 to 145	x			½	2 to 3	15 to 20	16 to 36
Shallot	50 to 85	65	45 to 85	a,d	—	na	90 to 110	x			1[a]	2 to 4	4 to 10	9 to 36
Spinach	50 to 65	60	40 to 75	d	5 to 12	na	40 to 65	x			½	3 to 6	5 to 10	6 to 16
Malabar	50 to 85	75	50 to 95	d	8 to 10	na	70			x	½	8	5 to 10	2 to 3
New Zealand	50 to 85	75	50 to 95	c	7 to 10	4 to 6 wk.	70 to 80			x	½	12	5	1
Squash summer	65 to 85	75	50 to 90	c	4 to 11	4 to 8 wk.	45 to 65			x	1	12	1 to 2 per type	1
Squash winter	65 to 85	75	50 to 90	c	4 to 11	4 to 8 wk.	80 to 110			x	1	12 to 24	1 to 2 per type	1 or more
Sweet Potato	65 to 85	85	65 to 95	a,d	na	na	120			x	see text	12 to 18	2 to 3	1 or more
Tomato	65 to 85	75	65 to 80	b	5 to 12	5 to 7 wk.	55 to 90			x	½	18 to 30	1 to 2	1 or more
Turnip	50 to 65	60	40 to 75	d	4 to 10	na	35 to 60	x			½	2 to 3	15 to 30	16 to 36
Watermelon	65 to 85	80	65 to 90	c	3 to 14	4 to 6 wk.	80 to 100			x	1	12	1	1

[a] Start from root cuttings, slips, crowns, or tubers. [b] Transplant seedlings into the garden [c] Transplant or direct seed. [d] Sow seed directly into the garden
na Not applicable, see text

APPENDIX E

Seed Catalog Sources

1 Allen Farm
Route 2, Box 243
Scottsville, NY 42164

8½ by 11. Selected list of vegetables.

2 Allen, Sterling & Lothrop
181 US Route #1
Falmouth, ME 04105

Over 10 pages, 8½ by 11. Price list only, no vegetable descriptions.

3 Brittingham Plant Farms
P.O. Box 2538
Salisbury, MD 21801

Over 25 pages, 6 by 9. Features asparagus and a good list of strawberry plants.

4 Brown's Omaha Plant Farms Inc.
P.O. Box 787
Omaha, TX 75571

4 pages, 8½ by 15. Folder offers broccoli, cauliflower, cabbage, collards, brussels sprouts plants; sweet potato slips or plants.

5 Burgess Seed and Plant Co.
P.O. Box 3000
Galesburg, MI 49053

Over 30 pages, 8½ by 11. Catalog features many unusual varieties, Burgess exclusives, and collections.

6 W. Atlee Burpee Co.
P.O. Box 6929
Philadelphia, PA 19132
or
Clinton, IA 52732
or
P.O. Box 758
6350 Rutland Ave.
Riverside, CA 92506

Over 170 pages, 6 by 9. This is the "Sears" catalog of the seed business. The Burpee catalog probably offers more individual items than any other.

7 D. V. Burrell Seed Growers Co.[r]
Rocky Ford, CO 81067

Over 95 pages, 4 by 8½. Provides extensive planting and growing advice.

8 Comstock, Ferre & Co.[r]
263 Main St.
Wethersfield, CT 06109

Over 30 pages, 8½ by 11. Good descriptions of varieties listed. This company offers a good selection of herbs and a special herb list.

9 The Conner Co.
P.O. Box 534
Augusta, AR 72006

Over 20 pages, 5 by 8. Catalog features mainly strawberries.

10 De Giorgi Company
Council Bluffs, IA 51501

Over 11 pages, 8½ by 11. This is a large catalog with many varieties. Good planting information for gardeners.

11 J. A. Demonchaux Co.
225 Jackson
Topeka, KS 66603

8 pages, 8½ by 11. Offers French varieties, gourmet vegetables. The company has a special book catalog.

12 Dixie Plant Farms
P.O. Box 327
Franklin, VA 23851

Over 15 pages, 4 by 8½. This catalog lists field grown varieties of cabbage, collards, egg plant, onions, sweet peppers, and tomato plants.

13 Earl Ferris Nursery & Garden Center[r]
Hampton, IA 50441

Over 45 pages, 8½ by 11. Large catalog lists asparagus and rhubarb but no other vegetables.

14 Earl May Seed & Nursery[r]
6032 Elm St.
Shenandoah, IA 51603

Over 80 pages, 8½ by 11. This company has a wide choice of varieties and a special midget selection.

15 Evans Plant Company
Tifton, GA 31794

Two pages, 11 by 17½ fold-out sheet. Has many varieties of vegetable plants.

16 Farmer Seed & Nursery
Faribault, MN 55021

Over 80 pages, 7½ by 9½. A very complete catalog. Special attention to midget vegetables and early maturing varieties for northern states.

17 Henry Field Seed & Nursery Co.
407 Sycamore St.
Shenandoah, IA 51602

Over 100 pages, 8½ by 11. One of the most complete catalogs available. Good tips for gardeners.

[r]Retail seed store. Shop from displays of seeds and garden supplies.

Seed Catalog Sources *(continued)*

18 Dean Foster Nurseries
Hartford, MI 49057

Over 75 pages, 5½ by 8½.
Features many varieties for
northern climates.

19 Fred's Plant Farm
P.O. Box 410, Route 1
Dresden, TN 38225

20 Glecker's Seedmen
Metamora, OH 43540

Two pages, 8½ by 14. Brief
descriptions of unusual
vegetables.

21 Grace's Gardens
Autumn Lane
Hackettstown, NJ 07840

Sixteen pages, 5 by 8½.
Grace's catalog features the
biggest and the most
unusual.

22 Gurney Seed &
Nursery Co.ʳ
1448 Page St.
Yankton, SD 57078

Over 75 pages, 10 by 13.
This is an extremely
complete catalog with
many extras and special
items. Emphasis on short
season North country
varieties.

23 Joseph Harris Co.ʳ
Moreton Farm
Rochester, NY 14624

Over 80 pages, 8½ by 11.
A very complete high-
quality catalog with good
descriptions.

24 The Chas. C. Hart
Seed Co.
Wethersfield, CT 06109

Over 25 pages, 7 by 10.
This catalog offers a good
choice of vegetables.

25 H. G. Hastings Co.
P.O. Box 4274
Atlanta, GA 30302

Over 45 pages, 8½ by 11.
Specializes in varieties for
South. Has back-to-the-
good life and other
unusual sections.

26 Herbst Brothers
Seedsman Inc.
1000 N. Main St.
Brewester, NY 10509

Over 70 pages, 8½ by 11.
Contains the best variety
charts I've ever seen.

27 Holmes Quisenberry
4626 Gleve Farm
Sarasota, FL 33580

Three by 5 card. Features
unusual tomato variety.

28 Jackson & Perkins Co.
Medford, OR 97501

Over 30 pages, 8½ by 11.
Catalog features vegetables,
flowers, berries, dwarf fruit
trees.

29 J. E. Miller Nurseries Inc.
Canadaigua, NY 14424

Over 40 pages, 8 by 10.
Catalog covers asparagus
and rhubarb. Features a
good selection of fruit
trees.

30 J. L. Hudson, Seedsman
P.O. Box 1058
Redwood City, CA 94604

Over 90 pages, 5½ by 8½.
A world seed service. Has a
selection of mexican and
oriental vegetables.

31 Johnny's Selected Seeds
Organic Seed and Crop
Research
Albion, ME 04910

Over 45 pages, 7½ by 9.
Features high-quality seed
with emphasis on organic
gardening. A very fine
catalog with lots of
information, and a nice
personal touch.

32 J. W. Jung Seed Co.ʳ
Station 8
Randloph, WI 53956

Over 70 pages, 9 by 12.
Emphasis on northern
grown and experiment
station introductions. A
good catalog.

33 Kelly Bros. Nurseries Inc.
Dansville, NY 14437

Over 75 pages, 8½ by 11.
Catalog offers a limited
selection of vegetable seed.

34 Keystone Seed Co.
P.O. Box 1438
Hollister, CA 95023

Over 27 pages, 8½ by 11.
Emphasis on quality.

35 Kilgore Seed Co.
1400 W. First St.
Sanford, FL 32771

Over 45 pages 8½ by 11.
Emphasis on Florida
vegetable varieties. Has
reference tables for Florida
gardens.

36 Kitazawa Seed Co.
356 W. Taylor St.
San Jose, CA 95110

Four pages, 5½ by 8½.
Lists oriental vegetables
only.

ʳ Retail seed store. Shop from displays of seeds and garden supplies.

Seed Catalog Sources *(continued)*

37 Lakeland Nurseries
   Hanover, PA 17331

   Over 60 pages, 8½ by 11.
   Features many novelties,
   giant vegetables.

38 Le Jardin du Gourmet
   West Danville, VT 05873

   Fifteen pages, 5½ by 8½.
   Seeds from France,
   gourmet vegetables.

39 Mellingers
   2310 W. South Range Rd.
   North Lima, OH 44452

   Over 90 pages, 8½ by 11.
   This is by far the best
   catalog for garden
   accessories.

40 Metro Myster Farms
   Route #1
   P.O. Box 285
   Northhampton, PA 18076

   Eight pages, 5½ by 8½.
   Offers a selection of grain
   and soybeans.

41 The Meyer Seed Co.
   600 S. Caroline St.
   Baltimore, MD 21231

   Over 65 pages, 8½ by 11.
   Catalog has a vegetable
   planting guide.

42 Midwest Seed Growers Inc.
   505 Walnut St.
   Kansas City, MO 64106

   Over 20 pages, 8½ by 11.
   Presents vegetable varieties
   in a straightforward,
   factual manner.

43 The Natural Development
      Co.
   P.O. Box 215
   Brainbridge, PA 17502

   Over 30 pages, 8½ by 11.
   Seeds for organic
   gardeners.

44 Nichols Garden Nursery [r]
   1190 North Pacific Hwy.
   Albany, OR 97321

   Over 60 pages, 8½ by 11.
   An unusual catalog that
   features many unusual
   vegetables and herbs. Also
   an herbal tea list,
   winemaking supplies and a
   rural bookstore section.

45 L. L. Olds Seed Co. [r]
   P.O. Box 7790
   Madison, WI 53707

   Over 80 pages, 8 by 10.
   This is a well written
   catalog that contains many
   vegetable varieties.

46 Geo. W. Park Seed Co.
   Greenwood, SC 29647

   Over 120 pages, 8½ by 11.
   This is the best illustrated
   of all the seed catalogs. It
   contains a midget vegetable
   section.

47 Piedmont Plant Co.
   P.O. Box 424
   Albany, GA 31702

   Over 15 pages, 5½ by 8.
   Offers a good selection of
   plants.

48 Porter and Son Seedmen
   1510 E. Washington
   Stephenville, TX 76401

   Over 30 pages, 5½ by 8½.
   This is a good small catalog
   that offers many unusual
   varieties.

49 Reuter Seed Company
   320 N. Carrollton Ave.
   New Orleans, LA 70119

   Over 30 pages, 7½ by 10½.
   Catalog features a good
   selection of vegetables.

50 The Rocky Mountain
      Seed Co. [r]
   1325 15th St.
   Denver, CO 80217

   Over 55 pages, 8 by 11.
   Vegetables for high
   altitude gardens of the
   rocky mountain area.

51 Roswell Seed Company [r]
   115–117 South Main
   Roswell, NM 88201

   Over 25 pages, 6 by 9.
   Special attention to
   varieties suited to the
   Southwest.

52 Seedway Inc. [r]
   Hall, NY 14463

   Over 30 pages, 8 by 10½.
   Includes many new items
   each year. A good source
   for elephant garlic.

53 S & H Organic Acres
   Montgomery, CA 96065

   One page, 8½ by 11.
   Features garlic, shallots,
   egyptian onions, comfrey,
   horseradish.

54 R. H. Shumway Seedsman
   Rockford, IL 51101

   Over 90 pages, 10 by 13.
   This is a delightful catalog
   with an old-time
   agricultural look. Every
   gardener needs a copy of
   this one.

55 Springhill Nurseries
   11 W. Elm St.
   Tipp City, OH 45366

   Over 80 pages, 8 by 8. This
   catalog contains many
   plants besides vegetables.

56 Spruce Brook Nursery
   Route 118
   P.O. Box 925
   Litchfield, CT 06759

[r]Retail seed store. Shop from displays of seeds and garden supplies.

Seed Catalog Sources *(continued)*

Over 55 pages, 6 by 9. A good catalog but contains few vegetables.

57   Stanford Seed Company
560 Fulton St.
Buffalo, NY 14240

Fourteen pages, 6 by 9. Catalog offers beans, corn and peas and features a good planting chart.

58   Stark Brother's Nurseries
and Orchards
Louisiana, MO 63353

Over 60 pages, 8½ by 11. Contains mostly fruit, but also a few vegetables.

59   Steele Plant Company
Gleason, TN 38229

Sixteen pages, 8½ by 11. A good source for sweet potatoes.

60   Stokes Seeds Inc.
P.O. Box 548
Main Post Office
Buffalo, NY 14240

Over 150 pages, 5½ by 9. This catalog has the voice of authority with over 500 vegetables. The emphasis is on short-season northern strains.

61   Geo. Tait and Sons, Inc.
900 Tidewater Dr.
Norfolk, VA 23504

Over 60 pages, 8 by 11. This firm has been in business over 100 years and specializes in vegetables for the South and the tidewater areas. Has a planting guide for eastern Virginia and North Carolina.

62   Texas Onion Plant Co.
P.O. Box 871
Farmersville, TX 75031

Three by 4½ card. Sells onion plants.

63   Thompson and
Morgan Inc.
P.O. Box 100
Farmingdale, NJ 07727

Over 160 pages, 6 by 9. This is the Cadillac of all the catalogs. The firm was founded in 1855. Their catalog features varieties from all over the world.

64   Tsang and Ma
International
1306 Old Country Rd.
Belmont, CA 94002

Twenty pages, 5½ by 8½. This catalog has only oriental vegetables. Each is illustrated with a photograph.

65   Otis S. Twilley Seed Co.
Salisbury, MD 21801

Over 60 pages, 8½ by 11. A very professional catalog.

66   Vermont Seed Co.
Way's Lane
Manchester, VT 05255

Forty pages, 5 by 8. Beans, beans everywhere; this company offers more beans and peas than any other catalog firm.

67   W. H. Perron and Co.
515 Labelle Boulevard
City of Laval
Que. Canada H7V 2T3

Over 120 pages, 8½ by 11. This is a high-quality catalog that contains a great deal of useful information. It also has a superior garden accessory section.

68   Whilhite Melon Seed
Farms
Weatherford, TX 76086

Over 40 pages, 7½ by 10½. If you're getting ready for a watermelon growing contest, this is the catalog for you. Also has other vegetables.

ʳRetail seed store. Shop from displays of seeds and garden supplies.

APPENDIX F

Retail Seed Stores

Agway Inc.
Syracuse, NY 13221

Harris Seeds West
1313 East Powell Blvd.
Gresham, OR 97030

Lagomarsino Seeds Inc.
5116 Folsom Blvd.
Sacramento, CA 95819

Charles B. Ledgerwood Seeds
3862 Carlsbad Blvd.
Carlsbad, CA 92008

Lockhart Seeds Inc.
3 N. Wilson Way
Stockton, CA 95201

P. L. Rohrer & Bro. Inc.
Smoketown, PA 17576

Seattle Garden Center
1600 Pike Place
Seattle, WA 98101

Tillinghast Seed Co.
Morris and Maple Sts.
La Conner, WA 98257

Wyatt-Quarles Seed Co.
Box 2131
Raleigh, NC 27602

APPENDIX G

Cooperative Extension Services

ALASKA
Cooperative Extension Service
University of Alaska
Fairbanks, AK 99701

ALABAMA
Cooperative Extension Service
Auburn University
Auburn, AL 36830

ARIZONA
Cooperative Extension Service
University of Arizona
College of Agriculture
Tucson, AZ 85721

ARKANSAS
Cooperative Extension Service
University of Arkansas
P.O. Box 391
Little Rock, AR 72203

CALIFORNIA
Agricultural Extension Service
University of California
College of Agriculture
Berkeley, CA 94720

COLORADO
Cooperative Extension Service
Colorado State University
Fort Collins, CO 80521

DELAWARE
Cooperative Extension Service
University of Delaware
College of Agricultural Sciences
Newark, DE 19711

DISTRICT OF COLUMBIA
Cooperative Extension Service
The Federal City College
1424 K Street, N.W.
Washington, DC 20005

FLORIDA
Cooperative Extension Service
University of Florida
Institute of Food and
  Agricultural Sciences
Gainesville, FL 32601

GEORGIA
Cooperative Extension Service
University of Georgia
College of Agriculture
Athens, GA 30601

HAWAII
Cooperative Extension Service
University of Hawaii
2500 Dole Street
Honolulu, HI 96822

IDAHO
Cooperative Extension Service
University of Idaho
College of Agriculture
Moscow, ID 83843

ILLINOIS
Cooperative Extension Service
University of Illinois
College of Agriculture
Urbana, IL 61801

INDIANA
Cooperative Extension Service
Purdue University
West Lafayette, IN 47907

IOWA
Cooperative Extension Service
Iowa State University
Ames, IA 50010

KANSAS
Cooperative Extension Service
Kansas State University
Manhattan, KS 66506

KENTUCKY
Cooperative Extension Service
University of Kentucky
College of Agriculture
Lexington, KY 40506

LOUISIANA
Cooperative Extension Service
State University
A & M College
University Station
Baton Rouge, LA 70803

Cooperative Extension Services *(continued)*

MAINE
Cooperative Extension Service
University of Maine
Orono, ME 04473

MARYLAND
Cooperative Extension Service
University of Maryland
College Park, MD 20742

MASSACHUSETTS
Cooperative Extension Service
University of Massachusetts
Amherst, MA 01002

MICHIGAN
Cooperative Extension Service
Michigan State University
East Lansing, MI 48823

MINNESOTA
Agricultural Extension Service
University of Minnesota
Institute of Agriculture
St. Paul, MN 55101

MISSISSIPPI
Cooperative Extension Service
Mississippi State University
State College, MS 39762

MISSOURI
Cooperative Extension Service
University of Missouri
Columbia, MO 65201

MONTANA
Cooperative Extension Service
Montana State University
Bozeman, MT 59715

NEBRASKA
Cooperative Extension Service
University of Nebraska
College of Agriculture and
   Home Economics
Lincoln, NB 68503

NEVADA
Cooperative Extension Service
University of Nevada
College of Agriculture
Reno, NV 89507

NEW HAMPSHIRE
Cooperative Extension Service
University of New Hampshire
College of Life Sciences and
   Agriculture
Durham, NH 03824

NEW JERSEY
Cooperative Extension Service
College of Agriculture and
   Environmental Science
Rutgers–The State University
New Brunswick, NJ 08903

NEW MEXICO
Cooperative Extension Service
New Mexico State University
Box 3AE, Agriculture Bldg.
Las Cruces, NM 88003

NEW YORK
Cooperative Extension Service
Cornell University
State University of New York
Ithaca, NY 14850

NORTH CAROLINA
Cooperative Extension Service
North Carolina State University
P.O. Box 5057
Raleigh, NC 27607

NORTH DAKOTA
Cooperative Extension Service
North Dakota State University
   of Agriculture and Applied
   Science
University Station
Fargo, ND 58102

OHIO
Cooperative Extension Service
Ohio State University
Agriculture Administration
   Bldg.
2120 Fyffe Road
Columbus, OH 43210

OKLAHOMA
Cooperative Extension Service
Oklahoma State University
201 Whitehurst
Stillwater, OK 74074

OREGON
Cooperative Extension Service
Oregon State University
Corvallis, OR 97331

PENNSYLVANIA
Cooperative Extension Service
The Pennsylvania State
   University
College of Agriculture
323 Agricultural
   Administration Bldg.
University Park, PA 16802

RHODE ISLAND
Cooperative Extension Service
University of Rhode Island
Kingston, RI 02881

SOUTH CAROLINA
Cooperative Extension Service
Clemson University
Clemson, SC 29631

SOUTH DAKOTA
Cooperative Extension Service
South Dakota State University
College of Agriculture
Brookings, SD 57006

TENNESSEE
Agricultural Extension Service
University of Tennessee
Institute of Agriculture
P.O. Box 1071
Knoxville, TN 37901

TEXAS
Agricultural Extension Service
Texas A & M University
College Station, TX 77843

UTAH
Cooperative Extension Service
Utah State University
Logan, UT 84321

VERMONT
Cooperative Extension Service
University of Vermont
Burlington, VT 05401

APPENDIX H

Suppliers of Predator Insects

VIRGINIA Cooperative Extension Service Virginia Polytechnic Institute Blacksburg, VA 24061	

VIRGINIA
Cooperative Extension Service
Virginia Polytechnic Institute
Blacksburg, VA 24061

WASHINGTON
Cooperative Extension Service
College of Agriculture
Washington State University
Pullman, WA 99163

WEST VIRGINIA
Cooperative Extension Service
West Virginia University
Morgantown, WV 26506

WISCONSIN
Cooperative Extension Service
University of Wisconsin
412 N. Lake Street
Madison, WI 53706

WYOMING
Agricultural Extension Service
University of Wyoming
College of Agriculture
University Station, Box 3354
Laramie, WY 82070

Supplier	Insects
Allan's Aquarium & Exotic Birds 845 Lincoln Blvd. Venice, CA 90291	Ladybugs
Bio-Control Co. Route 2, Box 2397 Auburn, CA 95603	Ladybugs Praying mantises
W. Atlee Burpee Co. Philadelphia, PA 19132 Clinton, IA 52732 Riverside, CA 92502	Ladybugs Praying mantises
California Green Lacewings Inc. P.O. Box 2495 Merced, CA 95340	Lacewing flies Trichogramma wasps
Connecticut Valley Biological Supply Co. Valley Rd. South Hampton, MA 01073	Damselfly nymphs Dragonfly nymphs
Eastern Biological Control Co. Route 5, Box 379 Jackson, NJ 08527	Praying mantises
Gothard Inc. P.O. Box 370 Canutillo TX 79835	Praying mantises Trichogramma wasps
King Labs P.O. Box 69 Limerick, PA 19468	Praying mantises Green lacewing
Lakeland Nursery Sales 340 Poplar Hanover, PA 17331	Ladybugs Praying mantises
Organic Control Inc. P.O. Box 25382 W. Los Angeles, CA 90025	Ladybugs Praying mantises
Rincon Vitova Insectaries Inc. P.O. Box 95 Oak View, CA 93022	Fly parasites Lacewing flies Ladybugs Scale parasites Trichogramma wasps
Robert Robbins 424 N. Courtland St. East Stroudsburg, PA 18301	Praying mantises

APPENDIX I

Insect Control Using Biological, Botanical, and Chemical Insecticides

VEGETABLE	SYMPTOM	PEST	Diazinon	Malathion	Pyrethrum	Rotenone	Ryania	Sabadilla	Sevin	Thuricide
Artichokes	Colonies of insects on leaves and buds.	Aphids		x	x	x	x			
	Trails of silver slime	Slugs, Snails		see text						
Asparagus	Shoots channeled, leaves eaten by larvae of beetles.	Asparagus beetle		x	x	x		x		
Beans	Colonies of black sucking insects on leaves.	Aphids		x	x	x	x			
	Circular holes eaten in leaves.	Bean leaf beetles	x	x	x	x	x		x	
	Hopping, running insects that suck sap from leaves.	Leafhoppers		x	x	x	x		x	
	Lower surface of leaves eaten between veins skeletonized.	Mexican bean beetles	x	x	x	x			x	
	Scale nymphs on underside of leaves; white adults flutter when disturbed.	Whiteflies		x		x				
Beets	Leaves eaten leaving trail of slime.	Snails, Slugs		see text						
Broccoli, Brussels Sprouts, Cabbage, Cauliflower	Colonies of small insects on leaves.	Aphids		x	x	x	x			
	Plants sickly, maggots attack underground parts of plant.	Cabbage maggots	x							
	Holes eaten in leaves by larvae.	Cabbage worms, Loopers		x		x			x	x
	Small plants cut off at soil level.	Cut worms	x	Use cardboard collars around plants, below ground level.							

Insect Control Using Biological, Botanical, and Chemical Insecticides *(continued)*

VEGETABLE	SYMPTOM	PEST	INSECTICIDE							
			Diazinon	Malathion	Pyrethrum	Rotenone	Ryania	Sabadilla	Sevin	Thuricide
Corn	Silks cut off at ear; kernels destroyed by large larvae.	Corn earworms					X		X	
	Ears and stalks tunneled by larvae.	Corn borers							X	
	Small plants cut off at soil level.	Cutworms	X							
Cucumber	Colonies of small insects on underside of leaves.	Aphids		X	X	X	X			
	All parts eaten.	Cucumber beetles	X	X		X			X	
	All parts of vines eaten.	Pickleworm		X	X	X				X
Eggplant	Plant defoliated. Beetle black, striped; larvae brick red.	Colorado potato beetle			X	X	X		X	
	Colonies of small insects on undersides of leaves.	Aphids		X	X	X	X			
	Colonies on underside of leaves.	Eggplant lacebug		X			X			
Lettuce	Colonies of small insects on leaves.	Aphids		X	X	X	X			
	Leaves eaten by pincer bugs.	Earwigs	see text							
	Wedge-shaped insects found on leaves, tips of leaves turn brown.	Leafhoppers		X	X	X	X		X	
	Leaves eaten leaving trails of silver slime.	Snails, Slugs	see text							
Kale	Colonies of small insects on leaves.	Aphids		X	X	X	X			
	Small pin-sized holes chewed in leaves.	Flea beetles	X		X	X	X		X	

Insect Control Using Biological, Botanical, and Chemical Insecticides *(continued)*

VEGETABLE	SYMPTOM	PEST	Diazinon	Malathion	Pyrethrum	Rotenone	Ryania	Sabadilla	Sevin	Thuricide
Melons	Colonies of insects on underside of leaves.	Aphids		x	x	x	x			
	All parts eaten.	Cucumber beetles	x		x	x	x		x	
Mustard greens	Colonies of insects on leaves.	Aphids		x	x	x	x			
	Leaves with holes eaten by larvae.	Cabbage worms				x		x		x
	Plants sickly; maggots attack roots and stem underground.	Root maggots	x							
Onions	Older leaves wither; small yellow insects feed at base of leaves.	Onion thrips		x	x	x	x			
	Plants sickly, maggots attack parts below ground.	Onion maggots	x							
Okra	Holes eaten in pods.	Corn earworms					x		x	
Peas	Terminals deformed, colonies of small insects on leaves.	Aphids		x	x	x	x			
	Beetles feed on blooms; larvae bore through pod and enter young peas.	Pea weevils	x	x		x				
Peppers	Colonies of small insects on leaves.	Aphids		x	x	x	x			
	Plants defoliated by orange- and yellow-bodied beetles.	Blister beetles			x	x	x		x	
	Small plants cut off at soil level.	Cutworms	x						x	
	Small pin-sized holes chewed in leaves.	Flea beetles	x	x	x	x	x		x	
	Leaves and fruit eaten.	Pepper weevils	x	x		x			x	

Insect Control Using Biological, Botanical, and Chemical Insecticides *(continued)*

VEGETABLE	SYMPTOM	PEST	INSECTICIDE							
			Diazinon	Malathion	Pyrethrum	Rotenone	Ryania	Sabadilla	Sevin	Thuricide
Radishes	Plants sickly, maggots attack plants below ground.	Root maggots	x							
Spinach	Colonies of small insects on leaves.	Aphids		x	x	x	x			
	Larvae tunnel through leaves.	Leaf miners	x	x						
Squash	Colonies of small insects underneath leaves.	Aphids		x	x	x	x			
	All parts eaten.	Cucumber beetles	x		x	x	x		x	
	Plants wilted, brownish flat bugs.	Squash bugs			x	x	x	x	x	
	Sudden wilting of runners, holes in stem near base.	Squash vine borers							x	
Swiss chard	Colonies of small insects on leaves.	Aphids		x	x	x	x			
Tomatoes	Colonies of small insects on leaves.	Aphids		x	x	x	x			
	Small plants cut off at soil level.	Cutworms	x						x	
	Many shot-sized holes in leaves.	Flea beetles	x		x	x	x		x	
	Leaves eaten (large green worms with horn).	Tomato hornworm			x	x			x	x
	Scalelike nymphs attached to underside of leaves; white adults flutter.	Whiteflies		x	x	x				
Turnips and Rutabagas	Holes eaten in leaves by larvae.	Cabbage loopers		x	x	x		x	x	
	Plants attacked below ground.	Root maggots	x					x		

APPENDIX J

Vegetable Disease Control

CROP	DISEASE	DESCRIPTION	REMEDY
Beans	Anthracnose	Dark, sunken, circular, or oval pod spots; brown borders, salmon colored ooze in spots; leaves and stems infected.	Spray with Maneb at the first sign of disease and weekly thereafter; also use Bordeaux mixture.
	Bacterial blight	Brown or tan spots or blotches with a yellow border on leaves; pods may have brick red or brown sunken blotches.	Use disease-free seed.
	Damping off	Seeds fail to grow, young plants die.	Treat seed with Captan dust or apply Captan to soil at planting time.
	Root and stem rot	Plant wilts and dies; plant is decayed on lower roots and stems	Apply Captan to soil at planting time.
	Rust	Brown spots (pustules) on leaves.	Use Maneb. Sulfur dust can be applied at weekly intervals.
Broccoli, brussels sprouts, cabbage, cauliflower, and other "cole" crops	Club root fungus	Roots become enlarged; plants wilt and finally die.	Grow only in well drained soil.
	Yellows	Leaves turn yellow; plants often deformed.	Choose resistant varieties.
	Black rot	Infections make leaves yellow or tan; leaf veins and vascular ring in stem may be black; head may decay.	Rotate cabbage with other crops; plant disease-free seeds, use Bordeaux mixture.
	Blackleg	Stems decayed and blackened at about ground line.	Keep garden tools clean; remove debris, follow crop rotation.
	Damping off, Stem rot	Seeds may rot, young plants die.	Treat seed with Captan dust; work Captan into soil in accordance with instructions.
Corn	Bacterial wilt	Long pale green or tan dead streaks on leaves, may cause stunting and death of plants.	The bacteria is carried by flea beetles, use insecticides to control; use resistant varieties.
	Smut	Galls on leaves, stems, ears, or tassels continue to enlarge, turn black, and break open.	Remove and destroy galls before they break open; rotate corn in garden.

Vegetables Disease Control *(continued)*

CROP	DISEASE	DESCRIPTION	REMEDY
Cantaloupe, cucumber, pumpkin, squash, watermelon	Anthracnose	Dark, sunken, circular, or oval pod spots; brown borders and salmon-colored ooze in center, on fruits, stems, leaves.	Spray with Maneb at first sign of disease and continue weekly as needed.
	Bacterial wilt	Vines wilt and die.	The bacteria is transmitted by cucumber beetle, use insecticide to control the beetle.
	Blossom end rot	Flowers become rotted, deformed.	Spray blossoms with Maneb.
	Fruit rot	Rotted fruit, gray moldy growth, decay at blossom end.	Prevent by growing on black plastic. Spray with Maneb at first sign of disease.
	Leaf spot	Dried brown spots on leaves soon become holes.	Spray with Captan.
	Powdery mildew	White powdery growth on surface of leaves and stems.	Spray with Benomyl or sulphur dust.
	Scab	Brown holes in fruit.	Spray with Maneb.
Peas	Damping off	Seeds fail to grow, young plants die.	Buy treated seed; treat seed with Captan dust or apply to soil at planting time.
	Downy mildew	White mold on underside of leaves.	Grow resistant varieties.
	Fusarium wilt	Seedlings wilt and die, growth of older plants is stunted.	Grow resistant varieties.
Pepper	Bacterial spot	Irregular tan or dark brown spots on leaves.	Spray with fixed copper at first sign of disease, then weekly.
Potato	Black leg	Stems decayed and blackened at or below ground line, tops grow poorly.	Plant disease-free tubers. Do not plant cold potatoes into cold soil.
	Late blight	Dead areas on leaves—brown or dark purple; white or gray moldy growth on leaf underside.	Plant disease-free tubers, spray foliage at first sign of disease with Maneb.
	Scab	Black, rough, scabby patches appear on skin.	Grow resistant varieties.
Sweet Potato	Scurf	Irregular purple-brown discoloration.	Use only disease-free tubers or slips.

Vegetables Disease Control *(continued)*

CROP	DISEASE	DESCRIPTION	REMEDY
Tomato	Blossom end rot	Leathery black or dark brown decay on the blossom end of fruit.	Can be cut down or eliminated by maintaining a uniform soil moisture.
	Early blight	Dark brown spots with concentric rings on leaves, stems, and fruits.	Spray foliage with Maneb at first signs of disease, weekly intervals from then on.
	Fusarium and Verticillium wilt	Leaves turn yellow and fall on one side of the plant before the other; vascular tissue may have dark discoloration, leaves wilt.	Use resistant tomato varieties, rotate garden crops.
	Late blight	Brown or dark purple dead areas on leaves, white or gray moldy growth on leaf underside.	Use partially resistant varieties. Apply Maneb at first signs of disease.
Vegetables in general	Nematodes	Galls and swellings on roots. Plants grow poorly, may be stunted and wilt. Tubers and fleshy roots may show lumps and swellings. Affects a wide range of vegetables.	There are several nematicides available; see your nursery.
	Southern stem blight	Decay of stem near ground line; often heavy white fungus growth.	Rotate crops.
	Virus	Mottling, mosaic yellowing leaves or fruits; some malformation in shapes of leaves or fruit.	Use resistant varieties; clean up weeds and garden residue.

APPENDIX K

Big Yield/Small Space Trouble Shooting Checklist

SYMPTOMS	POSSIBLE CAUSES	POSSIBLE CURES
GENERAL Dying young plants.	Fertilizer burn.	Mix fertilizer thoroughly with soil. Possibility is minimized by the use of time-release fertilizer.
	Disease (damping off).	See disease chart.
Stunted plants (pale to yellow).	Low soil fertility.	Mix up soil according to instructions in text.
	Poor soil drainage.	Add organic matter as recommended.
	Insects or diseases.	See insect and disease charts for identification and control.
Stunted plants (purplish color).	Low temperatures.	Protect from frost.
Spots, molds, darkened areas on leaves and stems.	Disease.	Identify disease from disease chart, control.
	Fertilizer burn.	Can sometimes occur if some time-release fertilizers come in contact with leaves. Keep fertilizer off plants.
Holes in leaves.	Lack of phosphorus.	Add an organic phosphorus source, see text.
	Insects.	Identify the insect from charts and control.
	Hail.	Many vegetables, especially corn, will recover on their own.
Wilting plants.	Dry soil.	Water.
	Excess water in soil.	This won't happen if the soil is made up according to instructions in text.
	Disease.	Identify disease from chart and take corrective control measures.
Weak, spindly plants.	Too much shade.	Take measures to increase the light.
	Too much water.	See wilting above.
	Plants too thick.	Space according to instructions.
Failure to set fruit.	High temperatures.	Fruit set will improve as weather cools.
	Low temperatures.	Use protective devices to increase temperatures.
BEANS Bean seeds won't germinate.	Planted in the spring before the soil warmed up.	Wait until soil warms up to plant. Start inside in individual peat pots, transplant after the soil warms up. Start earlier in the spring using protective devices.
	The soil crust is too hard for the bean seedlings to break through.	This probably won't happen in vegetable factory soil. If it does add more organic material.

Big Yield/Small Space Trouble Shooting Checklist (continued)

SYMPTOMS	POSSIBLE CAUSES	POSSIBLE CURES
Vines don't produce well, ends of the pods shrivel.	This is a watering problem. The soil should never dry out while beans are growing.	Water deep and consistently. Do not let the soil dry out completely.
	Old beans left on the vines. This cuts the production of new beans.	Pick regularly.
BEETS Beet seed doesn't germinate well.	The seedbed dried out while the beets were germinating.	Cover with a sheet of black plastic. Remove as soon as the plants start to show.
Beets never become very big.	You didn't thin.	Thin out the plants to a 2- to 3-inch spacing. Never leave two plants together. Use the thinings in cooking.
Beets taste woody.	This is a watering problem. Beets must grow full blast to maturity.	Don't let your beets dry out.
BROCCOLI Broccoli flowers before the heads are ready to harvest.	Too much heat.	Try planting in midsummer for a fall crop. In mild winter areas you can plant broccoli from early fall through late winter.
CABBAGE Cabbage heads split badly.	This is a watering problem. Any time watering is irregular, the growth becomes irregular and causes the cabbage heads to crack.	Don't let your cabbage dry out. You can delay growth and halt cracking by holding off water when the cracking begins.
Roots become swollen and knobby.	Caused by the disease club root.	Rotate your crops. Don't grow any cole crops on the same site twice.
Young plants bolt, overwintered plants fail to form heads.	Young plants will bolt if they are exposed to temperatures below 50 degrees for several weeks. Large transplants that are overwintered will flower in the spring.	Plant later in the spring or use protective devices. Plant smaller transplants for overwintering.
CARROTS Few carrot seeds germinate.	Carrots are shallow planted (½ inch). Often in hot weather the soil dries out and they won't germinate.	Place a black plastic sheet over the top of the bed to hold in moisture. Remove to water. When the seeds start to show, remove the plastic.
Carrots split badly.	Due to uneven watering. When the soil dries out carrot growth slows down; when they receive more moisture, growth speeds up and carrots split.	Don't let the soil dry out completely.

Big Yield/Small Space Trouble Shooting Checklist (*continued*)

SYMPTOMS	POSSIBLE CAUSES	POSSIBLE CURES
CORN The ears don't seem to fill out when only a few plants are grown.	Corn is a wind pollinator. Pollen from the tassels must fall on the silks to produce a mature kernel. This doesn't always happen with a few scattered plants.	Plant in blocks.
CUCUMBER Plants flower but don't produce cucumbers.	The first 10 to 20 flowers produced on any plant are males, after that there are 10 to 20 male flowers for every female. Cucumbers come only from female.	Wait for the female flowers or plant the modern gynecious varieties; they produce only female flowers.
Plants just stop producing fruit.	Cucumbers left on the vine to mature can stop a plant from setting new fruit.	Pick cucumbers as soon as they reach useable size.
LETTUCE Lettuce goes to seed before it's big enough to eat.	The lettuce is getting too much heat.	Plant earlier in the spring before hot weather, or plant in late summer for fall harvest. You can shade your garden with lath.
The tips of the lettuce turn brown.	This is tip burn due to heat.	You can solve the problem as above. You can also plant heat-resistant varieties.
Poor head formation or no heads.	This is due to lack of growing space.	Thin to the recommended spacing.
MELONS Melons taste bitter.	Bitterness occurs when there is cold, wet weather during the ripening period.	Plant to ripen in the hottest part of the season, or if the weather is unseasonable try again next year.
ONIONS Tough, flabby, nearly hollow bulbs.	A certain percentage of onion sets go to seed, using the nutriments for seed instead of bulb production.	Harvest as soon as you detect flower stalks and use as green onions, or cut off the flower stalks and take your chances that you'll have useable bulbs.
PEAS Some of the peas fail to come up.	This may happen when you plant in cold soil.	Wait and plant a little later, or start inside in individual peat pots and transplant outside.
PEPPERS Blossoms drop off.	Fruit setting is poor when the night temperatures fall below 55 or rise above 75 degrees F.	Wait for a change in temperature.
	Peppers won't blossom when the plants have all the fruit they can handle.	Pick the fruit as soon as it becomes big enough.

Big Yield/Small Space Trouble Shooting Checklist (continued)

SYMPTOMS	POSSIBLE CAUSES	POSSIBLE CURES
POTATOES Potatoes become knobby.	Potatoes need a steady supply of moisture. If the soil drys out then becomes moist, growth starts resulting in knobby potatoes.	Don't let the soil dry out.
RADISHES Radishes taste like hot peppers.	This is a watering problem. Radishes become hot when the soil dries out, then they are watered again.	Don't let the soil dry out.
Radishes produce many leaves, few bulbs.	The plants are planted too close together.	Thin to the recommended spacing.
SQUASH Winter squash rots from the stem end after picking.	If you pull the stem off a winter squash it will rot fairly quickly.	Use that particular squash right away instead of trying to store.
TOMATOES Blossoms drop without setting fruit.	Most tomatoes set blossoms in a very narrow *night* temperature range of between 55 and 75 degrees F. If the night temperature in a particular year stays below normal, blossoms don't set. During a heat wave, most blossoms fall off.	To increase night temperatures use plastic covers over tomato cages.
All vine, no fruit.	Plants that receive too much water and too much nitrogen tend to produce more vines and fewer flowers.	Cut down watering. Use a tomato formula fertilizer.
Blossom end rot.	This seems to be tied to soil moisture. If the soil is intermittently wet and dry, it seems to promote blossom end rot.	Don't let the soil dry out.
Misshapen fruit.	Often young plants exposed to temperatures below 55 degrees F. will produce deformed fruit. The low temperature seems to interfere with normal fertilization.	Pick off and wait until the temperature warms up.
Yellow or white patches on the plant or fruit.	Sunscald due to burning. This happens when a plant has poor foliage cover.	Grow in a wire cage.

RECOMMENDED READING

Dole, Louise E. *Herb Magic and Garden Craft.* New York: Sterling, 1973.

Faust, Joan Lee. *The New York Times Book of Vegetable Gardening.* New York: A & W Publishers, 1975.

Fox, Helen. *Gardening with Herbs for Flavor and Fragrance.* New York: Sterling, 1970.

Hertzberg, Ruth, Beatrice Vaughn, and Janet Greene. *Putting Food By.* Brattleboro, Vt.: Stephen Green Press, 1973.

Hobson, Phyllis. *Garden Way's Guide to Food Drying.* Charlotte, Vt.: Garden Way Publishing, 1980.

Jeavons, John. *How to Grow More Vegetables Than You Ever Thought Possible on Less Land Than You Can Imagine.* Berkeley: Ten Speed Press, 1974.

Newcomb, Duane. *The Postage Stamp Garden Book.* Los Angeles: J. P. Tarcher, 1975.

———. *The Apartment Farmer.* New York: Avon Books, 1977.

———. *The Complete Vegetable Gardener's Sourcebook.* New York: Avon Books, 1980.

Powell, Betty, and Thomas Powell. *The Avant Gardener.* Boston: Houghton Mifflin, 1975.

Ray, Richard M. (ed.). *Gardening Shortcuts.* San Francisco: Ortho Books, Chevron Chemical Company, 1976.

Ray, Richard M. (ed.). *All About Tomatoes.* San Francisco: Ortho Books, Chevron Chemical Company, 1976.

Raymond, Dick. *Down to Earth Vegetable Gardening Know How.* Charlotte, Vt.: Garden Way Publishing, 1975.

Seabrook, Peter. *The Complete Vegetable Gardener.* New York: A & W Publishers, 1976.

INDEX

Page reference in *italics* refer to illustrations in text.

GROWING VEGETABLES
THE BIG YIELD/SMALL SPACE WAY